PHILIP'S COUNTY GUIDES

EAST SUSSEX

PHILIP'S COUNTY GUIDES

SURREY	General Editor Keith Spence
HAMPSHIRE	General Editor Robin Dewhurst
EAST SUSSEX	General Editor Keith Spence
WEST SUSSEX	General Editor David Arscott

PHILIP'S COUNTY GUIDES

EAST SUSSEX

GENERAL EDITOR
KEITH SPENCE

WRITERS
John Lloyd
Helen Mount
John Skinner
Keith Spence

Photography by John Bethell

ACKNOWLEDGEMENTS
The publishers would like to thank the following
for their advice and assistance during the
preparation of this book:
Eastbourne Tourism & Leisure
East Sussex County Council
East Sussex Tourist Attractions Association
    (Robin Symington)
Hastings Borough Council
National Rivers Authority
Rother District Council
South East England Tourist Board (Gillian Pope
    and Priscilla Chapman)
Wealden District Council

FURTHER READING
AA/Ordnance Survey South Downs Leisure Guide
    (AA/Ordnance Survey, 1988)
J. R. Armstrong A History of Sussex (Darwen
    Finlayson, 1967)
Hilary Arnold Sussex (Cadogan Books, 1984)
David Arscott Curiosities of East Sussex
    (S.B. Publications, 1991)
Garth Christian Ashdown Forest (1917)
Jim Cleland Visitors' Guide to Sussex
    (Moorland, 1985)
Ben Darby Journey Through the Weald (Robert
    Hale, 1986)
John Godfrey The New Shell Guide to Sussex
    (Michael Joseph, 1990)
Edna & Mac McCarthy Sussex River, 3 vols
    (Lindel, 1975 and 1977)
E. V. Lucas Highways and Byways in Sussex
    (Macmillan, 1912)
Arthur Mee The King's England: Sussex (Hodder
    & Stoughton, rev. edn 1971)
Ian Nairn and Nikolaus Pevsner The Buildings of
    England: Sussex (Penguin, 1965, repr. 1991)
Charles A. Robertson Hailsham and its Environs
    (Phillimore, 1982)
Keith Spence Companion Guide to Kent and Sussex
    (Collins, new edn 1989)
Warden Swinfen & David Arscott Hidden Sussex;
    People of Hidden Sussex; Hidden Sussex Day by
    Day; Hidden Sussex – the Towns (BBC Radio
    Sussex, 1984–90)
Rupert Taylor The East Sussex Village Book
    (Countryside Books, 1990)
John E. Vigar Exploring Sussex Churches
    (Meresborough Books, 1986)

British Library Cataloguing in Publication Data

Spence, Keith
 East Sussex. – (Philip's County Guides)
I. Title II. Series
914.22504

ISBN 0–540–01268–8

Text and maps © George Philip 1993
Pictures © John Bethell
Series Editor: Theresa Wright
Design: Peter Burt
Page design: Jessica Caws

First published by George Philip Limited, Michelin
House, 81 Fulham Road, London SW3 6RB.

Mapping based upon Ordnance Survey maps with
the permission of the Controller of Her Majesty's
Stationery Office
© Crown copyright

Printed in Hong Kong

CONTENTS

INTRODUCTION

Sussex was a county single and indivisible for many centuries – at least since the 8th century, when it was called *Suth Seaxe*, 'the land of the South Saxons'. This unity was sundered into East and West Sussex, by the simple expedient of drawing a line across it from north to south, following a bureaucratic decision of the 1960s. All the same, there are differences between the two halves. East Sussex has the lion's share of the seaside resorts, from Brighton and Hove, through Eastbourne and Bexhill, to Hastings. West Sussex has the cathedral city of Chichester; but as compensation East Sussex can offer the magnificent and breezy town of Lewes, not to mention Rye, perched on its hill – a little town for which the word 'picturesque' might well have been coined.

The two halves have a subtly different social feel about them. West Sussex is a county of large estates and still keeps a faint whiff of feudalism. Further from London, it is less a county of commuter-based towns and villages. Opera at Glyndebourne in East Sussex, polo at Cowdray in West Sussex – these very different pursuits symbolize the differences between them. In addition, West Sussex is more heavily wooded and has no area of wilderness to compare with the bleak expanse of Ashdown Forest. The underlying geology is also different. East Sussex has far less chalk downland than West Sussex, but much more iron-rich sandstone.

EARLY HISTORY
Historically speaking, it is nonsense to talk of East and West Sussex as though they were two separate counties; but an introduction to a book on one of the halves must make the attempt.

Prehistoric Sussex goes back to the Palaeolithic period, about 400,000 years ago, though few human remains have been found from this period. The most notorious is the fragment of an ancient skull unearthed at Piltdown in 1908, which formed the basis for the elaborate archaeological hoax known ever since as 'Piltdown Man'. Widespread human settlement began around 3000 BC, as Neolithic peoples colonized the chalk downs – at that time the only feasible route for crossing Southern England from east to west, as the valleys to the north were choked by the impenetrable forest of the Weald.

Neolithic immigrants from Europe, followed a few centuries later by Bronze Age peoples, arrived about 2000 BC, leaving behind the burial mounds which are being steadily diminished in number as today's farmers deep-plough more and more of the chalk downland. Most of these remains are concentrated in West Sussex, as are the Iron-Age hill-forts, though East Sussex has Mount Caburn, outside Lewes. The lanky, chalk-cut figure of the Long Man at Wilmington is said by some authorities to date from the Bronze Age, though its date is disputed.

Turning to Roman remains, East Sussex has nothing to compare with the splendid palace at Fishbourne outside Chichester, or with the fine Roman villa at Bignor. Here the Romans' main contribution was the fortress at Pevensey, whose outer walls, built with rock-hard mortar bonded with tiles, have lasted for 1700 years. Inland, around Ashdown Forest, they mined and smelted iron, using slag from the workings as hardcore for their roads.

SAXONS AND NORMANS

The first definite date in East Sussex history is AD 490, when the Saxons attacked Andredscaster ('Anderida' was the Roman name for Pevensey) and butchered its defenders. From then on East Sussex enters the Dark Ages, which were darker than they were in much of the rest of England. Sussex lay between dense woodland to the north and a hostile sea to the south, and had little to recommend it during several centuries of internal turbulence and sea-raids – first by Saxons and later by Danes.

However, it was during this period that Sussex was converted to Christianity, which radiated through the county from Selsey in West Sussex (where St Wilfrid had arrived in 681 to convert the South Saxons). The earliest Saxon churches were no doubt temporary and flimsy wooden structures, liable to be burnt down by the Danes on their hit-and-run raids. From late in the Saxon period, parts of a few churches survive in West Sussex; in East Sussex, the most noteworthy Saxon relic is an 8th-century carved stone in Old Bexhill church.

The main legacy of the Saxons was administrative. They divided the county into territorial units known as 'hundreds', possibly because it contained a hundred families, or could contribute a hundred men-at-arms in time of war. Old Bexhill church contains a copy of a charter dating from 772, signed by King Offa of Mercia and detailing grants of land connected with the church's foundation in that year.

East Sussex was the setting for the epoch-making events of 1066, possibly the most famous date in English history. Duke William landed his troops at Pevensey, marched them inland from Hastings to the place now called Battle, and defeated Harold of England there. The Hastings hinterland formed the bridgehead from which his Normans marched north to conquer the whole country.

This stretch of coast might seem an unpromising place for an invasion but in the 11th century the East Sussex coastline was very different from what it is today. Pevensey Castle was right on the coast, instead of a mile inland as it is now, and dominated a flat expanse of tidal marsh, now the wide area of reclaimed agricultural land known as Pevensey Levels. Further to the east, Hastings had a harbour on the River Bourne, blocked with shingle centuries ago, while William's bridgehead was protected by three rivers (the Brede, Tillingham and Rother). Nowadays these are hardly more than placid streams, but in Norman times they were tidal rivers, meeting to form a wide estuary at Rye.

CASTLES, ABBEYS AND CHURCHES

Like the Saxons before them, the Normans imposed their own territorial organization on Sussex. Duke William divided the county into five north–south divisions known as 'rapes', each controlled by a powerful baron and running inland from a port fortified with a castle. This was at first a simple wooden stockade on an artificial earth mound (the 'motte and bailey'), soon superseded by the typical medieval castle with its stone keep and curtain wall. Three of these rapes are located in East Sussex – Lewes, Pevensey and Hastings. The castles at Lewes and Pevensey still give an idea of their medieval grandeur although that at Hastings was largely destroyed in the 13th century, when the promontory on which its stands was washed away by the sea.

Apart from these three great castles, by far the most impressive of the Normans' major buildings was the magnificent Benedictine Battle Abbey, begun soon after the Conquest and still well-preserved. (The Cluniac priory at Lewes is said to have been equally splendid, but only fragments of it now remain.) Along with these major foundations went a number of lesser abbeys, among them Robertsbridge, founded by the Cistercians in 1176, Michelham Priory and Bayham, the most beautiful of East Sussex ruins, in a tranquil setting by the River Teise.

The Normans devoted a vast amount of time and resources to building ordinary parish churches, nearly all of which were enlarged as the Middle Ages proceeded. These were neglected from Tudor times until the 19th century, then grossly mishandled and reshaped by the Victorians. Especially interesting is a group of three round-towered churches – St Michael's in the centre of Lewes and the village churches of Southease and Piddinghoe in the Ouse valley near by.

In Winchelsea, East Sussex has a very early example of a new town planned from scratch, as it was laid out after a great storm destroyed the old town in 1288. Its church is still a marvel, but less than half of the building that once stood there remains as it suffered constant French attacks along with the rest of the town in the following century. Winchelsea, like neighbouring Rye, was an 'Ancient Town', equal in status to the Cinque Ports and similarly responsible for providing ships for the navy. Both towns still have plenty of medieval remains, though Winchelsea has the feeling of a ghost town in comparison with the tourist bustle of Rye.

Among later medieval buildings, the finest survival is Bodiam Castle, whose stone outer walls still rise to their full height, reflected in the waters of a broad moat. Bodiam dates from the late 14th century and is the final flowering of the pre-artillery castle. Half a century later the giant Herstmonceux Castle was built of brick and still intended for defence although its walls would have quickly crumbled under bombardment from cannon balls.

From Henry VIII's time comes Camber Castle, standing low and squat among the grassy levels below Winchelsea. When built, it had some strategic significance, but the build-up of shingle has left it stranded far inland. Like the Martello towers of Napoleonic times, found dotted along the East Sussex coast from Eastbourne's Wish Tower round to Rye Harbour, it never had to prove itself against an enemy, and was soon abandoned.

NEW PROSPERITY

The invention of cannon, and the need for enormous quantities of iron, led to a great increase in prosperity in Tudor times. The old Roman iron-workings were reopened and new ones started. Streams were dammed to form hammer-ponds, whose water turned the water-wheels that provided power for huge drop-hammers. Forges worked day and night to turn out guns for the ships of Henry VIII and his successors. Tiny villages like Penhurst, remote and rural today, resounded with the clang of hammer on iron, while the night sky glowed with the fires of hundreds of furnaces.

This industry lasted well into the 19th century – the only time East Sussex has ever had any real industrial production. It left behind fine houses built by the ironmasters, like the half-timbered Hogge House at Buxted, whose builder was supposedly the first man to cast cannon in England.

Although East Sussex has any amount of minor half-timbered houses, followed in the 17th and 18th centuries by weather-boarding and brick-work, it cannot boast of many major country houses. The most substantial of them is Firle Place, tucked away below the downs – an unusual example of a Tudor house clad in a classical 18th-century skin. Glynde Place is a grand Elizabethan house. The village of Northiam has two fine old half-timbered houses – Great Dixter, basically a 15th-century hall house with later additions, and the 17th-century Brickwall.

THE COAST

In the middle of the 18th century came the discovery that the seaside was not just a place for the hard work of boat-building and catching fish. It could be made into a pleasure-ground for jaded city-dwellers to splash around in salt water or drink it as a tonic, to breathe in the sea air, and to gamble, dance and generally enjoy themselves. First came Brighton, then Hastings, followed by Eastbourne and Bexhill – until now, with a further century of infilling by bungalows and caravan sites, there is hardly a mile of coast unbuilt-on from Hove round to Camber Sands.

Seaside mania began around 1750, but it was not until Brighton was popularized by the Prince Regent, thirty years later, that the coast really took off. With the bizarre mock-Orientalism of the Prince's Royal Pavilion as its centrepiece, Brighton grew from a small fishing village into a town of spacious squares, laid out by the leading architects of the day. The bow windows of tall town houses, as dignified as any in London, looked out to sea and caught the sun

9

throughout the day while their occupants sipped sea-water, floundered into the sea from huts on wheels known as 'bathing machines', or gossiped at the lending library or assembly rooms.

By about 1800, the old Cinque Port of Hastings had followed Brighton down the holiday road; Eastbourne and Bexhill developed later, laid out by aristocratic landowners (the Cavendishes and De La Warrs respectively) in Victoria's reign. Opulent hotels, like the Grand and Metropole in Brighton and the Grand in Eastbourne, catered for wealthy visitors who came down from London by the newly-built railways. A host of smaller hotels and boarding-houses coped with the thousands of less well-off holidaymakers, bringing their families on a hard-earned bucket-and-spade seaside holiday.

At the same time the permanent populations went up by leaps and bounds. Brighton, for example, had about 7000 inhabitants in 1800, which by the end of the century had climbed to 100,000, and is now about a quarter of a million.

The seaside resorts are still the only substantial towns in East Sussex. Brighton and Hove now form a major conurbation, with their tide of building lapping up the south slope of the downs and only prevented from swirling down the other side by tight planning controls. Eastbourne extends as far inland as Polegate, while Bexhill and Hastings are linked by housing along the A259. The only substantial stretch of coastline left as countryside are the cliffs of Seaford Head, the Seven Sisters and Beachy Head – which run for 7 miles or so, cut only by the lazy meanders of the Cuckmere River, which slices through the chalk to meet the sea at Cuckmere Haven.

Fortunately for East Sussex, this fine coastal strip is now safeguarded for the future, with much of it forming the Seven Sisters Country Park. The park centres on the graceful, chalk folds of the Seven Sisters themselves, which feature in every 'Beautiful Sussex' type of calendar. Hastings has its own Country Park: a good deal smaller but more varied with its sandstone cliffs and ravines filled with trees, flowers and birdsong. Further east again, the Rye Harbour Nature Reserve covers a wide expanse of grass-covered shingle, and is a paradise for bird-watchers.

LANDSCAPE AND GARDEN

Walkers who love the wide-open spaces can have their fill of far-ranging views from the South Downs Way, a long-distance bridleway that runs for almost 100 miles from Eastbourne to Winchester, about a quarter of it in East Sussex. Its high points are Ditchling Beacon, behind Brighton, and Firle Beacon, inland from Newhaven. On the way, it takes in some of the finest chalk downland in the whole of Sussex, passing ancient burial mounds and clumps of trees planted as eye-catchers by 18th-century landowners.

Inland, the largest open space is the 14,000-acre Ashdown Forest, a high, wide tract of sandy heathland, criss-crossed by rides and footpaths and dotted with clumps of tall Scots pines. Though the cantankerous William Cobbett, writing in the 1820s, called it 'the most villainously ugly spot in England', the thousands of walkers and riders who flock there on fine weekends would certainly not agree with him. Lovers of watery pursuits, such as dinghy-sailing and fishing, can give full rein to their enthusiasms on Bewl Water reservoir, the largest man-made sheet of water in the whole of Sussex.

East Sussex has any number of fine gardens, many of them open to the public. The most extensive of them is Sheffield Park, laid out by Lancelot 'Capability' Brown in the 18th century and greatly extended in the early 1900s. It is now a superb arboretum, where trees from all round the world are reflected in tranquil lakes.

Sheffield Park is also the East Sussex terminus of the Bluebell Line, whose trains, pulled by steam-engines rescued from the scrapyard, potter for a few miles through the countryside to Horsted Keynes. On the other side of the county, the Kent and East Sussex Railway, formerly the hop-pickers' line, runs mainly in Kent, although it has a newly restored station at Northiam, and there are plans to revive it at least as far as Bodiam.

Museums are legion, and cover everything: vintage cars (Bentley, uniquely combined with a wildfowl sanctuary), art-nouveau furniture (Brighton), archaeology (Barbican House, Lewes), costume (Bexhill), and re-creations of the past such as the smuggling tableaux in St Clement's Caves, Hastings, and the Victorian shop interiors of Buckley's Yesterday's World, Battle.

ARTISTS IN EAST SUSSEX

The natural beauty of East Sussex has inspired writers and artists down the years to live there. Prominent among them was Rudyard Kipling, who lived in Rottingdean from 1897 to 1902, before moving inland to Bateman's, an old ironmaster's house near Burwash where he lived for the last thirty years of his life. The artist Burne–Jones, related to Kipling by marriage, also lived in Rottingdean.

There could hardly be a greater contrast with the extrovert Kipling than the tormented writer Virginia Woolf. She lived in the small Monk's House in Rodmell for more than twenty years until her suicide by drowning in 1941. Her sister, the artist Vanessa Bell, lived at Charleston Farmhouse, not far from Rodmell, and turned it into a country outpost of the 'Bloomsbury Group' of between-the-wars intellectuals. Berwick church near by is decorated with wall-paintings by Vanessa Bell and her lover, Duncan Grant painted during World War II and something of a curiosity in the world of church decoration.

Rye was the birthplace in 1579 of the playwright John Fletcher, and was the chosen retreat of the American-born novelist Henry James, who lived in Lamb House, the town's grandest Georgian mansion, in the years round 1900. E. F. Benson, author of the *Mapp and Lucia* stories set in and around Rye, was mayor of the town in the 1930s and also lived in Lamb House. Ashdown Forest entered the world of children's classics in the *Winnie-the-Pooh* books of A. A. Milne. Milne lived in the heart of the forest, and all Pooh's adventures were set there. At the opposite literary pole, the great 18th-century historian Edward Gibbon wrote much of his *Decline and Fall of the Roman Empire* while staying at Sheffield Park.

The first of the great artists to visit East Sussex was Van Dyck. He drew Rye as it was in his day, almost surrounded by water. In the 19th century, Sir John Millais used Rye's sister town, Winchelsea, as the backdrop to his open-air portrait *The Blind Girl*, and also used the interior of Winchelsea church as the setting for several of his pictures. Many recent artists, such as Graham Sutherland, Paul Nash and John Piper, have found inspiration in Rye and the country round about.

Among the composers, Debussy stayed at Eastbourne's Grand Hotel while writing his seascape *La Mer,* and Dvořák swam from the beach near Brighton's West Pier. Frank Bridge, a composer far less-known than his star pupil, Benjamin Britten, was born in Brighton, lived in Friston, and died in Eastbourne. But East Sussex's most famous contribution to the world of music is a place, not a person. The country mansion of Glyndebourne, below the downs, is where John Christie built himself an opera house and in 1934 began the annual summer opera seasons which continue to this day.

It would be futile to attempt any prophecy as to the future of East Sussex. By now the coast is as built up as it is ever likely to be, and inland the impetus to build on fields dotted around the countryside has died, because of the stagnation in new house-building projects. Due to the E.C. grain and meat mountains, farmers have been largely relieved of the pressure to produce as much food as possible from their land. The more enlightened among them may even stop grubbing up their hedges, or ploughing up untouched downland, and the encouragement of 'set-aside' land may encourage them to devote more of their acres to wildlife and general conservation.

Like the housing programme, road-building has almost ground to a halt, with most main roads, like the appalling A21 to Hastings, virtually unchanged over the past 40 years and now totally inadequate for today's heavy traffic. However, a few towns such as Uckfield and Robertsbridge have been relieved from congestion by recent bypasses.

For the foreseeable future, the outlook seems to be 'little change'. This is perhaps just as well, as the fragile beauty of East Sussex is in danger of vanishing without trace, unless the 21st century shows more restraint and common sense than the 20th century has so far done.

KEITH SPENCE
1992

LISTINGS & SYMBOLS

LISTINGS

The A–Z of Towns & Villages lists all settlements as well as some other places (e.g. Beachy Head, the South Downs Way) which do not fall into the categories covered by the Days Out listings.

Cross references to entries in the A–Z are given in SMALL CAPITALS. Cross references to the Days Out section are given in the form 'see p. ...'. A note at the end of some of the Days Out listings will direct you to other places of interest which appear in the A–Z. **Bold type** is used to highlight important buildings or other features, but does not imply that they are open, or even accessible, to the public.

Details of access and telephone numbers have been provided wherever possible. While every effort has been made to ensure these are up to date, they are subject to change. If you are planning a special trip to visit one of the places listed, it is best to check with the local tourist office in advance.

All information in this guide is believed to be correct at time of going to press. However, the publishers will welcome any comments or suggestions for improvements, which can be incorporated into any further edition.

STAR RATINGS

All entries, and sub-entries within the A–Z, have been rated from 0–3 stars as follows:

★★★	major attraction
★★	general interest
★	local or specialist interest

SYMBOLS

Days Out		A–Z of Towns & Villages	
⊕£	Admission fee	⋔	Church
☞	Refreshments	⛫	Castle
Ⓢ	Shop	⚑	Historic building
✗	Guided tours	🏛	Museum
⚲	Disabled access	Ⓜ	Monument
₤	Mother and baby facilities	〰	Viewpoint
✗	No dogs	♣	Park or open space
ⓘ	Information centre	≋	Pond, river or lake
		⚲	Pub or inn
		ⓘ	Information centre

HISTORIC HOUSES

ASHBURNHAM PLACE * *
Map p.146, B1
5 miles W of Battle; entrance gates on the B2204

Now owned and run by an interdenominational Christian trust, Ashburnham consists of a complex of buildings of all periods, from a medieval parish church to modern residential and conference accommodation. They stand in a magnificent 200-acre park, laid out by Lancelot 'Capability' Brown in the mid 18th century.

Centrepiece of the buildings is a red-brick house set above a wide grass terrace, and looking across a pair of lakes to a glorious sweep of trees on the hillside opposite. This curious-looking building, consisting of a central two-storey section with a single-storey wing on either side, is all that is left of the once-vast mansion of the Ashburnhams, built in the 17th century and cut down from three storeys to its present size in 1959.

St Peter's Church, behind the house, is still in use, though there are no longer any villagers in Ashburnham. The Ashburnhams made their money from iron (see PENHURST), and the church is full of splendid grilles, presumably made locally. In the chapel leading off the chancel are two huge monuments to 17th-century Ashburnham brothers – John, who rebuilt the church in the 1660s, and William – both of whom were court officials to Charles I and II.

Though the park suffered greatly in the 1987 hurricane, it still has plenty of magnificent old trees, among them the giant cedars guarding the stone bridge below the house. In summer the lakes are covered in waterlilies and fringed by yellow-flowered irises, while the waterbirds to be seen there include Canada geese, moorhens, mallard, and even the occasional cormorant.
Visits by prior arrangement. Tel (0424) 892244.

BATEMAN'S * *
Map p.150, C3
³/₄ mile SW of Burwash off the A265

£ ☕ Ⓢ

Bateman's is the house Rudyard Kipling lived in from 1902 until his death in 1936. The house was built in 1634 by John Brittan, a wealthy ironmaster and, appropriately, the stone has rusted in parts where iron ore runs through it. The stone house, though once symmetrical, no longer has its right wing. Its windows are mullioned and the chimney stacks are brick.

Inside, the Jacobean panelled house is much as it was when Kipling and his family lived in it. He moved here at the age of 37 when he was at the height of his fame. One can step into the study where he wrote *Puck of Pook's Hill, Rewards and Fairies* and the *Sussex Poems*, and see his ink-wells and pipe-cleaners lying on the table. Kipling's diminutive stature is illustrated by his chair which is supported on blocks. Other mementoes include portraits of Kipling and a set of terracotta plaques carved by his father, Lockwood, which were used to illustrate Kim.

The lovely gardens slope down to the banks of the River Dudwell where Kipling installed a water-mill to generate electricity. The mill, which contains the oldest water-turbine in Britain, was restored by the Sussex Industrial Archaeology Study Group and now grinds flour which is sold in the National Trust shop at Bateman's.
Good Friday and April–Oct, Sat–Weds 11am–5.30pm Tel: (0435) 882302

BUXTED PARK
Map p.149, C2
2 miles E of Maresfield on the A272

Ⓢ

Buxted Park is an elegant country-house hotel, conference centre and health club situated in beautiful gardens with deer

---

Bateman's, near Burwash. This fine Jacobean house was Kipling's home from 1902 till 1936.

HOUSE
&
GARDEN
OPEN
1100-530
EXCEPT Thur & Fri

ENTRANCE

park and lakes. Until the hurricane of October 1987, the park was renowned for its ancient trees and avenue of limes, but the storm had a particularly devastating effect here. The original house was demolished in the early 18th century and a lake dug on its site. The present house was completed in 1725.

Buxted's owner from 1931 was architect Basil Ionides. He rebuilt much of the house after it was damaged by fire in 1940 and incorporated elements from other houses which were being demolished or which had been bombed in World War II. Examples of additions from elsewhere include the front door and a chimney piece from Clumber, Nottinghamshire, the 18th-century staircase from 30 Old Burlington Street, London, a fireplace from Queensberry House, Richmond, and architectural elements from houses in Essex and Buckinghamshire.

Since Ionides' death in 1950, the house has had several owners including the President of the United Arab Emirates. It is now available for recreational purposes including clay-pigeon shooting, hot-air ballooning or fishing, and can be hired for weddings and other social events. *Tel: (0825) 812711*

CHARLESTON FARMHOUSE * * *
Map p.144, B2
6 miles E of Lewes; near Firle, on the A27

Approached from the main road on a narrow track, Charleston lies below Firle Beacon on the South Downs and dates from the 18th century. From 1916 it was the home of the remarkable 'Bloomsbury Group' of artists, which included Duncan Grant, Vanessa and Clive Bell and their family. Eminent visitors to the farmhouse included John Maynard Keynes, Giles Lytton Strachey, T. S. Eliot and Leonard and Virginia Woolf.

The house is profusely decorated with wall-paintings, stencils, painted furniture, textiles, ceramics and other artefacts from the prolific group of artists who made this their home, and whose collection of books, furnishings and works of art remains untouched. Maynard Keynes wrote his

Economic Consequences of the Peace in 1919 while a visitor, and his bedroom may be seen on the first floor. The group of artists were commissioned in 1940 to paint the murals at nearby Berwick Church, whose opening hours are timed to coincide with those of Charleston.

Particularly evocative are the Studio, added in 1925, containing many of Duncan Grant's paintings and memorabilia, and Vanessa Bell's bedroom, a former dairy with her bath concealed by a folding screen.

To the rear of the farmhouse is a walled garden, in the English cottage style, with shrub roses and a pond. Mosaics and sculptures near by decorate the area. Occasional art exhibitions by contemporary artists are staged at the house. *April–Oct, Wed, Thurs and Sat 2–6pm, only with guided tours; Suns and BHs unguided, 2–6pm. Kitchen open Thurs only. Tel: (0323) 811265*

FILCHING MANOR AND MOTOR MUSEUM * *
Map p.144, C4
4 miles NW of Eastbourne off the A22

The timber-framed 15th-century manor house is also, surprisingly, the home of the K3 Blue Bird hydroplane in which Sir Malcolm Campbell set the world water-speed record in 1937 and 1938.

The 'Campbell Memorial Hall of Speed' houses a collection of relics and memorabilia associated with the Blue Birds and Malcolm and Donald Campbell, including the K7 Vickers Beryl turbo-jet engine which helped set seven world water-speed records in the 1950s. Model, vintage and veteran cars (including Bugattis, a 1931 Alfa Romeo and a 1904 Peugeot), similar types of motor-cycles, and personal effects are also exhibited.

Part of the manor house is open to the public and contains furnishings, armour and antiques. It is a fine example of mid 15th-century architecture, with a large hall open to the roof, solar and minstrel's gallery.

Formal and woodland gardens surround the house. A path leads through the gardens to the sheds above the house where the K3 Blue Bird hydroplane is kept. As the only surviving Blue Bird boat, it is undergoing gradual restoration work after over 55 years

of inactivity. Speed racing of a different kind takes place in the nearby chalk-pit which has been converted into a karting track.
Easter–Oct, phone for opening times.
Tel: (0323) 487838

FIRLE PLACE ✳ ✳ ✳
Map p.144, B1
4¹/₂ miles SE of Lewes off the A27

🅰

Firle Place, close to the village of West Firle and originally built around 1475, has been the home of the Gage family since Tudor times. Though the heart of the house dates from that period, the exterior was largely remodelled in Caen stone during the Georgian period.

Several of the family have held responsible positions in their time, including Sir John Gage, a commissioner for the dissolution of the monasteries under Henry VIII, Sir Edward Gage, Sherriff of Sussex at the time of the Lewes martyrs, and General Thomas Gage, Governor of Massachusetts and commander-in-chief of the British forces in America at the time of the American War of Independence in 1775. The family was also responsible for introducing greengages to Britain around 1725.

Inside, the house is a treasure trove of fine art and furniture, housing part of the celebrated Cowper Collection with paintings by Reynolds, Van Dyck, Bartolommeo, Corregio and Guardi among others, Sèvres porcelain and French furniture of the Louis-Quinze and Louis-Seize periods.

The deer park in which the house stands was carefully landscaped in the 18th century in the style of Lancelot 'Capability' Brown. Dotted with trees, it boasts an ornamental lake and a castellated tower built in 1819 as accommodation for the estate's gamekeeper.
Easter–Sept, Weds, Thurs, Sun and BH Mons 2–5pm. Tel: (0273) 858335

GLYNDEBOURNE ✳ ✳
Map p.143, C4
1 mile S of Ringmer off the B2192

'Well, that's that!' was how Sir George Christie brought the curtain down on the 1992 opera season at Glyndebourne Opera House. The next day, bulldozers demolished

the theatre to make way for a new one.

In the grounds of a stately Tudor manor house, set in downland countryside between Ringmer and Glynde, the opera house was built by John Christie, a former Eton science master whose family had owned Glyndebourne since 1617. Blending in well with its surroundings and with seating for 300 people, it opened on 28 May 1934, giving six performances in two weeks of both *Le nozze di Figaro* and *Così fan tutte*.

Despite uncomfortable seating and poor acoustics, Glyndebourne quickly gained a reputation on a par with national institutions such as Wimbledon, Ascot and Henley, and has attracted many international artistes. Part of the enjoyment for the audiences, who are obliged to wear evening dress, are the champagne picnics held on the lawns during the long intervals. The house itself is not open to the public and the grounds are only open to opera-goers.

The ambitious new opera house of brick and concrete, with seating for 1150 people, is due to re-open on May 28th 1994, on the 60th anniversary of the original opening, with a performance of *Le nozze di Figaro*.
May–Aug, days and times vary.
Tel: (0273) 812321.

GREAT DIXTER ✳ ✳ ✳
Map p.152, C1
8 miles W of Rye off the A28

🅰 Ⓢ 𝑘 ✖

This superb 15th-century timber-framed hall house is unusual in that it stands in an equally superb garden, integrated with the house by more than 80 years of dedicated restoration and planting. The huge barns to one side of it and the large horse pond beside the approach road still give it something of the look of a traditional East Sussex farm.

Built on top of a hill on the fringe of the village of NORTHIAM, it has wide views northward across the Rother valley. It was largely created by the architectural writer Nathaniel Lloyd, who bought the near-derelict house in 1910. Lloyd was a close friend of the architect Edwin Lutyens, and during the following years the two worked closely on the house, adding a tile-hung extension at the side, and finally incorporating a complete yeoman's hall brought timber by timber from Benenden in Kent, eight miles away. The Lloyd family still lives there.

Great Dixter's magnificent hall, built about 1460, is over 40ft long and open to the rafters, which soar 30ft above the floor. The huge central tie-beam supports a massive king-post, and the hammer-beams are carved with the arms of the Echyngham family, who built the house. Upstairs is the long and comfortable solarium, with a small window looking down into the hall. It is full of old furniture, from an antique gaming-table to a 17th-century spinet, still playable, and contains small treasures like the painted glass panel by Dürer, signed and dated 1518.

The garden, presided over by the gardening writer Christopher Lloyd, was largely laid out by Lutyens. It consists of a series of outdoor 'rooms' leading into one another and crammed with carefully planted flower-beds. The elaborate topiary yew is clipped into peacocks, coffee-pots and other complex shapes. With its subtle changes of level, and variety of terraces and lawns separated by high hedges, it is a garden of constant surprises, and seems far larger than its actual size.
Apr–early Oct, Tues–Sat and BH Mons 2–5pm Tel: (0797) 253160

HAMMERWOOD PARK * *
Map p.154, C2
3 miles E of East Grinstead on the A264

The lane to Hammerwood Park is long and pot-holed. It passes some lovely old houses including the half-timbered Bower House and Bower House Cottage. The countryside opens out to rolling sheep-clad hills which provide a beautiful backdrop to the house, a large stone Georgian stately home designed in classical style by Benjamin Latrobe. It was built in 1792, just before he emigrated to America where he became one of the country's most famous architects, responsible for the Capitol and the White House in Washington D.C., and Baltimore Cathedral.

Its classical feel is enhanced by the Doric columns of the attached pavilions which look like small Greek temples. The present owners bought the Grade I listed building in 1982 as a ruin, and have spent a decade restoring it. The place has a delightful air of decaying gentility, and houses family collections including musical instruments and photography, and a replica of the Elgin Marbles which adorns the Tea Room.

A visit includes a fully guided tour, conducted by the family, and a video showing the restoration of the property. A break is taken in the middle of the tour when you are served a delicious cream tea. A guidebook has just been produced of which the owners guarantee, 'If you can put it down without getting engrossed, you can have your money back.' Monthly concerts take place in the library.

There is no village at Hammerwood, but St Stephen's Church, right beside the main road and with sweeping views south, is a very pretty Victorian building in golden stone with tower and spire.
Easter Mon–end Sept, Weds, Sat and BH Mons 2–5.30pm. Tel: (0342) 850594

MICHELHAM PRIORY * * *
Map p.144, A4
Near Upper Dicker, 1 mile off the A22

This outstanding group of monastic buildings, centred on the 13th–century moated Augustinian priory, has been the showpiece of the Sussex Archaeological Society since 1959. Founded in 1229 by Gilbert de l'Aigle ('the eagle'), the priory was dissolved in 1537, later becoming a farmhouse owned by the Sackville family, before being restored earlier this century.

Entered via the 14th–century gatehouse, faced in Eastbourne greensand and housing artists' studios upstairs, the visitor passes the dovecote and the outlines on the lawns of the cloisters, nave and choir of the original church. The main house, which has changing exhibitions of historical interest, has a fine vaulted undercroft, a medieval refectory with a large beamed inglenook fireplace and a Tudor wing with a collection of 17th- and 18th-century furnishings. Further displays include an 18th-century child's room, a collection of musical instruments and the Prior's Chamber on the first floor.

In the grounds, the large moat and stew pond (for keeping the monks' fish) are fed by the River Cuckmere and the restored Physic Garden contains some 100 plants originally used for medicinal purposes.

The 16th-century great barn of oak and elm, now tiled but originally thatched, is in the adjacent courtyard; it has a pair of wagon ways, larger on the north side to allow access for loaded carts. Also in the courtyard are the forge, the Wheelwrights' Museum, a museum of ropemaking (a traditional craft in the Hailsham area), a restaurant and a bakery. Near the car-park is a working water-mill of 13th-century origin, powered by water from the moat. *Late Mar–end Oct, daily 11am–5.30pm; Feb, Mar and Nov, Suns only 11am–4pm. Tel: (0323) 844224*

MONK'S HOUSE, RODMELL **
Map p.143, D3
3 miles S of Lewes off the A27

A small early 18th-century farmhouse in the middle of Rodmell, Monk's House became the second of two Sussex outposts of the Bloomsbury Set (the first was Charleston Farmhouse, p.16) when the writer Virginia Woolf bought the property with her husband Leonard in 1919. Virginia often wrote in glowing terms about the place. Their frequent visitors included many well-known artists and writers of the day such as Roger Fry, John Maynard Keynes, T. S. Eliot, Vanessa Bell (Virginia's sister) and Duncan Grant.

The Woolfs spent much time there, Virginia writing in the garden lodge, Leonard spending his time gardening. Tragically, the idyll came to an end in March 1941 when Virginia, who was prone to worry and depression, walked down the lane and drowned herself in the River Ouse.

Leonard continued to live at Monks House until his death in 1969 when it became the property of the National Trust. Some of the couple's personal items and furniture, much of it decorated by Vanessa Bell and Duncan Grant, can be seen in the ground floor rooms and there are a large number of Vanessa's paintings on the walls.

The garden, looking out on the church and divided into walled areas with ponds, statues and an orchard, is a mass of hollyhocks, dahlias and hydrangeas in summer, and contains busts of the Woolfs. *Apr–Oct, Weds and Sat 2–5.30pm. Tel: (0892) 890651.*

See also: ALFRISTON, The Clergy House; BRIGHTON, Royal Pavilion, Preston Manor; GLYNDE Place; NORTHIAM, Brickwall; RYE, Lamb House; WILMINGTON Priory.

CASTLES & ABBEYS

BATTLE ABBEY * * *
Map p.146, B2
6 miles NW of Hastings on the A2100

♿ Ⓢ ♿ ✈

On October 14, 1066 – perhaps the most crucial day in English history – the Normans under Duke William defeated the Saxons under King Harold of England, on a sloping site a few miles inland from the seaport of Hastings. It was on the ridge overlooking the battlefield that the Saxons took up their defensive position, and it was here that William built the great Benedictine Abbey of St Martin, to atone for the slaughter that had taken place.

The abbey (English Heritage) was begun a few years after the Norman Conquest, but little survives of the original foundation. The outline of the first Norman church, which had an apsidal east end with three radiating chapels, is marked out in the turf. The high altar stood on the spot where Harold was killed. The magnificent gatehouse, looming over the little town of Battle and closing the vista at the southern end of the High Street, dates from about 1338.

At least as impressive as the gatehouse are the remains of the 13th-century monks' dorter (dormitory), built over a beautifully vaulted series of common rooms. The undercroft parallel to the ridge, with its pair of towers, was built in Tudor times by Sir Anthony Browne, who was granted the abbey by Henry VIII. A panoramic model in one of the cellars, fitted out with hundreds of tiny soldiers, shows the opposing forces drawn up ready for battle.

The abbot's great hall, with its magnificent timbered ceiling, now forms part of a girls' school, but is open during the school summer holidays.

The course of the battle can be followed *in situ* from a signposted walk of about 1 mile round the battlefield, and is explained on plans placed at regular intervals.

Several of the gatehouse rooms were opened for the first time in 1992 and have been turned into a fascinating museum on the abbey's history. It has such hi-tech features as a 'Monastic Life Computer Station', with short videos on every aspect of life in a monastery.
Apr–Sept, daily 10am–6pm; Oct–March, daily 10am–4pm. Tel: (0424) 63792.

BAYHAM ABBEY * * *
Map p.155, D4
4 miles E of Tunbridge Wells off the B2169 Lamberhurst road

♿ ♿

Bayham Abbey is situated in a beautiful position in the valley of the River Teise, a tributary of the Medway famous for its trout. It is a ruined monastery which dates from the very early 13th century. Its grassy cloisters and substantial stone ruins give a good idea of the imposing complex which once stood here. Bayham was one of the early victims of the Dissolution, when Cardinal Wolsey stripped its assets to finance colleges at Oxford and Ipswich. Its pretty gatehouse survived to form an integral part of a romantic vista created by influential landscape designer Humphrey Repton in 1800.

Some of the stone carving is remarkably well preserved, particularly the gatehouse arch and faces on the corbels of what remains of the huge church. The aisles are carpeted with grass, while in the chancel the roots of a massive beech tree curl around the old stones. The north transept still has its dramatic vaulting although the south transept is fairly ruined.

The abbey is just on the Sussex side of the Kent/Sussex border. Up the hill on the Kent side, facing the ruins, is the present Bayham Abbey, not an abbey at all but a large Victorian stone mansion.
Good Friday or 1 April (whichever is earlier)– end Sept, daily 10am–6pm. Tel. (0892) 8900381.

The ruins of the thirteenth-century Bayham Abbey, near Tunbridge Wells.

BODIAM CASTLE * * *
Map p.151, B4
10 miles N of Hastings off the A21

⊞ ➡ Ⓢ ♿ ✈ *(castle)*

This superb National Trust-owned castle is set in the quiet valley of the River Rother, surrounded by a moat full of ducks and moorhens. It is everyone's idea of the perfect medieval fortress. With its round corner towers, square-cut gatehouse and powerful walls, it still looks strong enough to stand up to a prolonged siege – though, fortunately perhaps, its defences were never put to the test.

It was built by Sir Edward Dalyngrige in 1385, soon after the French had burned Rye and Winchelsea, when there were fears that a French fleet might sail up the River Rother, then fully navigable, and attack far inland. A model in the small museum near the castle entrance gives an idea of what it looked like in the days when it was fully armed and ready for action. Bodiam was one of the last medieval castles to be built, as by the 1380s the development of artillery had made them largely obsolete.

The entrance is through the great north gatehouse, carved with the shields of Sir Edward and other notables. Inside it is far better preserved than most medieval castles, with buildings round all four sides, among them the garrison kitchen, the chapel and the great hall. In one of the towers you can see a film of the different aspects of castle life, from dancing and music to the pageant of the tournament. In the base of another tower is a replica of the 'Bodiam bombard', found in the moat; this fearsome piece of artillery fired stone shot weighing 160lb and is similar to those used in 1346 at the Battle of Crécy.

The flat space south of the castle (now a car-park) is thought to have been the tilt-yard where tournaments were held.

The castle was 'slighted' or dismantled by the Roundheads during the Civil War, and later passed through a good many owners, including 'Mad Jack' Fuller (see BRIGHTLING) and Lord Curzon, Viceroy of India, who left it to the National Trust on his death in 1925.

All year, daily (closed Suns Nov–Mar) 10am–6pm (or sunset if earlier). Tel: (0580) 830436

HERSTMONCEUX CASTLE * * *
Map p.145, A2
2 miles S of Herstmonceux on Flowers Green Rd, off the A271

The construction of this beautiful moated castle, one of the earliest to be built of brick in England, was started in 1440 by Sir Roger Fiennes, son of Sir William (d. 1402) whose brass memorial is in HERSTMONCEUX Church. The Fiennes family, later to become the Dacres, were descendants of Normans who fought with William the Conqueror and had acquired the manor through marriage into the de Herst Monceux family. Sir Roger brought craftsmen over from Flanders, skilled in making the distinctive pink bricks; the castle set a trend for the use of bricks in larger English buildings thereafter.

The castle, which is some 200ft square with a magnificent gatehouse to the south, fell into disrepair in the 18th century and was partly demolished to build nearby Herstmonceux Place in 1777.

It was partly restored by Colonel Claude Lowther in 1913 and more completely (and successfully) in 1933 by Walter Godfrey, the architect working for its then owner, Sir Paul Latham. In 1948, the castle became the home of the Royal Observatory, which moved from Greenwich in London to get a clearer view of the skies. To the east of the castle is the remarkable Equatorial Group of six steel and copper domes which once housed the powerful astronomical telescopes. They were completed in 1958, three for reflector instruments and three for refractors. The Royal Observatory left Herstmonceux in the 1980s to relocate its main telescope on the Spanish island of La Palma.

There is no public access to the castle. It can best be seen by following the signposted footpath and bridleway just to the south-east of Herstmonceux Church, and walking for a quarter of a mile down through the former administrative buildings, to the immediate south of the castle.

A good view can be had of the gatehouse, towers, chimneys and battlements across the fields and lawns. By continuing on the uphill footpath to the east for a further quarter of a mile, the Equatorial Group of domes can be clearly seen.

The future of Herstmonceux Castle is uncertain, as at time of going to press it is on the property market.

PEVENSEY CASTLE * * *
Map p.145, B2
4 miles NE of Eastbourne on the A259

£

Pevensey Castle's massive perimeter walls and keep are a landmark for miles around. Originally built around AD 340 by the Romans, who called the place 'Anderida', the fort was situated on a peninsula before the sea receded and was one of the defensive chain of Saxon-shore fortresses along the south coast of England. Its strategic position has been exploited down the centuries, from the time of the Armada in 1587 to World War II. Presented to the nation in 1925 by the Duke of Devonshire, the castle is now in the care of English Heritage. The main entrance is from the Roman east gate by the car park.

Soon after the Normans landed at Pevensey in 1066, William the Conqueror's half-brother, Robert of Mortain, began the construction of the inner bailey and keep, with its massive circular supports, within the outer Roman walls which enclose some 10 acres. The gatehouse and east and north towers were added in the 13th century. The castle was besieged in 1088, 1147, 1264 and in 1399 but was never taken; it fell into disuse after the defeat of the Spanish Armada, and the reclamation of the shore by the shifting coastline sealed its fate as a fortress.

During World War II defensive positions were built within the castle, which housed an observation and radio direction post, and some of these can be seen on the south-east side of the keep. Within the inner bailey, which has a fine basement room in the north tower, are the stone outlines of an early Norman chapel; below the gatehouse is a deep and often damp dungeon. The postern lies to the north west and the Roman west gate leads to Westham Church, one of the earliest Norman churches in England.
Apr–Sept, daily 10am–1pm, 2–6pm; Oct–Mar, Tues–Sun 10am–1pm, 2–4pm. Tel: (0323) 762604

See also: HASTINGS Castle; LEWES Castle

GARDENS & PARKS

DITCHLING COMMON **
Map p.143, A1
2¹/₂ miles N of Ditchling on the B2112

Ditchling Common is an open area of common land, freely accessible to the public and designated a Country Park. Over the past few years, paths have been created, the pond (almost a small lake) has been cleared of choking reeds, and a 1¹/₂-mile nature trail has been marked out. Informative signs indicate areas of interest and there is an accompanying leaflet available. There is a large car-park, lavatories and a ranger service. The heathland covers some 185 acres and is home to a wide variety of birds and several rare species of butterfly. When the bluebells are in flower in spring, it is a sheet of colour.

In Norman times, the common was called The Chase because it was used as a royal hunting-park. Its history goes back centuries to the Bronze Age when its chalybeate (iron-impregnated) spring was used. The common has, like Ashdown Forest, seen many disputes over commoners' rights: it still has a Reeve and regular meetings of local farmers. The paths criss-crossing the common are popular with dog-walkers and pony-riders.

HASTINGS COUNTRY PARK **
Map p.147, C1
Due E of Hastings off the A259

[i]

For some 3 miles east of Hastings, the cliff-top has been turned into a country park, preserved from any future development. Much of it has been designated a Site of Special Scientific Interest. Its 600 acres are a glorious, mixed open space of wood, grassland, heath and cliff, deeply cut by glens and full of bird and plant life.

The sandstone cliffs consist of some of the oldest rocks in the south-east, and are rich in fossil animals and plants. Unfortunately, their strata of sand and clay are being steadily eroded, in some places at the rate of about 4ft each year.

Heading along the coast from East Hill, on the edge of Hastings, you come first to Ecclesbourne Glen, a wooded valley popular with smugglers two centuries ago. Its damp atmosphere encourages moisture-loving plants, while the thick undergrowth provides perfect nesting sites for tits, warblers and other small birds.

Fairlight Glen, at the half-way point, gets its name from the cliff-top village of FAIRLIGHT. Its centuries-old woodland is carpeted in spring with bluebells, wood anemones and many other flowers. A stream runs between huge boulders under the trees, and the glen has the country park's only access to the beach.

The main car-park and visitor centre are at the eastern end of the park, down a lane beside Fairlight church. A memorial plaque here commemorates Archie Belaney (1885–1938), an early ecologist who lived for years as a Red Indian in Canada and wrote under the name of 'Grey Owl'. His books did much to publicize the fate of the Indians, and the threats to the beaver and other animals on which they depended for their survival.

From the car-park, paths lead down to the Firehills, an open area of heathland, bright in summer with yellow gorse. The coast of France can be seen from here on a clear day.
Visitor centre: *Easter–Sept, Sat, Sun and BH Mons 2.30–5pm. Tel: (0424) 813225*

SEVEN SISTERS COUNTRY PARK ***
Map p.144, D3
2 miles E of Seaford on the A259

🍴 ♿ *Living World:* [S] [i]

The 692 acres of the Park extend from Exceat on the main road down the lower meanders of the River Cuckmere to CUCKMERE HAVEN and along the westernmost Seven Sisters. Clearly marked trails, with the Valley Walk specially designed for easy access for the disabled, start at the Interpretation Centre housed in the converted 18th-century brick and flint farm buildings at Exceat Farm. This has an excellent exhibition on man and his impact on the surrounding countryside since prehistoric times. Leaflets describing the Park Trail and the Valley Walk are available here.

The 3-mile Park Trail explains the changing face of the landscape (chalk, shingle, meadows, downland and scrub) and the variety of wildlife habitats it hosts, including badgers and rabbit warrens, longer grasses which support birds, butterflies and grasshoppers, and permanent pasture grazed by sheep.

Fine views can be had of the River Cuckmere as it meanders across the valley, while below Haven Brow (low tide only) chalk erosion and the drift of the shingle from west to east may be seen. The trail returns via an artificial lake, for birds to nest and feed on, and the salt marsh area with indigenous plants and grasses.

The 2-mile Valley Walk similarly explores the history, wildlife and vegetation of the Park and follows a path running south of the Interpretation Centre to Foxhole.

The Living World**, which is also housed in the Exceat Farm complex, is an informative and well-designed natural history exhibition, with particular emphasis on smaller insects and marine life, and is especially suitable for children. From locusts, stick insects, butterflies and moths to anemones, crabs, and many of the local fish found in nearby rockpools, there is much to keep the visitor amused and intrigued.

Park: Easter–Oct, daily 10.30am–5.30pm; Nov–Mar, Sat–Sun 11am–4pm. Tel: (0323) 870280

The Living World: Mid Mar–Nov, daily (also weekends, and school holidays in winter) 10am–5pm. Tel: (0323) 870100

SHEFFIELD PARK GARDEN **
Map p.148, C3

Just E of the A275, midway between Lewes and East Grinstead

£ ● &

At the southern edge of Ashdown Forest, in the picturesque village of Fletching, an impressive Gothic-style gateway faces the church. This used to be the main entrance to Sheffield Park, but today, public access

is through the 'back gate', off the A275 East Grinstead–Lewes road. Sheffield Park is familiar to children and steam train enthusiasts because it is the station for the Bluebell Line (see p.32). Half a mile up the road from the station, however, is a superb National Trust Garden.

Modelled by Lancelot 'Capability' Brown in the 18th century, the gardens and woodlands cover 100 acres with a chain of lakes on different levels, linked by cascades and waterfalls. Trees and shrubs of every imaginable shape, size and colour grow in profusion and are reflected in the peaceful lakes.

In the Middle Ages the manor of Siffele (as Sheffield was spelt then) was held by Simon de Montfort. After he defeated Henry III at the Battle of Lewes in 1264, he became England's king, in all but name, until he was killed at Evesham the following year. Some 500 years later, in the late 18th century, the manor was bought by John Baker Holroyd, a politician, who commissioned James Wyatt to build him a new mansion in fashionable Gothic-Revival style, and Brown to lay out the garden.

Brown formed two lakes, linked by a cascade, and planted the garden in informal style. These two lakes are known as the Upper and Lower Woman's Way, as the ghost of a headless woman is said to drift along the path beside them. Two more lakes were added by the Earl of Sheffield in the 1870s which are linked to each other and the lower pair of lakes by waterfalls. It is the water, rarely out of sight, that gives Sheffield Park its unique appeal.

Not many of the original shrubs and trees survive, and the glorious display today is mainly the work of Arthur Soames, who bought Sheffield Park in 1909 and devoted 25 years to planting trees from all over the world. The National Trust continued this work when it bought the park in 1954. (The house is privately owned.) The gardens were devastated by the hurricane of October 1987, but since then, over 400 trees have been planted, and there is now little evidence of the storm.

April–early Nov, Tues–Sat 11am–6pm (or sunset if earlier), Sun and BH Mons 2–6pm; Sun in Oct and Nov 1pm–sunset. Tel: (0825) 790231 or 790655

ZOOS & WILDLIFE

BENTLEY WILDFOWL AND MOTOR MUSEUM ＊＊
Map p.149, E2
3 miles SE of Uckfield off the A22

⊞ ➴ Ⓢ ♿

Some 100 species of wildfowl inhabit the reserve at Bentley, created by the late Gerald Askew who bought the estate in 1937. It is now owned and managed by East Sussex County Council who received the estate as a gift to the people of East Sussex from Mrs Askew in 1978.

Ducks, geese and swans (including Hawaiian geese, trumpeter swans and the rare white-winged wood ducks) have been encouraged to breed in captivity. They can be viewed close to at the series of ponds, lakes and pens that form the reserve.

Bentley House★★, the core of which is an older farmhouse, is a post-war building in the Georgian style designed by Raymond Erith. The ground floor rooms to the front are interlinked and contain antique furniture and paintings. Of particular interest in the west wing is the Bird Room, with its collection of wildfowl paintings by Philip Rickman, and the Chinese Drawing Room in the east wing, decorated with 18th-century wallpaper. A formal garden, laid out in a pattern of 'rooms' hedged by yew, lies to the rear and features rose, kitchen and pool garden areas.

The **Motor Museum★★** houses a collection of veteran, Edwardian and vintage vehicles which changes periodically. Many of the items, which are meticulously polished and kept in good running order, are on loan from private collectors and include racing cars, military vehicles and production prototypes.

Among the other attractions on the Bentley estate are a woodland walk, children's adventure playground and an education room for group visits.

Apr–Oct, daily 10.30am–dusk; Nov–Mar (exc. Jan), weekends only.
House: *Apr–Oct, daily from 12am.*
Tel: (0825) 840573.

DRUSILLAS ZOO, ALFRISTON ＊＊＊
Map p.144, B3
3 miles W of Polegate, at the roundabout off the A27

⊞ ♿ ⚑ *(zoo)*

From its origins as tea-rooms in the 1920s, the award-winning Drusillas Zoo has become one of the most popular tourist attractions in East Sussex, with over 300,000 visitors a year. It is designed with children of all ages in mind.

Open all year round, the zoo park includes exhibits on the evolution of species, a farm display with cattle, pigs, sheep and poultry (where a life-sized artificial cow can be milked), a monkey sanctuary, meerkat mound (with domed viewing area in centre for children), and special enclosures for penguins, otters, owls and beavers. Throughout the zoo, the emphasis is very much on education and fun: children are encouraged to explore the animal kingdom through a comprehensive series of 'hands on' exhibits, games and quizzes.

The zoo also contains a Japanese Garden, flamingo pond and animals from the outback of Australia, such as emus and wallabies. A large adventure playground, miniature train ride and Drusillas Village, with working pottery and other shops, complete the visit for those with any stamina left after the zoo's attractions. Many special events are held throughout the year.

The **English Wine Centre**, on the Alfriston Roundabout exit from the park, is an associated attraction. It sells wines from Sussex (and other English counties), offering wine tastings. Educational tours and lectures can be arranged. An annual wine festival and regional food fair is held here. The Centre also has a small museum devoted to the history of winemaking.

Drusilla's Zoo: *All year (except Christmas Day), daily 10am–5pm (last admission) and 4pm in winter. Tel: (0323) 870234*
English Wine Centre: *Off-licence hours. Tel: (0323) 870164*

HAREMERE HALL **
Map p.151, B2
Near Etchingham, off the A265

🏛 🍴 Ⓢ ♿ ✕

Haremere Hall offers a splendid family day out with its working shire-horses, and the surrounding gardens and countryside. The Hall itself is a 17th-century manor house, the country home of Jacqueline, Lady Killearn; its stables and courtyard are now home to the massive, gentle work-horses: Shires, Ardennes, Suffolk Punches and cart-horses.

These horses have been integrated into the farming and forestry operations carried out on the estate. The horses are also being bred here, so the collection includes horses of varying ages as well as breeds. There are also usually a number of calves being reared for the Home Farm, and free-range chickens cluck around the paddocks and barns. With children in mind, the organizers have devised a worksheet, and set up an adventure playground.

Horse-and-cart rides are available in good weather, and the wagons take a rural ride through pretty farm lanes passing orchards, meadows and marshland ponds. Twice a day, at 11am and 3pm, there is a demon-stration of the horses' skills in the stable courtyard. If it is raining, the demonstrations are held under cover. Visitors are encouraged to bring picnics and are welcome to eat in the hay barns if it is wet. There is also a terraced cafeteria.

The admission fee includes access to the nature trail and 140 acres of lovely parkland surrounding the Hall. Work-horse courses and driving weekends are held throughout the year lasting from one to three days, and special one-day courses are offered for children. Telephone for information.
April–Oct, Tues–Sun and BH Mons 10.30am–4.30pm. Tel: (058 081) 501

HEAVEN FARM
Map p.148, B3
1 mile S of Danehill on the A275

🏛 🍴 𝕏 ♿

The present farm was built by a wealthy landowner in 1830 although the site has been farmed since the 14th century. The buildings include a barn, stables, slaughterhouse, granary, cowsheds, piggeries, forge and oasthouse – and have been preserved with their original contents as a museum of Victorian farming methods.

The owners have a modern farm 2 miles away, built in 1964. A combined tour of the two farms is offered to school parties, to illustrate the contrast in Victorian and today's farming methods.

In addition, there is a beautiful 1½ mile nature trail which holds a Conservation Award from the South of England Agricultural Society. In spring, the Sussex woodland is carpeted with bluebells and anemones and in summer there are clumps of foxgloves and other flowers. Ploughman's lunches and cream teas are available in the Stable Tea Rooms.
Apr–Sept, daily 10am–6pm. Tel: (0825) 790226

WILDERNESS WOOD
Map p.149, C3
Just S of the A272, in Hadlow Down village (12 miles S of Tunbridge Wells)

🏛 🍴 Ⓢ 𝕏 ♿ *(yard)*

Wilderness Wood, in the hills of the High Weald, is a family-owned and run working wood, covering about sixty acres and organized to show how English wood is grown. Traditional chestnut coppices and pine and fir plantations provide wood which has been harvested here for the past thousand years.

In the main yard, the harvested wood is made into garden furniture, fences and bird-tables, and in the adjoining barn, where refreshments are served, informative displays about growing and using wood can be found. Near the yard are picnic areas and barbecue stands for hire, and a children's play area, including an aerial ropeway.

A woodland trail of about three-quarters of a mile is illustrated with a clear explanatory leaflet. (You are advised to wear boots after wet weather.) A seasonal bluebell trail takes you through the best spring flowers while, as the seasons change, summer foxgloves are followed by a variety of autumn toadstools. A short tree-trail helps you identify the varieties grown and seasonal nature spotter sheets are available.
All year (except Christmas Day), daily 10am–dusk. Tel: (0825) 830509

BEACHES

BEXHILL BEACH * *
Map p.146, D2–3
5 miles W of Hastings off the A259

Bexhill beach is one of the few in England to be awarded the coveted European 'Blue Flag' for cleanliness and safe bathing – an award it won in 1989, 1990 and 1991. In a test of sea-water round the country (carried out by the Consumers' Association in 1991), Bexhill had the only water entirely free of any pollution. The foreshore consists of a shingle bank above a broad beach of sand and rock pools uncovered at low tide.

Beach activities include sailing, fishing, rowing, windsurfing, swimming and water-skiing. Among the summer events are rowing and sailing regattas. Dogs are not allowed on a specified stretch of beach at the centre of the 2-mile promenade.

At its western end, Bexhill beach shades into Cooden Beach. Here the gardens of inter-war private houses and small hotels fringe the shingle. At its eastern end, the secluded shingle beach of Glyne Gap, easily reached on foot from Galley Hill, has a fine viewpoint at the end of Bexhill's seafront.

BRIGHTON BEACH * * *
Map p.143, E1
52 miles S of London on the A23

Brighton became the first seaside resort 250 years ago after Dr Richard Russell extolled the virtues of bathing in the sea, and it has been attracting bathers ever since. Now on a sunny summer day it can be quite difficult to find a space on the beach. In more recent years, Brighton became the first major seaside resort to designate an area of the beach for naturists, at Black Rock.

Two miles long from Black Rock to the Hove boundary, the beach is mainly pebbles and shingle, though some sand is exposed at low tide. Amenities are excellent with frequent cafés, souvenir shops and toilets in the arches beneath the upper promenade, and a small fun-fair in Madeira Drive. There are also opportunities to hire windsurfers and jet-skis.

At one time Brighton had three piers but, although two remain, only the Palace Pier is still in use. Recently refurbished, it has a fun-fair, amusement arcades, bars, a restaurant and numerous stalls selling candy-floss, rock, pancakes and souvenirs.

CAMBER SANDS * * *
Map p.153, E1
4 miles E of Rye off the A259

The sprawling holiday village of Camber looks out on to a magnificent expanse of sand. Stretching for 2 miles east from the mouth of the Rother to the shingle of Dungeness, Camber Sands are backed by huge dunes, planted with marram grass to prevent erosion.

At low tide, the sea goes out for a ½-mile or more, leaving acres of gently ridged golden sand. Children playing on isolated sand-spits and unwary swimmers are often cut off by the fast incoming tide. Red flags are flown when swimming becomes too dangerous

Inland from Camber are the flat, sheep-covered water-meadows of Romney Marsh. The hulking blocks of Dungeness Atomic Power Station loom in the distance, 7 miles down the coast. Rye's championship golf course is just west of the village.

CUCKMERE HAVEN BEACH * * *
Map p.144, D2
3 miles E of Seaford off the A259

The shingled beach, with its defensive groynes, is best approached on the footpath (part of the SOUTH DOWNS WAY) which leads down by the banks of the meandering River Cuckmere. It is just over 1 mile from the car-park at the Seven Sisters Country

---

Brighton Beach, with the Palace Pier in the background.

Park (see p.24) to the beach. To the east lie the imposing cliffs of the Seven Sisters.

Bathing should only be attempted with caution, as the undertow is strong; lifelines are situated on the beach. The sea-shore walk east to Birling Gap should only be attempted on a falling tide and even then with care; at least 2 hours are required. The flint and chalk cliffs are liable to erosion and approaching the cliff edge is not advised.

The area is a nature reserve, in the care of East Sussex County Council, and a profusion of birds and wild flowers can be observed.

EASTBOURNE BEACH * * *
Map p.145, D1
15 miles SE of Hastings on the A259

The popular central beach, of shingle and sand, lies between the Pier and the Bandstand, below Grand Parade, and has won awards for its water quality. Swimmers are segregated from water-sports. There is safe bathing, supervised by a lifeguard service, and no dogs are allowed on this section. The beach is cleaned daily. Showers and changing rooms, with bathing costume and towel hire, are on hand; deckchairs, windbreaks, inflatable mattresses and beach umbrellas can also be hired for the day. High-water tables are displayed and a beach wheelchair is available.

Beyond the Wish Tower, to the west, is a more dangerous and rocky section where bathing four hours either side of low tide is not advised. Care is also needed to the east, beyond the Redoubt Fortress. Red warning flags are hoisted from points along the promenade when bathing is dangerous.

Boat trips to view BEACHY HEAD depart from both the beach and the Pier. There are telescopes along the front.
Boat trips: *Phone (0323) 412290.*

HASTINGS BEACH * *
Map p.147, C1
5 miles E of Bexhill on the A259

The combined promenades of Hastings and St Leonards run for about 3 miles along a shingle bank above a wide expanse of sand and rock-pools uncovered at low tide. These pools are rich in seaweed of various kinds, crabs, starfish and other marine life. At its eastern end, beyond the castle, Hastings' fleet of 40-odd fishing boats are winched up on the shingle out of reach of the waves, beside the tall black-tarred 'net-shops' where nets were once hung to be dried. The RNLI lifeboat-house by the harbour is open daily during the summer.

West of St Leonards, Bulverhythe beach was once a favourite landing-place for smugglers and adjoins Glyne Gap (see Bexhill Beach, above). The timbers of the *Amsterdam*, a Dutch merchant sail-boat, can sometimes be seen in the sand at exceptionally low tides.

Beach activities include swimming, fishing, rowing, windsurfing and water-skiing. A foreshore patrol keeps a lookout for swimmers in difficulties. Among regular annual events are a windsurfing championship in September and a sea-angling festival in November.

HOVE BEACH * * *
Map p.142, E4
1 mile W of Brighton on the A259

Although Hove's beach is a continuation of Brighton's, giving a combined length of 4 miles, in many ways it has advantages over its neighbour. It has the same pebbles and shingle with sand at low tide, but it doesn't have the same kind of 'kiss-me-quick' image. There are fewer souvenir shops, though also fewer cafés, and often it can be easier to find room to stretch out on the beach on a hot summer's day. Parking is easier too, and it's free.

One of the characteristics of Hove is the beach-huts which line up along the broad promenade, all painted a uniform sea-green, though other colours are permitted for the doors. Some are owned, but others can be rented.

There is no pier, but there are other forms of entertainment to be found on the lawns behind the promenade, among them tennis, bowls and mini-golf, while the Hove Lagoon is an excellent place to learn how to windsurf. Experts and jet-skiers have designated areas in the sea.

NORMAN'S BAY *
Map p.145, B4
2 miles E of Pevensey off the A259

This small resort lies below the open fields that form the southern extremity of the Pevensey Levels and borders on Hooe Level to the east. Access is either from Pevensey Bay or across the railway line, south of the main Eastbourne–Hastings road. In contrast to Pevensey Bay, its larger and noisier neighbour, Norman's Bay beach can be deserted even in the summer months. Amenities are few, save for the various camping and caravan sites. Mobile homes and seaside holiday cottages predominate. Swimming and windsurfing are possible from the shingle and sand beach, where the groynes make a brave attempt to prevent the ever-eastward drift of the shingle. Hastings and Bexhill can be viewed to the east, with Eastbourne and Beachy Head to the west.

PEVENSEY BAY *
Map p.145, C3
3 1/2 miles NE of Eastbourne on the A259

Pevensey Bay is a small but lively holiday resort nowadays, far removed from its origins 300 years ago as the small fishing community of Wallsend.

The shingle beach lies directly below the main car-park, for which you have to pay. On the beach, the defensive groynes mark the continuing battle to resist the advances of the sea and the eastward drift of the shingle. The beach is popular for swimming and windsurfing, and the water quality conforms to EC standards. To the east are views of Bexhill and Hastings; to the west are the remains of two Martello towers (nos. 60 and 61), constructed as part of the coastal defence chain during the Napoleonic Wars and later used by customs officials to prevent smuggling. In 1833 the 'Battle of Pevensey Sluice' marked one of the last encounters between local smugglers and members of the excise.

There is a wide range of holiday accommodation, from hotels, caravans and camping to bed-and-breakfast and self-catering, available in the area.

ROTTINGDEAN BEACH
Map p.143, F2
3 1/2 miles E of Brighton on the A259

It can be difficult sometimes to tell that Rottingdean has a beach at all. The only access is by The Gap, next to The White Horse Hotel which, with the modern apartments opposite, looks down on the concrete undercliff walk linking Brighton with Saltdean. At high tide, the sea crashes against the promenade, totally covering the beach which, as the tide recedes, reveals itself to be a mixture of shingle and sand with some rocky areas. The beach is sectioned off by several groynes.

Apart from the area around The Gap, the promenade is backed by chalk cliffs which, on a sunny day, can add a particular brilliance to the beach. There are no amenities other than a toilet block and the only cafés and shops are to be found in the village itself.

SEAFORD BEACH * *
Map p.144, D1
9 miles W of Eastbourne on the A259

Much less popular than it was during Victorian days, when the railway first arrived, Seaford has a similar pebble beach to its bigger neighbours, but few of their amenities. Quite a long beach, it sweeps in a curve for 2 1/2 miles from Seaford Head to Newhaven's eastern breakwater.

Rather scrappy in appearance, the seafront is backed partly by Victorian and modern apartments, and by open land at the western end. The beach is steeply banked and swimming at high tide is recommended only for strong swimmers. It is a popular beach with windsurfers, and water-skiers are often seen. Fishing is also quite common.

There are some beach-huts on the promenade, near the Martello tower, and there is a sports ground near by with a cricket pitch and tennis courts.

The western end of the beach, known as the Buckle after the 16th-century soldier Sir Nicholas Pelham, featured a pub called The Buckle until recently. Built like a stylized lighthouse, it is now a private residence.

SPECIAL INTEREST

BARTLEY MILL *
Map p.155, D4
*3 miles E of Tunbridge Wells off the B2169
Lamberhurst road*

⊞ ☕ Ⓢ

Bartley Mill, standing on the River Winn, dates from the 13th century. It was owned by the monks of Bayham Abbey (see p.20) a couple of miles away, and was the mill for the whole parish. It was used for grinding flour until World War I, when it was converted into an engineering workshop.

Today it is once more a working mill, having been bought in 1985 and lovingly restored by its owner. The extensive work has included re-excavating the mill-ponds and repairing the sluice-gates. The mill stands in some 180 acres of land which is farmed organically. The wheat grown on the farm is ground on site and sold to local bakeries to make stone-ground organic bread.

Refreshments are served upstairs in the mill, and a shop on the ground floor sells organic produce from the farm together with home-made jams and fudge. There are children's trout pools and a tea-garden. A guided tour covers the whole process of breadmaking, from the growing wheat to the baker's oven. Outbuildings house local craftsmen.
All year, daily 10am–6pm (milling can be seen at weekends at 2pm). Tel: (0892) 890372

BEWL BRIDGE RESERVOIR * *
Map p.156, E1
1 mile S of Lamberhurst off the A21, signposted as Bewl Water

☕ (no indoor seating) ♿

Bewl Bridge Reservoir is a beautiful lake in outstanding meadow and woodland countryside. Although close to the A21, it is not visible from the road. It was formed between 1970 and 1975 by damming the small River Bewl – a tributary of the River Teise – thereby flooding three small valleys. A little way downstream, the Bewl forms the moat of Scotney Castle.

The reservoir covers 770 acres, making it the largest inland water in the south-east. There are 17 miles of shoreline, and the reservoir holds 6,900 million gallons of water. It is a paradise for fly-fishermen, being well-stocked with rainbow and brown trout. Other recreational activites include bird-watching, walking and riding (there are 2 miles of marked trails as well as 13 miles of waterside footpaths and bridleways), and water-sports such as sailing, canoeing, rowing, windsurfing and diving.

There is a new children's adventure playground featuring a fort, Burmah bridge and 60ft curved slide. During the summer there are passenger-boat trips lasting about 40 minutes (weather permitting) on the SS Frances Mary, a beautifully restored wooden boat of 1916. During the summer, various events are held including lakeside concerts with fireworks, craft weekends and car-club meetings.
Reservoir: Recreational activites Apr–end Oct, daily 9am–sunset. Tel. (0892) 890661
Fishing Lodge: Apr–end Oct, daily 8.30am–6pm. Tel: (0892) 890352

BLUEBELL RAILWAY * * *
Map p.148, B2
Train leaves Sheffield Park Station, mid-way between Lewes and East Grinstead, on the A275

⊞ ☕ ♿

The Bluebell Railway recreates the romance and atmosphere of the great days of steam. Climb aboard the train and trundle up the gradient from Sheffield Park, north-west towards Horsted Keynes along the old railway line that passes through beautiful Sussex scenery – and plenty of bluebells in spring. The organizers plan to extend the line to East Grinstead and work to this end is already under way.

One of the Bluebell Line's historic steam locomotives.

The Bluebell collection of thirty historic steam locomotives is one of the largest in the country. Among the trains is a pair of little 'Terriers' built in the 1870s and a massive heavy freight engine of 1958. Walking into the engine shed at Sheffield Park is like stepping back in time with water-crane, inspection pit, ash, coal, the noise of hissing steam and the unforgettable smell of steam-engines. A museum of small exhibits has a display of old equipment, tickets, models and photographs.

There is a choice of places to eat: at Sheffield Park Station is Puffers, a self-service restaurant, and the Bessemer Arms, a replica of a Victorian pub and restaurant; at Horsted Keynes is a genuine 1882 station buffet, with bar and snacks; or you can eat on the train – many trains convey a buffet car. A recent addition is the 'Orient Express' style restaurant in beautifully restored Pullman Cars from the 1920s and 1930s.

Railway: *Jun–Sept, daily; Jan–Feb, Sundays; December, Santa specials; Mar–May and Oct–Nov, weekends; also Weds in May, half-term week in Oct. Tel: (0825) 722370 (talking timetable) or (0825) 723777.*
Pullman Car bookings: *All year. Tel: (0825) 722008.*

NUTLEY POST MILL
Map p.148, B4
2 miles NW of Uckfield off the A22

£

Nutley Post Mill is thought to be the oldest post mill in Sussex. It is a tiny construction made entirely of wood in a style known to to have been popular in the 12th century. It would have been used to grind corn for local smallholders. It was restored by the Uckfield and District Preservation Society and became fully operational in 1981 (although it is rarely used).

Unusually, there are no records of the mill in Sussex until 1840, and it is thought that it was brought here from Goudhurst in Kent. It stopped grinding corn in 1908 and was supported by steel joists and brick pillars, which prevented its collapse, until the comprehensive restoration programme began.

Easter–end of British Summer Time, last Sun each month and BH Suns and Mons 2.30–5.30pm. Tel: (0825) 712632, Mrs Long

PATCHAM WINDMILL*
Map p.142, C4
3 miles N of Brighton off the A23

✕

Built in 1885 by Joseph Harris, a baker in the village, Patcham Windmill was the last brick-built tower-mill to be built in Sussex and continued to operate until 1924. It changed hands several times after that and, in 1964, was converted into a home. It now houses the Musgrave Collection which, among thousands of exhibits, features paintings by George Musgrave, old English and Roman coins, toys, Victoriana and archaeological discoveries made in the Middle East during research on the travels of St Paul.

May–Aug, Weds–Sat 10–12am and 2–5pm. Tel: (0273) 501169.

POLEGATE WINDMILL
Map p.145, C1
4 miles NW of Eastbourne off the A22

£

Polegate Windmill is tucked away in a housing estate in Park Croft Rd, just off the main A22 road to the west. It is a large tower-mill, dating from 1817, and the only one of its kind in East Sussex open to public view. It is in the care of the Eastbourne Civic Society and was restored to working order in 1967.

The mill is built of brick; its 'sweeps' are turned into the direction of the wind by a fan-tail on the cap of the mill. Inside is a small museum. The wind-shaft in the grounds is from a smock-mill at Battle.

Easter–Sept, Sun and BH Mons 2–5pm; also Weds in Aug. Tel: (0323) 734496.

WEIR WOOD RESERVOIR **
Map p.154, D1
3 miles S of East Grinstead, via a turning left off the B2110

Weir Wood Reservoir was created in 1950 by damming one of the headstreams of the Medway (the Medway's valley forms the border between West and East Sussex).

The expanse of water covers 280 acres, and submerged in its depths are the remains of the Walesbeech Roman iron-bloomery. At its western end, tower the impressive Stone Farm Rocks, tree-clad sandstone crags which are popular with climbers. The setting for this beautiful stretch of water has led to comparisons with the Lake District, albeit on a minute scale.

The lake is a favourite with anglers, being well-stocked with trout (permits available), and bird-watchers come from miles around during autumn migration season. Among the wide variety of wildfowl that frequent the reservoir are curlews, great-crested grebes, barnacle and Canada geese, mallards and shelducks, and moorhens. Part of the reservoir is maintained as a nature reserve to protect rarer species and their habitat. There are two car-parks, one specially designed for disabled visitors.

WEST BLATCHINGTON MILL * *
Map p.142, D3
1¹/₂ miles N of Hove off the A2038

Built in 1820 on the site of an earlier mill, West Blatchington Mill is the oldest smock-mill in Sussex. Now surrounded by modern housing estates, it was once used to signal to smugglers. The timber cap, of hexagonal design rather than the more normal octagonal, is built on a square flint tower some hundred years older and is surrounded by small barns. In 1825, the mill was the subject of a John Constable pen and ink sketch.

The mill stopped working commercially in 1897, but has been restored with much of the original machinery surviving. Visitors can now see how grain is transformed into flour while, on the loading floor, there is a museum with milling and farming exhibits. *May–Sept, Sun and BHs 2.30–5pm. Tel: (0273) 775400, ext. 2257*

WILMINGTON LONG MAN* * *
Map p.144, C3
7 miles NW of Eastbourne off the A27

The origins of this massive figure cut into the chalk hillside are unclear. Historians' theories ascribe it to either the depiction of a Romano–British god or an elaborate 18th-century joke. Certainly, important archaeological discoveries have been made on Windover Hill, and ancient flint workings and burial barrows can be seen near to the Long Man.

The genderless giant holds a stave in each hand; it has been suggested this shows the early British sun god, Balder, opening the doors of darkness. Each stave is some 230ft high and the distance between them is half their height. The outline was restored in recent years with white blocks and has been described as 'the largest representation of the human form in Western Europe'. The figure was designed to be seen from a distance and incorporates a foreshortening effect. The best view is from the small public car-park below Wilmington Priory; a footpath leads up to the Long Man, which is in the care of the Sussex Archaeological Society.

See also: ASHDOWN FOREST Farm; BECKLEY, Great Knelle Farm; BODIAM, Quarry Farm; DANEHILL, Country Tours.

ALCISTON

Map p.144, B2   ******
4 miles W of Polegate off the A27

Thatched and timbered cottages, many incorporating local flint, line the small road which passes the Rose Cottage inn and the Old Postman's Cottage on the right, before reaching the medieval complex of monastic buildings at Court House Farm.

Alciston Church**, with its short spire and fish-shaped weather-vane, is reached by a track beside a paddock. It is built of flint, with a surviving Norman window and several Early English features. Excavations have revealed the presence of an earlier, pre-Conquest apse. Substantial restoration to the later additions was carried out in the Victorian period. Two bells hang in the tower, dated 1380 and 1400. A blocked-up priest's door and five scratch dials, which marked the time of the services, may be seen on the south exterior wall. The organ was originally at BERWICK Church nearby, and the belfry was restored in oak in 1985, to a 14th-century design, complementing the new west screen and the pews. The nave roof has heavy tie-beams and king-posts in three bays, and was restored in 1898.

The church is part of a group of buildings once owned by Battle Abbey (see p.20), which include the large tithe barn, some 170ft long with a steeply pitched roof and one of the biggest in Sussex, a 14th-century dovecote, fishponds and an early clergy house. These are clustered around the present working farm and may be viewed from the road. After the Dissolution the land passed to the Gage family, of nearby Firle Place (see p.17).

ALFRISTON

Map p.144, C3   *******
4 miles NE of Seaford off the A259

This is a picturesque village bustling with tourists, as it has a wealth of attractions. Ideally located, fronting the River

Cuckmere and below the South Downs, the village is a popular centre for walkers.

Alfriston Heritage Centre and Old Forge*, above the Dene car-park, is the best starting point; here the story of the original Saxon settlement and the importance of the village in medieval times, is told through a comprehensive exhibition. The layout of the village in 1890 is illustrated by a model; adjacent is the Blacksmith's Forge Museum with an interesting collection of artefacts.

From there, West St leads to the ancient Market Cross on the village square at the junction of North St with the High St. On the right is the Market Inn (known also as 'The Smugglers'), the former home of Stanton Collins, a notorious local smuggler.

The Star Inn* is further down the road, a black-and-white timber-framed building with 14th-century origins as a pilgrims' rest. It is roofed in Horsham tiles and has a profusion of carvings; St George and the dragon are depicted in colour above the entrance to the left. A strange ship's figurehead in red stands by the lane leading up to the South Downs Way. Opposite is the **George Inn**, proclaiming its 'first transfer of innkeeper's licence 1397'.

On the left, a lane (known in Sussex as a 'twitten') leads down to the Tye – or village green – past the United Reformed Church. The White Bridge over the River Cuckmere lies ahead, connecting with many local footpaths.

St Andrew's Church**, 'the Cathedral of the Downs', stands on a circular mound, probably of Saxon origin. Formed in the shape of a Greek Orthodox cross, it is built of flint (used to remarkable effect) and local greensand stone. The present church, which is surprisingly spacious, dates from around 1360; it has no aisles and the main entrance is from the west. The north window of the northern transept has ancient glass depicting St Alphege, Archbishop of Canterbury, next to a modern representation of St Andrew. The chancel contains a fine Easter Sepulchre with a carved human face and curled-up dog above, together with a sedilia and piscina. The roof timbers still carry the hooks used to support the Lenten Veil, used before the Reformation to separate the congregation from the proceedings at the altar.

🏠 **The Clergy House****, to the south of the church, was the first building acquired by the National Trust in 1896 (for £10, after the approach of the local vicar F.W. Benyon, whose efforts led to the creation of the National Trust itself). It is set in a pleasant cottage garden. A thatched timber-framed Wealden-style house of around 1350 with hall, solar and service area, it was the home of the priests who served under Michelham Priory.

From the Clergy House the path leads back to the High St via the Wingrove Inn, formerly a renowned racing stables.
Heritage Centre and Old Forge: Easter–Oct, daily 11am–5pm. Tel: (0323) 870303)
Clergy House: Apr–Oct, daily 11am–6pm. Tel: (0323) 870001)

ARLINGTON

Map p.144, B3   **
2 miles NW of Polegate off the A22 and A27

🏛 **St Pancras Church***** has a shady churchyard, approached down a small lane beside the village pub, and part of the recently introduced National Living Churchyard Scheme. This Scheme seeks to encourage wildlife and flora by not intensively mowing selected areas of land.

The flint-faced church, named after its associations with the former monastery of St Pancras at Lewes, is an outstanding Norman to Early English church but has earlier origins. Despite some Victorian restoration, the evolution of its distinctive styles up to the Reformation can be clearly seen.

The Norman Chapel has fine examples of dogtooth carving on the pillars and has a 13th-century pottery food-storage jar displayed behind glass. Stone coffin lids lie against the wall.

The walls of the nave bear the remnants of painted murals, some in a 'roses and crosses' pattern dating from the 14th century, with later murals showing signs of biblical texts. The screen and chancel seats were carved in Mayfield out of timbers taken from the old tower, where three 17th-century bells hang.

The shingled broach spire of the church is unusual as its base starts below the line of the nave roof. To the right of the porch entrance is a surviving Anglo-Saxon window with headers made from Roman tiles.

🌳 **Abbotts Wood*** is near the village. It is a Forestry Commission site with car-park, toilets (including disabled), picnic area, walks and trails. Dogs are allowed.

〰 **Arlington Reservoir** lies half a mile from the village, with footpath access for those wishing to walk around the water.

The peaceful setting of Arlington village is in contrast to the nearby Arlington Stadium: a national speedway racing venue for motorcycle events and the home of the Eastbourne Eagles and British League racing meetings.

ASHDOWN FOREST

Map p.154, E2 etc.   ***
Covering a rough triangle marked by Forest Row, Crowborough and Maresfield, via the A22 S of East Grinstead

Driving into Ashdown Forest is like entering another, much older world. It is essentially a large sandy heath covered with bracken, gorse, heather and rough grass. It covers an area of 14,000 acres, about half of which is freely accessible to the public. In the summer it is crowded with walkers, riders and picnickers but a clear autumn or winter day is the best time to come if you want to avoid the people and experience the area's unique sense of wilderness, solitude and space.

Ashdown Forest seems something of a misnomer (it is known by local children as 'Bashdown Forest' due to the absence of trees). Most of the great trees were cut down as fuel and to heat the iron foundry forges, but some forested areas do survive (such as Five Hundred Acre Wood). The clumps of Scotch pines crowning every high point are the forest's most prominent landmarks. These were planted last century by the Victorians to add interest to what they considered a monotonous landscape.

Historically, Ashdown Forest has been used by man from as far back as prehistoric times. The Romans were active here and cut their road from London to the South Downs straight through the forest, using slag from local iron-works for its surface. Villages grew up on its fringes and, by the middle ages, commoners were using the land for grazing cattle and pigs, digging peat, cutting wood for fuel and bracken for roofing their houses. The wealthy hunted deer here which resulted in a thriving poaching industry.

Ashdown Forest was a busy smuggling route and was scattered with numerous hideouts. **Cackle Street** was known as a smugglers' haunt, and another was **Duddleswell**. Duddleswell is an old name meaning Dudell's spring and it was the seat of a royal manor. The manor today is a 19th-century house, opposite which once stood a much older house. The hamlet is much as it was in the days of the early settlers, simply a collection of small farms. At Cackle Street is a beautiful lake called **Boringwheel Mill**, so called after a flour mill of the same name. The name Boringwheel suggests that cannons were bored here. This process took place once the cannons had been hollow-cast, using a special boring tool (one of which is on display at the Anne of Cleves Museum, Lewes).

Use of forest land was constantly in dispute: villagers claimed rights of grazing, while the rich wanted to enclose large areas and reserve them for hunting and 'improving'. In 1885, the Board of Conservators of Ashdown Forest was set up to administer the area and settle land ownership claims. This job was taken over by the East Sussex County Council in 1987 and administration is now run from the Ashdown Forest Centre at **Wych Cross** near Forest Row.

☑ The **Ashdown Forest Centre**★★ consists of three timber-framed barns, thatched with bracken in traditional style. One of the barns houses an information centre for visitors with explanations of the forest's history and details of its wildlife.

The volume of visitors gives the Conservators plenty to deal with, not least of which is the provision of car-parks and picnic areas, and the prevention of forest fires (which are often triggered by stray cigarette ends and overturned camping stoves). Preserving what is left of the forest's wildlife and rare plants is another priority.

The **Ashdown Forest Farm** is also at Wych Cross, where five roads meet at the heart of the forest. This is a family-run working farm and rare-breeds centre. There is an extensive collection of animals, from bantams to heavy horses. A tea shop, play area and gift shop make the farm a good family outing.

Camp Hill★, at 650ft, is the summit plateau of the forest over which ancient pack-horse trails used to run and can still be followed. At the edge of the plateau is the chain-link perimeter fence of the former Diplomatic Wireless Service Station – until recently a latticework of aerials – where embassy messages from all over the world were transmitted and received. The station, codenamed 'Aspidistra', was opened in 1942 to broadcast anti-Nazi propaganda. It closed in 1985. Just across the road from Camp Hill can be seen a short section of the old Roman road which has been exposed.

The perimeter of Ashdown Forest is marked by several places with 'gate' or 'hatch' names dating from the times when the forest was a royal hunting park. These include Highgate, Friars Gate, Coleman's Hatch, Chuck Hatch and Chelwood Gate.

At **Chelwood Gate**, there are a few houses, a garage, and the Red Lion pub. The former Prime Minister Harold Macmillan (Lord Stockton) lived at Chelwood Gate and, in 1963, President Kennedy visited him here. A memorial slab

The magnificent gatehouse of Battle Abbey dominates the town's high street.

and a clump of pines on the road out to Wych Cross commemorates the visit.

Coleman's Hatch is a scattered village of tile-hung cottages, farm-houses and some modern development. Its distinctive Church of the Holy Trinity was built in 1913 in Early English style; it has a five-sided baptistry and an unusual stone spire.

Ashdown Forest is most clearly and endearingly portrayed in A. A. Milne's *Winnie the Pooh* books and particularly in E. H. Shepard's well-observed illustrations. Milne lived at HARTFIELD and the surrounding countryside is the scene for his stories (with its sandy banks, streams, pine clumps and occasional oaks). Shepard's map which accompanies the stories shows the '100 aker wood', a 'floody place' and 'Eeyores gloomy place – rather boggy and sad'. A shop at Hartfield, 'Pooh Corner', specializes in all things related to the world of Christopher Robin and his friends.

Ashdown Forest Farm: *All year, daily 11am–6pm (or dusk). Tel: (0825) 712040.*
Ashdown Forest Centre: *Tel: (0342) 823583.*

original settlement, founded by villagers fleeing the plague. Today, it is a mix of Victorian and modern brick and tile-hung houses, with a pub, the Royal Oak, where maypole dancing is still performed on May Day, and a cricket green.

Near by, the hidden community of Barcombe Mills is at the site of a Roman crossroads. From Norman times up to 1934 it was continually milling flour. The last mill burned down in 1939. Since Edwardian days this delightful spot on the River Ouse, with its pools and weirs, has been popular for picnics, boating and fishing. A toll bridge here, originally built in 1066, was the first point at which tolls were levied in Sussex. It still has a sign showing the tolls charged in 1939.

♀ The former railway station is now a restaurant and tea-room, while next door is a pub, the **Angler's Rest**, which has pictures showing the mill in its working days. Hidden away up-river and reached by a lovely riverside walk is the **Anchor Inn**, a former bargees' inn dating from 1790.

BARCOMBE

Map p.143, B3 ∗∗
3 miles N of Lewes off the A275

Really three communities in one, Barcombe fragmented when villagers moved out of the original village to escape bubonic plague in the 17th century.

🏛 **St Mary's Church∗** is an isolated 11th-century building, with fine views to Offham Hill, overlooking a pond which is home to unusual ducks like the blue-billed, ruddy duck from North America. It stands amid a few scattered cottages and farms from the original village. Survivors from this early period include a 17th-century Sussex barn and a thatched round-house with horse-operated gin, which was used to operate machinery in the barn; behind them is the 16th-century court house. Inside the church is an unusual, modern glass memorial screen.

The main part of the village is now Barcombe Cross, 1 mile or so from the

BATTLE

Map p.146, A3 ∗∗∗
6 miles NW of Hastings on the A2100

Battle grew up at the gates of its magnificent Benedictine abbey (see p.20) which still dominates the village today. The High St slopes gently up from the abbey gatehouse, past a splendidly varied collection of buildings of all periods, ranging from 15th-century half-timbering to 1990s brickwork.

In front of the gatehouse, on the Abbey Green (now a tarmac car-park), a brass plate marks the spot where bulls were tethered for the old English sport of bull-baiting. The half-timbered Pilgrims' Rest, at the corner of the green, was a pilgrims' hostel as long ago as the 12th century.

🏛 **St Mary's Church∗∗** was built outside Battle's precinct walls in about 1115 by Abbot Ralph to cope with the growing population of the village. The original church was greatly enlarged at the end of the 12th century. The massive west tower dates from about 1450. Inside there are some fine Norman columns with carved capitals, and the font is also Norman.

Above the nave arches, on the north side, are the faded remains of a sequence of wall paintings from around 1300. They tell the life-story of St Margaret of Antioch, who lived in the 4th century and was executed by the Romans after being tortured in various ways, including being hung up by her hair. No one has yet explained why so obscure a saint should be commemorated in a church dedicated to the Virgin Mary.

Near the high altar is the sumptuous painted and gilded tomb of Sir Anthony Browne and his wife. Sir Anthony was granted Battle Abbey after the monasteries were dissolved, and died in 1548. The Battle of Hastings is commemorated by the modern Senlac Window, and by a copy of the Roll of Battle Abbey, which records the names of all the knights who sailed to England with Duke William in 1066.

🏛 **Buckley's Yesterday's World★** is near the church and gives a vivid insight into everyday life in Victorian and Edwardian times. This three-storey medieval building is crammed with reconstructions of every type of shop, from a grocery store to a photographer's studio, displayed to the accompaniment of the music of the day.

🏛 **Battle Historical Museum** is a few doors away, with a more conventional style of display. It features a copy of the Bayeux tapestry, a diorama of the Battle of Hastings, and old local industries such as iron and gunpowder-making.

Going up the High St from the abbey, there are plenty of outstanding old buildings. On the left is the former Bull Inn (now called Inglenooks), built in 1688 with stone taken from the abbey kitchens. The nearby George Hotel has a dignified façade of about 1812, while the stables at the back still have their ostlers' quarters.

🏛 **The Almonry** is a mainly Tudor building, near the top of the High St, with beautifully planted walled gardens at the side and back. Now the local council offices, it contains a detailed town model, continuously updated, which shows every building in Battle.

Beyond The Almonry is a large brick-built complex, very much of the 1990s. Raw-looking, capped by an odd, spindly, brick-and-tile spire, it houses the public library and social services department. A market is held on Fridays in the brick-paved area behind.

For centuries Battle has been famous for its Bonfire Night celebrations, which take place on the first Saturday in November. In May the town holds a 10-day festival of music, plays and art.

Buckley's Yesterday's World: *All year, daily 10am–15.30pm. Tel: (04246) 4269*
Historical Museum, *Easter–early Oct, daily 10am–1pm, 2–5pm. Tel: (04246) 2044*
The Almonry, *Easter–Sept, Mon–Sat 10am–5pm; Oct–Easter, Mon–Sat 10am–4pm, Sun 12am–4pm. Tel: (04246) 2727*
Tourist Information Centre: *88 High St. Tel: (04246) 3721.*

BEACHY HEAD

Map p.144, E4   ★ ★ ★
1 mile SW of Eastbourne off the B2013

The highest chalk cliffs in Britain, at 534ft, command stunning views to Eastbourne directly below and west towards BIRLING GAP and the SEVEN SISTERS beyond. Clear days give views of up to 30 miles away. The 4200 acres of surrounding countryside were bought in 1929 by Eastbourne Borough Council and are maintained as farmland and open leisure space. Over 1 million visitors a year come to enjoy the walks, views and variety of wildlife, which includes nesting birds, rare butterflies and plants.

From the car-park by the hotel, the Peace Path Walk leads down to a viewing point, from where the **lighthouse★★★** can be seen, with its distinctive red and white bands. The tower, constructed in 1902 of Cornish granite, is 153ft high and has been operated automatically since 1983. Its beam is visible from up to 25 miles away.

41

From the cliff-tops, where caution is advised at all times, much birdlife can be observed below, including terns, waders, gulls and fulmars as well as wheatears, warblers and other inland birds. Rare butterflies, such as the Adonis Blue, can be glimpsed in some of the more sheltered areas below the cliff-top.

A small brick seating-area marks the site of the Lloyds Corporation watch-tower which, between 1877 and 1904, was a signalling operation for Channel shipping. West of the hotel is the former Signalman's Cottage, now sadly vandalized.

🛈 A **Countryside Centre★** lies beside the hotel, maintained by the Sussex Wildlife Trust and Eastbourne Country Rangers. It has an exhibition area and gift shop.

There are many walks and bridleways which will reveal more of the geology, archaeology and wildlife in this conservation area. West to Shooters Bottom and beyond, lies the Belle Tout lighthouse (see BIRLING GAP) and a walk below the cliffs leads to Cow Gap. There is a Youth Hostel near by.

Admission to the countryside centre is free, although there is a charge to use the car-park; the proceeds are used to help conserve the downland countryside. Dogs are allowed, but care should be taken on the cliffs. There are toilets (not disabled) and. refreshments are available. There is only limited access for the disabled, except on the Peace Path Walk which has a concrete path.
Countryside Centre: Daily 11am–4.30pm.
Tel: (0323) 411145

BECKLEY

Map p.152, C2   *
10 miles N of Hastings on the B2088

This long village straggles east from its church, meeting up with the London–Rye road at the hamlet of Four Oaks. King Alfred the Great (d. 900) referred in his will to 'the manor of 'Beccanleah'.

🕍 **All Saints Church★**, at the western end of the village, must have had a Saxon predecessor. The stumpy tower, capped by a fine broach spire, dates from the 11th century, and may well be pre-Norman. The church's homely character is emphasized, rather than spoiled, by the domestic-looking dormer windows, added around 1800.

The chancel arch and arcades are Early English, while the ornate tracery of the great east window is 15th-century. Worth hunting out are the stone 'jack-in-the-green' corbels, below two of the aisle arches; such grotesque heads, with leaves growing from their mouths, may well be of pre-Christian origin. In the north aisle is a huge dug-out chest made from a single tree-trunk, and banded with iron, which is thought to be more than 800 years old.

To safeguard Beckley church's treasures, 'electronic intruder protection' has been installed. Valuable items have been photographed and electronically marked – an idea that should surely be adopted by other churches.

The church forms an attractive grouping with the elegant 18th-century brick house across the lane, and the splendid Church House, decorated with carved brickwork pilasters, on the other side of the main road.

The great days of the Sussex iron industry are recalled by Beckley Furnace, lost in the lanes south of the village. It is impossible to believe that this cluster of cottages above the little River Tillingham was once an industrial centre, though the records show that it was.

Great Knelle Farm, on the A268 north of Four Oaks, runs a children's farm on part of its 600 acres, where young visitors can get acquainted with farm animals at first hand by helping to feed them and trundling round the fields on a tractor-drawn train. There are also nature trails, and a working blacksmith's shop. The attractions include conservation areas and a 'talking' scarecrow.
Farm: Easter–end Oct, Sun–Fri 10.30am–5.30pm; also Sats in Aug. Tel: (079726) 321

The little village of Beddingham, with Mount Caburn beyond.

BEDDINGHAM

Map p.143, D4   *
2¹/₂ miles SE of Lewes off the A26

In the shadow of Mount Caburn,
Beddingham would be an attractive village
if it hadn't been divided by the A26/A27
road junction. A row of flint and thatched
cottages runs along the A27, while the
church and a farm lie in a cul-de-sac
between the A26, A27 and Glynde Reach,
a tributary of the River Ouse now
controlled by a pumping station.

St Andrew's Church★ has Norman
origins, but its castellated tower was not
built until the 16th century, using stones
from the demolished Lewes Priory. Inside,
as well as traces of medieval wall paintings,
there is a font with an intricately carved lid
commemorating Queen Victoria's Diamond
Jubilee in 1897 and, on the wall, an armorial
tablet to Sir Thomas Carr, who was knighted
by George III for congratulating him on his
escape from an assassination attempt.

The writer Virginia Woolf lived in the
village at Asham House for seven years
until she moved with her husband to
RODMELL in 1919. For years within the
Beddingham Landfill Site, the house was
due for demolition in 1992, but there are
plans to incorporate parts of it in a new
camping barn to be built as accommodation
for passing walkers on the nearby South
Downs Way. The footpath crosses
Beddingham Hill, site of a radio transmitter.

BERWICK

Map p.144, B2   * * *
3 miles W of Polegate off the A27

Berwick is a pretty village with several
thatched cottages and the Cricketer's Arms
inn. Its greatest attraction, however, is its
remarkable church.

The **Church of St Michael and All
Angels★★★** is reached by a path from the

small car-park and has Saxon origins, with
the present building dating from the 12th
century. It was much restored by the vicar
Edward Boys Ellman (1815–1906),
author of *The Recollections of a Sussex
Parson*, who was devoted to his parish; he is
buried in the churchyard where, to the
south, a small mound marks a probable
Saxon burial site.

The church has a magnificent series of
murals commissioned by Bishop Bell of
Chichester in the early years of World War
II from the group of artists then living at
Charleston Farmhouse (see p.16), which
included Duncan Grant, Vanessa Bell and
Quentin Bell.

The paintings were completed in 1942,
following earlier bomb damage to the
church, and include Vanessa Bell's *Nativity*
on the north wall, which shows local features
such as a Sussex barn and trug; Duncan
Grant's *Christ in Glory*, over the chancel
arch, with the kneeling figures of a soldier,
sailor and airman; and his *Victory of Calvary*,
on the west wall, for which the artist Edward
Le Bas posed. Smaller paintings show the
four seasons and the cycles of life.

An ancient font, believed to be Saxon,
and a 14th-century Easter Sepulchre with a
canopy, used to relate the story of the
Passion to medieval congregations,
complement the modern murals which now
dominate the interior. The clear glass of
the low windows offers fine views of the
countryside. The church has been struck
several times by lightning and suffered
considerable damage (now repaired) in the
Great Storm of 1987.

The church is normally open at the
same times as Charleston Farmhouse, near
by, for a voluntary donation. Access is
difficult for disabled people.

BEXHILL

Map p.146, D2   * * *
5 miles W of Hastings on the A259

Smaller and less bustling than its seaside
neighbours Eastbourne and Hastings,
Bexhill feels like a resort that time has

The harbour at Bexhill.

passed by. For most of the 19th century it was little more than a small summer extension of the inland village of Old Bexhill. Then, in the 1880s, it was developed by Lord De La Warr, who owned the land between Old Bexhill and the sea. Although it does not have any grand Regency or Victorian squares, and never got round to building a pier, it still keeps much of the informal charm of late Victorian and Edwardian times.

♁ The long, low **De La Warr Pavilion**★★ is the seafront centrepiece and is unique among South Coast buildings. With its giant sea-facing bow window and expanses of white-painted concrete, it still looks remarkably modern and would be unlikely to get accepted by any planning committee today, although it was built as long ago as 1935. The winning entry out of 230 in an architectural competition, it was designed by the German architect Erich Mendelsohn, who had fled from Nazi Germany, in partnership with the British-born architect Serge Chermayeff. While it was under construction, and its steel structure was still exposed, it was nicknamed 'King Kong's Meccano Museum'. Now a Grade I Listed Building, it is an up-to-the-minute entertainment centre, with a 1500-seat theatre, restaurant, reading room and conference hall. During the summer it puts on everything from comedy to collectors' fairs, and from tea dances to jazz concerts.

Next door, by way of contrast, is the Oriental-looking Marina Court Avenue, which consists of small seaside homes adorned with flattened onion domes, and windows shaped like Moorish casements.

One block back from the seafront is Egerton Park, a wide expanse of grass and flowerbeds, with a boating lake for days when the sea gets rough.

🏛 **Bexhill Museum**★, on the edge of the park, is a single-storey Edwardian building, with a brightly-painted iron framework, which was originally a 'shelter hall'. It is crammed with displays on local history and archaeology, including cases on the iguanodons and other giant reptiles which once roamed the area.

One display is devoted to the only contact Bexhill had with international affairs: soldiers of the King's German Legion were stationed there during the Napoleonic Wars. These were men from Hanover, who had fled from their homeland after its occupation by the French and formed themselves into a regiment. On their way back to Germany, they fought under Wellington at Waterloo.

Also on view is the detailed architects' model for the De La Warr Pavilion, showing that the original design included a large, round open-air swimming-pool and a graceful pier, ending well out to sea at a pair of diving-boards.

Old Bexhill★★ is at the top of a steep hill, leading up from the front along Sea Rd and Upper Sea Rd and past the station. Here a group of old houses, some brick and some weather-boarded, cluster below the church.

♁ **St Peter's Church**★ has its original foundation dating from 772, when King Offa of Mercia declared its site a 'holy hill' and paid for a church to be built. The present sturdy battlemented tower was built about 1070, and there is still a good deal of Norman stonework inside, including unusually broad, round-headed arches in the nave.

The church's oldest survival is the 'Bexhill Stone', kept in a case below the tower. This roughly rectangular sandstone slab, about 3ft long by 18in wide, is carved with interlaced Celtic designs of a type found in the North of England and goes back to the 8th century. It was almost certainly the lid of a reliquary that contained the bones of a saint, placed in the church when it was consecrated. Also under the tower is a copy of King Offa's charter of 772.

A striking mural over the arch into the north chapel, showing saints with angels flying overhead, was painted in 1951 by Alan Sorrell, better known for his reconstructions of scenes and buildings of the past than for his church wall-paintings. One of the saints shown is St Richard, Bishop of Chichester in the 13th century, who must have come to Bexhill often, as its manor house, opposite the foot of Church St, was the home of the bishops when they visited East Sussex.

The **Manor Gardens**★★ have an entrance where some fragments of these medieval walls survive. They consist of a series of terraces falling away to a pond. The garden is beautifully laid out and planted, with various small buildings dotted about, including an aviary.

🏛 The **Museum of Costume and Social History**★ is housed in the single-storey manor stable. It is lined with tableaux displaying clothes mainly of the period round 1900, from evening dresses to officers' uniforms. Mixed up with the clothes are old typewriters, bicycles, sewing machines and photographs, along with a kitchen complete with mangle, bathtub, sink and cooking range.

Bexhill's western end shades into Cooden, an upmarket resort of hotels and houses with well-tended gardens above the shingle. At its eastern end, the seaside housing continues without interruption to St Leonards.

Bexhill Museum: All year, Tues–Fri and BH Mons 10am–5pm, Sat–Sun 2–5pm. Tel: (0424) 211769.
Museum of Costume and Social History: Apr–end Oct, Tues–Fri (and Mon, June–Oct) 10.30am–5pm (4pm, Oct), Sat–Sun 2–5pm. Tel: (0424) 210045.
Tourist Information Centre: De La Warr Pavilion, Marina. Tel: (0424) 212023.

BIRLING GAP

Map p.144, E4   ★ ★ ★
1 1/2 miles S of East Dean off the A259

Outstanding views of the SEVEN SISTERS, lying proudly to the west, may be had from the observation platform, where a staircase leads down to the shingled beach.
The cliffs, and surounding 700 acres of downland on the Crowlink estate, have belonged to the National Trust since the 1930s and are part of the Heritage Coast national conservation scheme. It is

easy to see why the area has a long history of smuggling and shipwrecks.
There are cliff-top walks, starting from the parking area beside the coastguard station and the Birling Gap Hotel. A National Trust information board, outside in the car park, relates the history of the surrounding countryside. The walks to CUCKMERE HAVEN (to the west) and to Cow Gap (to the east) should, however, only be attempted at low tide, allowing several hours for each. The strong undertow of the tide on the beach makes it particularly hazardous for swimming.
Many tumuli are scattered along the hilltops. An Iron-Age embankment is close to the Belle Tout lighthouse, built in 1831 of granite but abandoned when a new one was built at BEACHY HEAD. Bird life abounds and the area is a favourite breeding place for fulmars and gulls.
There is free parking, toilets and access for the disabled (to all areas except the beach). Refreshments can be bought at the hotel and cafeteria.

BISHOPSTONE

Map p.144, C1   ★ ★
1 1/2 miles NW of Seaford off the A259

This peaceful hamlet has views of the sea and is hidden in the downs at the edge of Seaford's modern housing estates. It shows signs of settlement in the surrounding fields going back to the early Bronze Age, 3500 years ago. A Saxon settlement and cemetery was also discovered in the late 1960s.
For nine hundred years, up to the 17th century, Bishopstone was a retreat for the Bishops of Chichester and, according to records, it was the bishops who built the first windmill in England here in 1199. The mill has long gone, but you can still see a fine example of Saxon and Norman architecture, St Andrew's Church.

♰ **St Andrew's Church**★★ is probably the finest church of its age in the area. It has a rare Saxon sundial bearing the name 'Eadric', a square flint Norman tower and, inside, a 12th-century coffin lid

47

carved from stone. At one time, the bishop's grange stood near here and, in 1324, it is said that Edward ll was entertained here.

Behind the church are some charming 18th-century almshouses. Near by are located Bishopstone Manor (now three dwellings dating from 1688 and bearing a carved Pelham buckle) and pretty cottages grouped around a green known locally as the Egg. Other interesting houses are Norton farmhouse, which has mullioned windows and dates from 1597, and Barrack Cottage, which recalls the time when large numbers of soldiers were billeted in the area as a defence against possible Napoleonic invasion. Nearby Seaford Bay was considered a very likely landing point.

Just below Bishopstone, off the main Newhaven–Seaford Road, are the few remains of an old tide-mill, built in 1762. It was huge, probably the largest industrial building in Sussex at the time, and operated until 1884, harnessing the power of incoming tides to grind corn. Living conditions in the community which supported the mill were terrible, but it survived until World War II when the workers' cottages were flattened to allow unobstructed views of the coastline. Members of the Catt family, who operated the mill, are buried in the churchyard.

BLACKHAM

Map p.154, C4
7 miles E of East Grinstead on the A264

The hamlet of Blackham is a little group of houses and farms, just north of Withyham, scattered round the main A264. All Saints' Church, built in 1902, is a small building with lancet windows and unusual bell-turret.

The surrounding countryside is very pretty with gently rolling hills, high beech hedges, large oaks and unspoilt hedgerows full of wild flowers. Straggling southwards from the main road is another hamlet, Balls Green, with picturesque cottages and round Sussex oasts.

BODIAM

Map p.151, B3   *
10 miles N of Hastings off the A229

Apart from its magnificent castle (see p.22), there is little to see in this small village down by the River Rother.

A pretty red-brick bridge across the river leads to the village, which consists of the Castle pub and a cluster of houses round a small green edged with horse-chestnut trees. The slope above the castle has been turned into a neatly planted vineyard.

From late March to early September, a small cruise boat, the *Elsie May*, chugs down the River Rother to Newenden, taking about 45 minutes to do the journey.

St Giles' Church (usually kept locked) is up a steep hill north of the village, tucked away at the end of a path beside the Sandhurst road. The knoll on which it stands looks man-made, and may have been a fortified motte or earth mound. The Early English chancel, with its lancet windows, is 13th-century, while the battlemented west tower is 15th-century Perpendicular.

The 200-acre **Quarry Farm**, across the river from the village, entices visitors with a superb crimson-painted steam traction-engine at its entrance. The farm calls itself the 'Rural Experience', and is especially geared to children. A walk round 'four seasons on a farm' passes pens of rare farm animals such as Tamworth pigs, and gives an insight into the farmer's year, with displays on bee-keeping, sheep-shearing and other rural activities.

One of the yards is full of steam-powered road-rollers and other monsters, brilliant in gleaming brass and paint, which snort into life when Quarry Farm holds its periodic steam-fairs.
Quarry Farm: Easter–end Sept, Weds–Sun and BHs; late July–early Sept, daily 11am–5pm. Tel: (0580) 830670.

The gatehouse, Bodiam Castle.

BOREHAM STREET

Map p.145, A3
7 miles E of Hailsham on the A271

From the main road which runs along a ridge there are extensive views of the Weald to the north and Pevensey Levels to the south; it is hard to believe that the village was once on the edge of the sea before it retreated. Edward I passed through the hamlet in 1302 on his way to Battle Abbey.

There are several fine brick houses in the village, some in the 18th-century classical style, and a choice of tea-rooms and restaurants. Adjacent to one of these is an old stone mounting-block. Boreham Street Farm, on the main road, has a circular oast-house with twin cowls and an adjacent barn, both converted into private dwellings. The White Friars hotel has 16th century origins.

Windmill Hill is 1 mile to the west, where a much dilapidated post-mill stands on the northern edge of the village, past the green. There is a modern, residential tennis training-centre in the village.

BREDE

Map p.147, A1   ******
6 miles N of Hastings on the A28

Brede is a pretty, compact village of brick and weather-boarded houses, built round a small Y-shaped layout of roads. It gets its name from the Anglo-Saxon word meaning 'broad', referring not to the place, but to the river which runs along the valley to the south. In earlier times, the Brede was a tidal arm of the sea, navigable inland as far as Sedlescombe. It filled the valley, joining the River Rother and the River Tillingham to form a wide estuary at Rye. In 1297 it was still wide enough for Edward I to inspect his Channel fleet only 1 mile east of today's bridge over the river.

⛪ St George's Church** stands in a commanding position looking across the valley to the ridge behind Hastings.

Basically a Norman church of about 1140, it was greatly enlarged from the 13th century onwards. The low battlemented tower dates from about 1450. The interior is crammed with monuments and has plenty of stained glass, giving it a very busy feel.

The south chapel was the chantry of the Oxenbridge family, and is full of their tombs. The finest of them, complete with effigy in armour, commemorates Sir Goddard Oxenbridge, who died in 1537. Known locally as the 'Brede Giant', he is said to have been 7ft tall, and was popularly supposed to eat children for supper. His daughter, Lady Tyrwhitt, was governess to the young Princess Elizabeth, later Queen Elizabeth I.

Near by is a tall, slender sculpture of the Madonna and Child, carved in oak by Clare Sheridan, first cousin of Sir Winston Churchill, in memory of her son, who was drowned at sea in 1937. She died in 1970 and is buried in the churchyard, across the path from the east window. Like the Oxenbridges, she lived at Brede Place, a 15th-century manor house 1 mile east of the village.

Towards the back of the church is a massive Flemish chest, dated 1633, decorated with carved panels of biblical and secular scenes. The grey panels showing the Stations of the Cross were painted by Sir W. T. Monnington, a former President of the Royal Academy.

Across the road from the church is a cottage whose proud builders signed their names and date, 'John and Mary West 1760', with blue headers in the brickwork.

BRIGHTLING

Map p.150, D3   ******
7 miles E of Heathfield off the B2096

Brightling is a tiny dog-leg of a village, consisting of the parish church, the manor house, and a handful of small houses on either side of the road. It is still haunted by the eccentric personality who lived there in the years around 1800 – John Fuller, known as 'Mad Jack' because of the follies he built in the neighbourhood.

The most obvious of these is the huge Pyramid tomb, 25ft high and made of sandstone blocks, which dominates the churchyard. Legend claimed that 'Mad Jack', who died in 1834 aged 77, was buried inside it wearing a top hat and holding a bottle of claret. Unfortunately, this has now been disproved. A little to the south of Brightling village is a hamlet with the strange name of Cackle Street; there is another one near Brede.

ⓣ The small **Church of St Thomas à Becket★★** is a pretty building which is still almost entirely medieval, as the Victorians seem to have ignored it. About the only addition since the 15th century is the entrance porch, tacked on in 1749. On the nave wall is a fine memorial bust of Fuller, showing a jovial, well-fed character. Opposite him is the bust of William Shield, a musician friend who is buried in Westminster Abbey. The north aisle walls are painted with biblical texts in elaborate script, dating from the 16th to 18th centuries.

Fuller's gifts to the church included the neat little gallery at the west end, together with the organ that sits on it. Though it looks like an ordinary church organ, it is in fact a barrel organ, the largest in Britain in fully working order. It has two barrels, each playing 12 tunes.

An unusual feature of the church is a 'listening point' where, for a small fee, you can listen to an account of its history.

The 18th-century façade of Brightling Manor (not open to the public) adjoins the churchyard and can be seen through the main gate on the road. In Fuller's time it was known as Rose Hill, so called by a Fuller ancestor who married a girl called Rose and commemorated her in this delightful way.

Ⓜ Brightling Needle is the most prominent of the follies built by 'Mad Jack', scattered in and around the village. This 40ft stone obelisk stands in the middle of a field 650ft above sea-level, and is the second highest point in East Sussex. During Napoleonic times it was the site of a beacon for warning of the arrival of French ships in the Channel.

Ⓜ The **Sugar Loaf★**, down the hill near Wood's Corner on the B2096, is a slender, hollow cone like a witch's hat, made of stone and reached along an overgrown path from a lay-by. It is said that Fuller wagered with a friend that the spire of nearby Dallington Church could be seen from the grounds of Rose Hill; realising that this was not the case he had the fake spire built nearer to home. His other follies are a temple in the grounds of Brightling Park, and an observatory, now a private house, neither of which can be visited. Fuller's building projects were more than mere eccentricity, as they gave local employment at a time when agriculture was severely depressed after the Napoleonic Wars.

BRIGHTON

Map p.142, E4 ★★★
8 miles W of Newhaven on the A259

It was in Brighton, 250 years ago, that the English love-affair with the seaside began when Richard Russell, a doctor who had recently moved there from Lewes, published a dissertation declaring how good bathing in the sea at Brightelmstone, as Brighton was then called, was for the health. George III's flamboyant son, the Prince Regent, was among those who went to find out for themselves, first making a visit in 1783. Over the years he made frequent visits to take the waters, as a result of which it became fashionable for the rich and famous to do likewise. When the railway arrived in 1841 many more people were able to reach Brighton on a cheap, day excursion from London. From those small beginnings, Brighton has grown into the largest and liveliest seaside resort in the south-east.

At the time of Dr Russell's pronouncement, Brighton was no more than a centuries old fishing village, ravaged by storms and French raiders. However, the Prince Regent liked the place so much, especially after he met Maria Fitzherbert there and secretly married her, that he decided to make it his home.

Ⓜ The Royal Pavilion★★★ was initially a small, rented farmhouse, which the Prince

Regent later bought and had enlarged into a classical country home. Over the years it was added to and then the architect John Nash was engaged to carry out a major transformation which was completed in 1822. Renamed the Royal Pavilion, the Prince Regent's fantasy became reality soon after he became George IV. It was a palatial extravaganza beside the sea, its exterior decorated in the Indian Moghul style with spires, minarets and onion domes, the interior in an opulent Chinese decor with hand-painted ceilings, enormous glass chandeliers, and magnificent golden dragons. After George's death, William IV and Queen Adelaide made just as many visits, but Victoria was not so keen and, after her last visit in 1845, faced with threats to pull the Pavilion down, the town bought it in 1850.

During World War I, the Pavilion served as a hospital, appropriately for Indian soldiers. More recently it has undergone massive restoration work, hindered at times by fire and storm damage, but by late 1992 the work was nearing completion, most of the main rooms returned to their fully furnished, original splendour. Among the most outstanding rooms are the Banqueting Room, the Great Kitchen and the Music Room.

Elsewhere, grand terraces and squares were being built. The first of these was Royal Crescent, built with black mathematical tiles in 1799, and this was quickly followed by Bedford Square and Regency Square.

Kemp Town* grew because more grand ideas were implemented as Brighton developed. In 1823, a local landowner called Thomas Read Kemp, who had originally rented the farmhouse to the Prince Regent, started work on Kemp Town, to the east of Brighton, inspired by John Nash's work around London's Regents Park. At the same time work had started on the squares of Hove to the west. Sussex Square, Lewes Crescent, Arundel Terrace and Chichester Terrace formed the nucleus of Kemp Town which, unlike Hove, never became a separate

entity. These days the name is applied to the much bigger area lying east of the Old Steine. Once the homes of dukes, the grand houses are more likely occupied now by actors, authors and television personalities. Brighton Racecourse is found on the downs behind Kemp Town and has been hosting flat-race meetings since 1783. It now holds 15 or so a year.

In the Victorian era, the town had no fewer than three piers, a fashion of the period, which gave a taste of strolling the decks of a ship at sea without being tossed about by the waves. The first was the Chain Pier, which was built like a suspension bridge in 1823 and destroyed by a storm in 1896. This was followed by the West Pier which opened in 1866 but was closed in 1975 following post-war neglect. Recently, part of the pier has been dismantled, though there are hopes to restore it fully by the end of the century. The **Palace Pier****, opened in 1894 just west of the Chain Pier, still draws thousands of visitors.

🏛 **The Brighton Museum and Art Gallery**** lies next to the Royal Pavilion, housed in what was the Prince Regent's indoor tennis courts. Amongst its extensive displays, the museum includes art-nouveau and art-deco furniture and decorative art, musical instruments, fashion displays (from cavemen's furs to outlandish punk), paintings by English and European masters, the famous Willett Collection of unusual 18th- and 19th-century pottery and porcelain, and sections on Sussex archaeology and Brighton history.

The Dome*, which became a theatre in 1935 and seats more than 2000 people, puts on numerous concerts, from pop to classical, and also has a summer programme of entertainment. This is situated next to the Museum in what used to be the Prince Regent's stables.

The Theatre Royal*, behind the Pavilion in New Rd, is another much-loved feature of the town. Originally built in 1807, but altered in Victorian times

Michelham Priory, near Upper Dicker.

53

when it inherited its red-plush interior, it often stages productions prior to their West End runs.

🏛 **Preston Manor★★**, along the A23 from the Royal Pavilion, dates from 1738, although there has been a house on the site since about 1250. Owned by the Stanford family for 138 years, and substantially altered by them in the early 1900s, it stands in a corner of Preston Park, preserved as a typical Edwardian country home with rooms containing silver, glass, china, clocks, pictures and period furniture. One room is decorated with leather squares brought to England by Catherine of Aragon. The servants' quarters are also on view, giving a unique view of life 'downstairs' as well as 'upstairs'. In the grounds there are lily ponds, a croquet lawn, a walled garden and a pets' graveyard.

⛪ **St Peter's Church★** is a 13th-century building adjoining the manor. It has some remarkable wall-paintings of the period depicting St Michael, the Nativity, the Last Supper and the martyrdom of Thomas à Becket. Damaged by a fire in 1906, they have since been restored.

🏛 **The Booth Museum of Natural History★★**, in nearby Dyke Rd, houses one of the finest collections of birds in Britain. More than 500 can be seen, mainly assembled between 1865 and 1890, in settings recreating their natural environment. Some are now quite rare. Other galleries have displays of butterflies from around the world and animal remains, including fossilized dinosaur bones, and a section on nature conservation.

The Sea Life Centre★★, housed underground in the Gothic galleries of the former aquarium and dolphinarium on the seafront, gives a fascinating insight into life beneath the sea. The largest attraction of its kind in Britain, it is full of fascinating marine life, both tropical and local. Touch-pools and a fish nursery are of special interest to children, while a glass tunnel enables the whole family to walk beneath the sea and watch sharks, giant conger eels and sting-rays drift silently by at close quarters.

🏛 **The Sussex Toy and Model Museum★** is another museum to fascinate the children. Located beneath the arches of Brighton railway station in Trafalgar St, its collections include cars, trains, aircraft, soldiers, forts, dolls and teddy bears.

The Lanes★★★ are one of Brighton's most popular attractions after the Pavilion. At the heart of the old town, and confined by North, East and West Sts with the seafront to the south, this maze of narrow, winding streets and alleys lined with Georgian bow-windowed frontages was once the home of fishermen. Now it is a must for antique lovers, but there are also fashion shops and a good choice of cafés, restaurants and pubs. Within the area stands the dignified town hall, built in 1830 on the site of a small priory linked with St Pancras in LEWES. In recent years the North Lane area between the Royal Pavilion and the station has been developing along similar lines.

Close to the Lanes, the Old Steine was where the fishing boats were hauled up on the beach and the nets left to dry. Now laid out with gardens and lawns, it is surrounded by several outstanding houses, including Marlborough House, designed by Robert Adam, and next door, Steine House. The latter, now occupied by the YMCA, was where the Prince Regent installed Mrs Fitzherbert, who never actually stayed at the Pavilion.

⛪ **St Peter's**, the parish church, can be reached from the Old Steine via Grand Parade. Built in the 1820s by Sir Charles Barry, one of the architects responsible for the Houses of Parliament, it is in neo-Gothic style and attains almost cathedral-like proportions.

⛪ **St Bartholomew's**, in nearby Ann St, is the largest brick-built church in England. Never completed, it was built in the late 1800s to the same dimensions as Noah's Ark.

⛪ **St Nicholas's**, in Dyke Rd, is Brighton's oldest church. Originally built in the 14th century, it suffered at the hands of the Victorian mania for major restoration.

Buried in the churchyard is Nicholas Tattersell who, for the sum of £60, took Charles II from Shoreham to exile in France in 1651. Tattersell later renamed the boat he used 'The Royal Escape'. The event is commemorated each year by the Royal Escape yacht race to Fécamp in Normandy, organized by the Old Ship Hotel, the oldest of the town's inns. Also buried at the church is Phoebe Hessel, who, in the 18th century, managed to serve undetected for 17 years as a soldier in the army, to be near the man she loved. She reached the ripe old age of 108. Martha Gunn, who died in 1815, was one of the original women bathing attendants, known as 'dippers', who helped people in and out of the sea across the pebble beach. She was a favourite of the Prince Regent and her portrait is said to hang in Buckingham Palace. Amon Wilds was the man who built much of Regency Brighton.

The Brighton Centre was built to meet Brighton's more recent needs as a major conference venue. Opened in 1977, this large, ugly concrete seafront edifice hosts major conferences, including party political conferences, as well as concerts and indoor sporting championships. Two of the town's top hotels, the Grand, with its iron balconies and glazed entrance, and the red brick Metropole, both products of the Victorian era and forerunners of the luxury hotels of the Riviera, are conveniently near by.

The **marina★** is the town's latest development, built beneath the cliffs at Black Rock. Originally opened in 1978, it has been beset by financial problems but to date has permanent moorings for around 2000 yachts, exclusive apartments, shops, pubs, restaurants and a multi-screen cinema. Future plans include a large hotel.

The Volks Electric Railway★ links Black Rock with the Palace Pier by 1¼ miles of track. Built by Brighton inventor Magnus Volk in 1883, and extended in 1901 after originally running from the aquarium to the Chain Pier, it was the first public electric railway in Britain.

Transport, especially early motor transport, has strong associations with Brighton and one of the best known events on the town's calender is the London to Brighton Veteran Car Run which takes place every November and commemorates the repeal of the 'red flag' Act. Lesser-known London to Brighton events include the Historic Motorcycles run in March and the Veteran Commercial Vehicles Rally in May, while in June the bike ride attracts more than 20,000 cyclists. All the events finish on the seafront beneath the cast-iron columns of Madeira Drive, scene of the famous speed trials every September.

The Brighton Festival★★, one of the most important international arts festivals in Britain (with more than 400 events), is held over three weeks every May. Entertainment includes theatre, dance, exhibitions, fireworks, concerts, opera, jazz and folk, poetry readings, cabaret, street parties and parades, and draws international and fringe performers as well as thousands of spectators from many miles around.
Royal Pavilion: June–Sept, daily 10am–6pm; Oct–May, daily 10am–5pm. Tel: (0273) 603005
Brighton Museum and Art Gallery: All year, Tues–Sat 10am–5.45pm, Sun 2–5pm. Tel: (0273) 603005
Preston Manor: All year, Tues–Sat and BHs 10am–5pm. Sun 2–5pm. Tel: (0273) 603005
Booth Museum of Natural History: All year, Mon–Weds and Fri–Sat 10am–5pm, Sun 2–5pm. Tel: (0273) 603005
Sea Life Centre: All year, daily 10am–6pm. Tel: (0273) 604234
Sussex Toy and Model Museum: All year, Tues–Sun 10am–5pm. Tel: (0273) 749494
Volks Electric Railway: Easter–end Sept, times vary. Tel: (0273) 681061
Tourist Information Centre: Marlborough House, 54 Old Steine. Tel: (0273) 23755.

BURWASH

Map p.150, C3　　　　　　　　★★
5 miles E of Heathfield on the A265

Burwash is one of the most beautiful villages in Sussex. It consists of a single High St of predominantly 17th- and 18th-century

timber-framed and weather-boarded houses. The houses are fronted by brick pavements and well-kept lawns and trees. There are two possible interpretations of the name Burwash: it is said by some to derive from Burghersh, the title of the Duke of Westmoreland's eldest son; or from the Anglo–Saxon *burgh* (meaning hill), and *woesse* (meaning bog or marshland). The latter explanation is quite likely, as the village stands on a hill surrounded by clay soil which is marshy during the wettest times of the year.

Burwash was a famous smuggling town in the 18th and 19th centuries: smuggling and sheep-stealing grew as the iron industry declined, upon which the area had depended since Roman times. Between 1820 and 1840, there were so many unsavoury characters in the area that Burwash was declared unsafe to travel through.

A walk along the High St passes some pretty cottages and a fine red-brick house with grey headers, Rampyndene, which was built in 1699 for a wealthy wool merchant. It has an ornate front porch carved with whimsical birds, flowers and cherubs.

St Bartholomew's Church is at the eastern end of the village. It has a Norman tower dated 1090 although much of the church was rebuilt by the Victorians. Among its monuments is what is thought to be the oldest cast-iron tomb slab in existence. Dating from the 14th century, it has a decorative cross and an inscription to John Colins. The font, and a small brass, date from the 15th century. In the south aisle is a tablet to Rudyard Kipling's son, John, who was killed in Loos in 1915, at the age of 18. The Kipling family lived near by at Bateman's (see p.14) for the last 30 years of Rudyard's life.

Burwash Common, 2 miles to the south-west on the A265, is strung out along the main road. Its church, St Philip's, is a solid Victorian building dated 1867. The chancel arch is very ornately carved with heavy foliage. A fine 17th-century brick house, called Holmshurst, is 1 mile north of the village.

BUXTED

Map p.149, C2
1 mile E of Maresfield on the A272

Buxted is a predominantly Victorian village built on two hills and centred on its station. This was not always so, however. The village originally grew up around the great house of Buxted Park (see p.14) and was a traditional English village with a parish church and villagers' cottages. But in the 1830s Lord Liverpool, the owner of Buxted Park, wanted more privacy and tried to move the village out of the park. The inhabitants understandably resisted relocation, so Lord Liverpool retaliated by ceasing maintenance work on their cottages. When these finally became uninhabitable, the villagers had no choice but to move out, and ended up in new houses near the railway line. In 1885, St Mary's Church was built for the new village by Father Wagner, a wealthy High Church priest who erected several churches around Brighton, particularly in poorer areas.

St Margaret's* 13th-century parish church, is the old village church and is thus in the park where the village once stood, just along the drive. It is dedicated, unusually, to St Margaret, Queen of Scotland (1045-1093) and there are marguerites carved in her name on the Jacobean pulpit. The same flowers are also moulded into the superb 17th-century chancel ceiling, along with hop motifs. The ceiling was a gift from a rector of the time in thanks for a splendid crop of hops. The church tower is medieval and its small shingled spire was added in the 18th century.

Among the monuments in the church are an ancient vestment chest, two small medieval brasses to rectors of the parish, and the Jacobean pulpit mentioned above, from which William Wordsworth's brother preached when he was vicar at Buxted. A white marble plaque commemorates Basil Ionides (d. 1950) who owned Buxted

The village of Ditchling, superbly set beneath the Downs.

Park from 1931, and rebuilt the house after it was gutted by fire in 1940. The park can be reached through a gate at the end of the churchyard.

Hogge House is near the entrance to the park. It is a black-and-white, half-timbered building, decorated with a panel showing a hog. This was the emblem of Ralph Hogge who owned the house. Hogge's foundry is thought to have been the first in England to cast cannons, in 1543, and his cannons are said to have been responsible for the defeat of the Spanish Armada in 1588.

CADE STREET

Map p.150, D1
1 mile E of Heathfield on the B2096

A roadside monument, just north of the Battle road, announces that Jack Cade, rebel, was killed here by Alexander Iden, Sheriff of Kent. Cade was the leader of the Kentish rebellion of 1450 and the inscription warns against his path: 'This is the Success of all Rebels, and this Fortune chanceth ever to Traitors.' In fact, Cade didn't actually die here but was found, mortally wounded, in a nearby garden and died on the way to London.

The **Independent Chapel**, 1767, is a simple symmetrical building with a graceful oval window above its south-facing porch. Inside the galleried chapel, and decorating headstones in the churchyard, are several pretty terracotta relief plaques made in the early 19th century by Jonathan Harmer of Heathfield, a potter whose work can be seen in several churches in East Sussex.

CAMBER

Map p.153, D1
4 miles E of Rye off the A259

Camber is a sprawling holiday village, made up of seaside bungalows, a holiday camp, caravan parks, putting greens, amusement arcades and all the usual summer paraphernalia. What sets it apart from similar resorts are the magnificent Camber Sands (see p.29), which stretch for 2 miles east from the mouth of the River Rother to the shingle of Dungeness, and are backed by huge sand-dunes. At low tide, the sea goes out for a half a mile or more, and unwary swimmers are often cut off by the fast incoming tide.

Camber Castle* (not open) is one of a chain of castles built round the South Coast during the 1530s: at a time of hostility between Henry VIII and France. Now stranded far inland, when it was built it stood on a spit of land guarding the Rother estuary and was right on the coast, as Kent's Walmer and Deal Castles still are. It is built to a cloverleaf plan, with a squat tower at its centre. The retreating sea soon made it useless, and it was dismantled in 1642. English Heritage are at present restoring it, and hope eventually to open it to the public.

Behind Camber stretches the flat, sheep-covered grassland of Romney Marsh, and 7 miles down the coast the hulking blocks of Dungeness Atomic Power Station loom in the distance. Rye's championship golf-course is just west of the village.

CATSFIELD

Map p.146, B2   *
3 miles W of Battle on the A269

Catsfield's name has nothing to do with animals. It derives either from a Belgic tribe called the Catti, or from St Cedd. The village centre is built round a small triangle of roads, and is dominated by a tall and oddly foreign-looking spire. This belongs not to the parish church, as you might expect, but to the Methodist church, built in 1912.

St Laurence's Church, at the top of a steep hill, south of the village, is an unpretentious medieval church which goes back in part to Norman or even Saxon times. The sturdy west tower was built before 1200 and the chancel is 14th-century.

The north aisle dates from the 1840s. Just inside the door is a rare type of holy-water stoup, cut into the stonework of the wall. In the nave is an unusual monument in encaustic tiles, showing a yacht outlined against the setting sun. It commemorates Lady Annie Brassey, an intrepid Victorian traveller, who died at sea in the Indian Ocean aboard her schooner *Sunbeam* in September 1887, and was 'committed to the deep at sunset'.

The tile-hung Queen Anne Manor House can be glimpsed over the churchyard wall.

CHAILEY

Map p.143, A3
8 miles N of Lewes on the A275

The name Chailey comes from the Saxon *chag,* meaning gorse, and *legh,* the word for field. Chailey is a big, scattered parish of three villages: North Chailey, Chailey and South Common. Its long parish boundary extends for 24 miles. Chailey's pretty village green is overlooked by a cluster of brick and tile cottages and St Peter's Church.

St Peter's Church has a squat 13th-century tower with an unusual shingled, pyramidal spire. The chancel is also 13th-century. It was all much altered by the Victorians.

Chailey Moat, near by, used to be the old rectory. It is a 16th-century house, hiding behind an 18th-century brick and tile-hung façade. The moat is said to have been dug by a resident parson.

South Common, a straggling hamlet with the common enclosed, was at one time famous for its pottery made from local Weald clay. Local street names, like Kilnwood Lane, bear witness to the village's pottery industry. Although the potteries have gone, there is a large Redland brickworks.

Chailey Common, around the junction of the A275 and A272, is 450 acres of wet and dry heathland with rare sphagnum bog, heather and gorse. It has been a nature reserve since 1966 and is privately owned and managed by Chailey Common Nature Reserve. The common has been designated a Site of Special Scientific Interest for its heathland plants, which include rare orchids, and its wide variety of insects and birds (such as the stonechat). During World War II, the common was used as an army camp and tank-training ground: remains of the trenches and gun emplacements can still be seen. It is open to the public all year round. There are two landmarks visible on the common: a restored old smock mill (not working) and a tall spire which belongs to the chapel of Chailey Heritage. The modern village of North Chailey is built around the common.

St Mary's is the village church of North Chailey. Built of sandstone in 1876, it has an unusual, saddle-backed central tower.

Chailey Heritage is an important school for handicapped children. It was founded in 1903, sentimentally titled 'The Guild of Brave Poor Things', for the victims of tuberculosis and other physically impaired children. Today there are over 200 children at the school which has facilities to cope with spina bifida and cerebral palsy. The school chapel was built by Sir Ninian Comper in 1913 and has a lovely, blue-and-gold wagon-roof. Hanging on one wall is a rope from Scott's last expedition – a symbol of co-operation.

CHALVINGTON

Map p.144, A3   *
5 miles W of Hailsham off the A22

St Bartholomew's Church is of 13th-century Decorated style, in flint and stone, with a shingled spire above a small wooden turret containing three early 17th-century bells. In the timbers of the roof, above the nave, can be seen two small, coloured panes of glass. The north-east window has a panel of an archbishop with crozier, inscribed S.TH/OM/AS and

59

may well be a 13th-century representation of St Thomas à Becket. At the top of the chancel's east window is some further stained glass, with an inscription to John Diliwyt, a late 14th-century rector of the parish, and the arms of Canterbury. The chancel, which has no arch, was restored in 1974 through the benefaction of Margaret Andrews, a parishioner; her initials are cut into the stone step to the right. By the altar is a memorial to Ann Fuller, daughter of the first Lord Heathfield; her hatchment is also within the church. The parish register which survives from 1538 is amongst the oldest such records in the county. To the left of the churchyard entrance stands a poignant tombstone to Job Guy 'departed this life by a kick from a horse' aged eight years.

CHIDDINGLY

Map p.149, F3   * * *
5 miles NW of Hailsham off the A22

 Chiddingly Church is built of sandstone and has late 11th-century origins, although it was much restored in 1864. It overlooks the cricket green. An octagonal 130ft stone spire, one of only three surviving in East Sussex (the others are at NORTHIAM and DALLINGTON), dominates the surrounding area. Pelham buckles are carved on each side of the west door of the 15th-century tower. To the left of the porch, which is roofed with Horsham slates, is a tombstone with a terracotta plaque by the Heathfield artist Jonathan Harmer.

On the south wall of the 17th-century transept is the remarkable alabaster memorial to Sir John Jefferay, Baron of the Exchequer to Elizabeth I, and Member of Parliament for Arundel and East Grinstead. He is shown lying with his wife, with his daughter Elizabeth in a hooped dress and her husband Sir Edward Montague in niches below. Next to it is a memorial to William Jefferay (d. 1611), and his wife Margaret together with their seven daughters, lined up in a row to the right.

A brass with black lettering to John Jefferay (*c.* 1480-1512) is in the floor of the centre of the church, which also contains a fine 18th-century pulpit.

 The Jefferay family seat was at **Chiddingly Place**, a short walk to the north-west of the village and now Place Farm. Remnants of the late Tudor–early Elizabethan features can be seen from the road and the large barn to the left of the farmhouse has several early windows, now blocked up with brick. The Wealdway and Vanguard Way, long-distance footpaths, intersect near the village.

COOKSBRIDGE

Map p.143, B3
2¹/₂ miles N of Lewes on the A275

This small village, grouped around its railway station, is said to have got its name when Simon de Montfort's army of Londoners stopped here on the way to do battle with Henry III at Lewes in 1264: breakfast was served to the men by cooks on the bridge. Whether the story is true or not is another matter. Another theory for the name is that the man who built the bridge was called Cook.

Today the village comprises mainly modern housing, but there are a few old flint and brick cottages and, at the southern end of the village, an old malthouse which is let at a peppercorn rent to the parish council. It is now used as the village hall.

 Shelley's Folly, a mansion of Flemish-bond brick built around 1700 in the style of Wren, is about 1 mile north of the village.

CROWBOROUGH

Map p.154, E4
7 miles SW of Tunbridge Wells on the A26

Situated at the eastern point of the rough triangle covered by Ashdown Forest, Crowborough really only began to develop

Formal flower-beds by the seafront at Eastbourne.

in the Victorian era, and is now a wealthy commuter town. It spreads over Beacon Hill and is the highest town in Sussex, with wide views of the surrounding countryside.

⌂ Beacon House, at 796ft above sea level, is the highest inhabited spot in the county. Dating from 1838, it is one of Crowborough's oldest houses which illustrates just how new the town is, by Sussex standards anyway. The front of the house is signed with the Abergavenny arms (see ERIDGE PARK), which emblazoned all the Abergavenny estate properties of the 19th century.

The modern town centre is at Crowborough Cross where two main roads intersect, and it has a comprehensive shopping centre and sports complex. At the heart of Crowborough is a triangular green overlooked by the oldest part of the town.

⛪ All Saints' Church was built in 1744 but so altered and enlarged in the 1880s, at the instigation of Lord Abergavenny, that all you can see of the original building is its tower. It is built in sombre, dark grey stone. Next door is the Vicarage, a particularly fine Georgian house, built at the same time as the old church, in 1744, and by the same man, Sir Henry Fermor, whose name is signed on the doorway.

Until Crowborough started to develop in the mid 19th century, the area was principally inhabited by smugglers and iron-smelters. The Victorians built a comfortable town of large detached houses with gardens and a railway station. At the turn of the century, Crowborough was advertised as 'Scotland in Sussex', because of its hills and its nearness to Ashdown Forest. Perhaps the advertising appealed to Sir Arthur Conan Doyle who moved here in 1909, building a large house called Windlesham Manor (now a hotel) near the golf course. Most famous for creating Sherlock Holmes, Conan Doyle also wrote some less well-known books which are set in the area, such as *The Poison Belt* (based on Rotherfield) and *When the World Screamed* (the South Downs). Conan Doyle died in 1930 at the

age of 71 and was buried in his garden before being moved, with his wife, to the family vault in 1935. Belief that his ghost haunted Windlesham Manor was so strong that the house was exorcized.

CROWHURST

Map p.146, B3
5 miles NW of Hastings off the A2100

This village stands at the head of a valley high above Bexhill and Hastings, straddling the railway, with woodlands behind.

⛪ St George's Church has a 15th-century tower, but is otherwise Victorian. Carved in the stonework on either side of the tower door is the 'Pelham buckle' – the emblem of the Pelham family, found on several Sussex churches. The badge was awarded to Sir John Pelham, who came from LAUGHTON, for his part in capturing King John of France at the Battle of Poitiers in 1356. The vast yew tree in the churchyard is said to date back to the time of King Harold.

The ruins of Crowhurst's 13th-century Manor House are in a garden below the church. They consist of a gable end of the hall, complete with window tracery, and other fragments.

CUCKMERE HAVEN

Map p.144, D3   ＊＊＊
½ mile S of Exceat off the A259

The River Cuckmere rises near Heathfield, 20 miles to the north, and its outflow to the sea is below Exceat Bridge at the unspoilt Cuckmere Haven, where its final passage is characterized by a series of spectacular meanders.

The Seven Sisters Country Park (see p.24) is the best place to view these meanders, by following the trail which lies to the east of the river's course. There are parking facilities at Seven Sisters Country Park, along with refreshments, toilets and an information centre.

For many hundreds of years, the mouth of the river has drifted gradually east owing to the encroachments of the shingle beach. A new cut was made in 1846 to prevent flooding of the valley and this is strengthened today by an automatic weir control. The beach shingle is kept in place to some degree by a system of groynes. A fish-way has been constructed by the National Rivers Authority to help the migrating parr of the sea trout pass between the river and the tidal section.

A group of old coastguard cottages stands on Short Cliff to the west of the estuary; the area was renowned in the 18th and 19th centuries as a landing place for smuggled goods. Several gangs operated from here, taking their booty to villages further inland. There were notable encounters on the shore in 1783 and 1788 with Excise officers.

Several shipwrecks have occurred on the coastline here, and occasional glimpses at low tide may be had of the remains of the German ship *Polynesia* which was wrecked in 1890.

The SOUTH DOWNS WAY reaches the coast at Cuckmere Haven and crosses the causeway before continuing its eastern route along the cliffs towards BEACHY HEAD.

DALLINGTON

Map p.150, D3 **

4 miles E of Heathfield off the B2096

The picturesque village has several attractive brick and tile-hung cottages and next to the church is a fine timber-framed house. Dallington Forest was once an important source of fuel for the iron-making industry of the Weald. In a field north of the B2096 is the Sugar Loaf, one of 'Mad Jack' Fuller's follies (see BRIGHTLING).

The original **Church of St Giles** was dismantled in 1864 and rebuilt with only the crenellated tower and spire surviving; the latter is a rarity in Sussex as it is tiled in stone. On the west face of the tower are carved shields and the buckle symbol of the Pelham family, awarded to Sir John Pelham who fought at the battle of Poitiers in 1356.

DANEHILL

Map p.148, B3

3 miles S of Wych Cross on the A275

Situated on the western fringe of Ashdown Forest, Danehill's position gives it some fine views across the heathland.

All Saints' Church dominates the crossroads as the village is approached from the north side, sitting broadside on a little hill, an impressive sight. It was built in Decorated Gothic style by Bodley in 1892 and has a solid battlemented tower at the west end, with a pyramidal spire on top.

The village pub is a beautiful 18th-century building called the Sheffield Coach House. Just outside the village going south on the A275 is an attractive group of golden sandstone buildings which form the nucleus of Heaven Farm (see p. 27).

A **Country Tour** can be taken from here, through countryside designated an Area of Outstanding Natural Beauty. Heaven Farm Country Tours will take parties in their own coach on a choice of two journeys. The East–West Sussex County Boundary Tour crosses and re-crosses the county boundary, linking a series of wonderful views as it follows the old ridge roads and passes the Weir Wood Reservoir (see p.34). The Ouse Valley Tour follows the riverside pastures of the Ouse valley to the county town of Lewes and returns through Sussex downland by Mount Caburn and Glynde. Each tour covers about thirty miles and takes 2 hours on average. The organizers suggest that your tour begins or ends with a meal in the Stable Tea Rooms at Heaven Farm. *Tours: All year. Tel: (0825) 790226.*

DENTON

Map p.144, C1 *

1 mile NE of Newhaven off the A259

Denton was a farm settlement in Saxon times, on the course of an ancient trackway from Newhaven to the Sussex Weald.

63

In recent years, however, it has been overrun by housing and become a suburb of Newhaven. Several old and interesting buildings remain, however.

St Leonard's Church is a 13th-century building which has a Norman font, similar to one at St Anne's in LEWES and carved in the shape of a woven basket. Following the Civil War, the church was reconcecrated after Parliamentarian soldiers had stabled their horses there.

Denton also has a small manor house, which bears the date 1724 and is said to be haunted, some attractive 18th-century flint cottages, and the Flying Fish Inn which is several hundred years old and has stocks in its garden.

Ralph Reader, of Gang Show fame, grew up in Denton where the local Scouts are known as Ralph Reader's Own.

THE DICKERS

Map p.144, A4   *
3 miles W of Hailsham off the A22

The Dickers consist of two villages, Upper and Lower, the latter strung along the busy Hailsham–Uckfield road. The area abounds in nurseries, garden and farm shops and from Upper Dicker there are views to the South Downs. Michelham Priory (see p.18) lies half a mile to the south-east of Upper Dicker.

St Bede's School, the mansion house of Horatio Bottomley, former MP for the area, dominates Upper Dicker; the bricks used in its construction allegedly came from Government stock. Bottomley, a flamboyant character, was jailed on numerous counts of fraud in 1922. Berwick railway station was built for his convenience and was formerly known as Dicker Halt. Many of the surrounding cottages were also built by him. Bottomley was a passionate racehorse-owner and remnants of his private racecourse and grandstand can be seen behind the farm shop below the school. The fine Stud farmhouse is now a school boarding house.

Holy Trinity Church, set at an angle to the road, was designed by W. J. Donthorne and completed in 1843. Built of stone and flint, it is in the Norman style and contains a 17th-century font.

Lower Dicker, 1 mile to the north, was renowned in the 18th and 19th centuries for its Dickerware pottery and bricks made from Wealden clay; chimney pots, drainage pipes and tiles were supplied from here to the growing towns of Brighton and Eastbourne. The last pottery closed in the late 1950s and the Potters Arms on the main road recalls a once-thriving industry.
Tourist Information Centre: Boship Farm Roundabout (A22). Tel: (0323) 442667.

DITCHLING

Map p.143, B1   * * *
7 miles N of Brighton, at the junction of the B2116 and the B2112

This picture-postcard village is set superbly beneath the downs, with its old church, pond and green, its former coaching inn and period shops around the central crossroads. It has a long association with artists, among the most famous being the sculptor and designer Eric Gill and the painter Frank Brangwyn. Other famous people who have lived there include Dame Ellen Terry, Rowland Emmett and Dame Vera Lynn.

St Margaret's Church★ is the oldest building in the village, dating from the 13th century and built of flint and Normandy stone. Inside are rare chalk carvings and a Norman treasure chest.

Wings Place★, opposite the church, is a beautiful Tudor house. It was once said to have been associated with Anne of Cleves, but the story is believed to have been invented by a Victorian estate agent hoping to improve the chance of a sale.

Ditchling Museum★ was the Victorian school house and features displays on the stage, crafts and photography as well as works by Gill and Brangwyn. Dioramas and tableaux are used to illustrate local history.

◆ **Ditchling Common Country Park★★**, 188 acres of open countryside with a lake, stream and nature trail, is to the north of the village. It supports a variety of wildlife, including reed buntings, dragonflies and damsel flies and fish such as perch, carp, roach and pike.

Close to the common is the **Sussex Border Path**, a long-distance footpath which roughly follows the border between East and West Sussex. It passes through the village and crosses the South Downs west of Ditchling Beacon. At 813ft, the highest point on the South Downs in East Sussex, the beacon is a popular beauty spot with spectacular views south over the sea and north to the Weald.

Ditchling Museum: Apr–Oct, Mon–Sat 10.15am–5pm, Sun 2–5pm; Nov–Mar, Sat and Sun only, same times. Tel: (0273) 844744

EAST BLATCHINGTON

Map p.144, D1　　　　　　　　*
1 mile NW of Seaford off the A259

Now taken over by the suburbs of Seaford, East Blatchington still retains a village feel with leafy lanes, pretty cottages and a pond. One of the most attractive buildings is Alces Place, originally a 17th-century farmhouse, but now converted to six dwellings.

⛪ **St Peter's Church** dates from about 1100 and has some Norman and Early English work but was considerably restored in Victorian times. Inside is a memorial to Henry Tracey Corwell, a balloonist who ascended to 7 miles above Wolverhampton in 1862, at that time the greatest height ever achieved by man. There is also a plaque thanking God for sparing the church after it was struck by lightning in 1879.

EASTBOURNE

Map p.145, D1　　　　　　★★★
15 miles SE of Hastings on the A259

Once described as 'the town for health', Eastbourne is the classic coastal resort, with a wealth of attractions for all seasons.

The coming of the railway in 1849 spurred William Cavendish, later the 7th Duke of Devonshire, to plan the town with his architect Henry Currey as an exclusive and refined development for the Victorian middle class. With its parks and gardens, theatres and pier, it retains its elegant and sophisticated superiority over other English seaside towns.

The modern resort has earlier origins and a visit to the Old Town 1 mile north-west of the railway station is worthwhile.

⛪ **St Mary's Church★★** in the High St has fine early Norman features; among the many memorial tablets is one to Henry Lushington who survived imprisonment in the 'Black Hole of Calcutta', only to be murdered 7 years later by Indian bandits – to 'his greater misery'. The ancient Lamb Inn stands next to the church.

🏛 **Towner Art Gallery and Local History Museum★★★** is across the road in Manor Park, housed in an 18th-century mansion. It is an outstanding collection of paintings and sculpture displayed on a rotating basis; the original bequest of works of art, made by local businessman J. C. Towner in 1920, has been much expanded over the years and includes many works with local associations. In the small museum are a Victorian kitchen display, local archaeological exhibits and the writing desk used by Lewis Carroll, author of *Alice in Wonderland*, a frequent visitor to Eastbourne in his later years.

The **Pier★★** is the focal point of the modern resort. Designed by Eugenius Birch, and opened in 1872, it contains all the amusements expected of a seaside resort. Boat tours to BEACHY HEAD depart from here and from the beach. Grand Parade is fronted by the 'Carpet Gardens', a glorious extravaganza of municipal garden design.

The central stretch of beach (see p.30), winner of awards for water quality, leads past the bandstand where regular concerts are held throughout the season.

🏰 **Martello Tower 73★★**, also known as the Wish Tower, is home of the British Model Soldier Society's collection of

military miniatures. Many of the exhibits show scenes from the Napoleonic era, when the defensive tower was built.

🏛 The **Lifeboat Museum** is near by and was the first of its kind in Britain, opening in 1937. Eastbourne's lifeboat service began in 1822, two years before the foundation of the Royal National Lifeboat Institution.

Behind the seafront are grouped the Congress, Winter Garden and Devonshire Park theatres, offering a full range of entertainments and conference facilities. A further theatre, the Royal Hippodrome, is near the pier. Devonshire Park is host to world-class tennis tournaments throughout the summer, including the pre-Wimbledon international ladies' championships.

Eastbourne Heritage Centre★★ stands opposite in Carlisle Rd. Originally the home of the Victorian manager of the Devonshire Park and Baths Company, it is the best starting point for a detailed appreciation of Eastbourne's history. An audio-visual programme explains the rise of the resort; upstairs in the tower is a collection of 'penny-in-the slot' machines (pennies supplied on request).

🏛 **'How we lived then' Museum of Shops★★** lies a short walk away in Cornfield Terrace. Over 50,000 items of merchandise and packaging ephemera are displayed on three floors, with accompanying nostalgic sound effects inside such shop façades as the grocer's, draper's, post office and chemist's. This eclectic collection includes a telephone exchange made by the 12-year-old John Logie Baird, inventor of television.

🏰 🏛 **Redoubt Fortress★★** lies on Royal Parade, to the east of the Pier. It was one of three built to command the defensive chain of Martello towers, during the threat of invasion from France (the others were at Harwich and Dymchurch). Within the massive circular forts are exhibits in the casemates of the Sussex Combined Services Museum and a small acquarium. During the season, ever-popular 1812

concert evenings (with fireworks) are held within the fortress.

Treasure Island is next door, a theme park with every possible facility for children's play. **The Butterfly Centre** is adjacent with free-flying butterflies in a tropical watergarden setting. **Princes Park** is further along Marine Parade, one of Eastbourne's many pleasant open spaces, with boating facilities. Opposite are two further 'themed' children's adventure playgrounds. **Eastbourne Park** is being developed inland, to the east of the town centre, and has a golf-driving range, cycle ways and a miniature steam-railway. **Sovereign Centre,** at the junction with Wartling Rd, is an all-weather water-sports centre with several pools and flumes. **Sovereign Harbour,** beyond, is one of the largest marina village developments in Europe, with moorings, shops and housing on the seafront.

Towner Art Gallery and Museum: All year, Sat 10am–5pm, Sun 2–5pm. Tel: (0323) 411688.
Martello Tower 73: Phone for opening times. Tel: (0323) 410440.
Lifeboat Museum: Phone for opening times. Tel: (0323) 30717.
Eastbourne Heritage Centre: Apr–Sept, Tues–Fri, Sun and BHs 2–5pm. Tel: (0323) 411189.
Museum of Shops: All year, daily 10am–5.30pm. Tel: (0323) 37143.
Redoubt Fortress: All year, daily 10am–5.30pm. Tel: (0323) 410300.
Butterfly Centre: Easter–Oct, daily 10am–5pm. Tel: (0323) 645522.
Sovereign Centre: All year, daily, times vary. Tel: (0323) 412444.
Tourist Information Centre: The Pier, Seafront. Tel: (0323) 411400.

EAST CHILTINGTON

Map p.143, B2　　　　　　　　　＊
5 ¹/₂ miles NW of Lewes off the B2116

A scattered village spreading north of the B2116, East Chiltington lies mainly in a cul-de-sac close to the Lewes–London

This natural rock formation at Eridge Park has been incorporated into a 'sublime' landscape.

67

railway. This is where the 13th-century church is to be found, along with a pub, the Jolly Sportsman, a one-time thatched building that has now been greatly modernized. Since the village hall was sold in the 1960s, the pub has been used for parish council meetings and elections. The road leading to the church is on the line of a Roman road which ran from Keymer to Barcombe Mills. At the far end of the village the road becomes a track which leads to the private Novington Manor.

Near the railway bridge is Brook House Farm, whose grounds contain strange metallic sculptures by Hamish Black.

EAST DEAN

Map p.144, D4   ******
5 miles W of Eastbourne on the A259

The older part of the village lies off the main road and surrounds a pleasant green. Above the green and the war memorial, Glebe Cottages have two firemarks, once used for insurance purposes, on their walls.

⛪ The **Church of St Simon and St Jude**** lies below the green, with its squat 11th-century tower, and is approached by a churchyard gate with a revolving, central swivel. The 13th-century chancel is built at a slight angle for truer orientation; an old aumbry and stoop, for the storage and washing of the holy vessels, are to the right of the altar. The carved pulpit is dated 1623 and has an inscription to two churchwardens of the time. By the door to the vestry is a broken tombstone to one of the Bardolf family of nearby Birling Manor. A modern organ spans the interior, reaching up towards the kingpost roof. The pedestal of the font is said to have been recovered in 1885 from the nearby Tiger Inn, where it had been used as a mounting-block. Jonathan Darby, an 18th-century vicar, was deeply involved in smuggling operations in the nearby Birling Gap area.

🍷 The **Tiger Inn****, with many low beams, is part of a group of flint cottages where the local militia were housed at one

time. The village used to have a telegraphic relay station for the underwater cable between France and England.

The Seven Sisters Sheep Centre**, 1 mile south of East Dean (at Birling Farm), is a working sheep-farm with over 30 breeds, many of them rare, and other small farm animals. An exhibition tells the history of downland sheep-farming over the centuries. Demonstration shearing and cheese-making take place regularly. The impressive 17th-century Dunwick Barn, some of whose timbers came from shipwrecks near by, houses further exhibits on wool, spinning and weaving. Outside are agricultural relics including a mobile shepherd's hut complete with bed and stove. *Sheep Centre: Mid-March–mid-September, daily 2–5pm (restricted opening during May). Group visits by appointment. Tel: (0323) 423302*

EAST GULDEFORD

Map p.152, D4
1 mile E of Rye on the A259

The best thing about this little hamlet is its situation, out on the levels, where larks soar overhead, and sheep graze on the grassland cut by a network of drainage ditches. Its name comes not from the Surrey town, but from the Guldefords, a local Sussex family.

⛪ The humble-looking **St Mary's Church**, usually locked, is reached via a grassy path beside a stream. Dating from about 1500, it is made entirely of red brick, dappled with the lichen of age, and has a hunched appearance due to its twin roofs, with a small bell-turret tucked between them.

EAST HOATHLY

Map p.149, E3   *****
6 miles NW of Hailsham on the A22

The new bypass for the busy main road will restore some tranquility to this mainly Victorian village. Older cottages can be glimpsed up the quaintly named Cider House Walk in the centre, beside the old village school, now a pottery centre. A plaque on a house opposite commemorates Thomas Turner (1729–1789) who was the local schoolmaster and diarist, given to repenting of his frequent drinking bouts.

The Parish Church** is at the north-west end of the village, off South St, and hemmed in by a housing estate. It has a squat 15th-century tower. The church was virtually rebuilt in 1855. To the right of the altar is a carved Norman piscina; the fine mosaic memorial on the east wall of the chancel was given by the children of the Revd Frederick Borradaile. Outside, on the west door of the tower, are the carved buckle symbol of the Pelham family, who lived near by at Halland, and shields with boars heads, of the Lunsford family.

Sir Thomas Lunsford was known as 'the Sussex Cannibal' for allegedly dining on children; he was tried in 1632 for assaulting his neighbour, Sir Nicholas Pelham, on this spot and a bullet-groove can be seen to the right of the door. He was fined £8,000 and later left England to live in the new colony of Virginia. A tombstone, below the east window, bears a terracotta plaque by Jonathan Harmer, the Heathfield artist.

Warnham Cottage*, at the far end of the village (opposite the King's Head pub), houses 'Specially for You'. This craft workshop centre produces modern interpretations of traditional 'round' smocks, once a local cottage industry. Skilled local needlewomen demonstrate their techniques in assembling a range of clothing designed by Julian Akers-Douglas. *Craft workshop centre: 10am–4pm (or by appointment). Tel: (0825) 840397.*

ERIDGE PARK

Map p.155, D2
2 miles SW of Tunbridge Wells off the A26

Eridge Park covers a roughly circular area of some 3 miles in diameter. It has been the family seat of the Nevills and their descendants, the Abergavenny family, for centuries. The Nevills first came to England with William the Conqueror.

In the late 16th century, Queen Elizabeth I stayed at the Abergavenny's hunting-lodge.

In the 18th century, the house was considerably enlarged and, in 1810, the 2nd Earl transformed it into a huge Gothic pile and renamed it Eridge Castle, making it his principal residence from Kidbrooke Park (see FOREST ROW). Just before World War II, Lord Abergavenny demolished the castle and built a modern house in its place, reinstating the name Eridge Park. In the south–west corner of the park is the Iron-Age Saxonbury Camp. Its defensive ditch can still be seen around the summit, and on top of the hill, surrounded by woodland and rhododendrons, is a folly of a round tower with arrow slits, dated 1838.

The village of Eridge Green is just south-west of the park on the A26. On the boundaries of the park, many of the cottages bear the Abergavenny monogram with which the family emblazoned its properties in the 19th century. It shows a large tasselled 'A', a bull, a Tudor rose and a portcullis.

ETCHINGHAM

Map p.151, B1
2 miles W of Hurst Green along the A265

Etchingham is a straggling village on the A265 which has grown around its station (built in 1852) on the main London–Hastings line. Where the station now stands was once the medieval fortified manor of the de Echyngham family. It guarded the crossing-place of the River Rother which was navigable as far as this point at the time. Nothing remains of the manor.

The Church of the Assumption and St Nicholas** is said to be the finest 14th-century church in Sussex. It stands virtually unaltered since it was built by Sir William de Echyngham in 1363.

The grey stone building is massively solid in appearance and its vast tower, topped with a pyramidal roof, still has its original 14th-century copper weather-vane. Inside, the stalls have misericords which tip up to reveal carvings on every one. Subjects include foliage, keys, fish, and two show foxes preaching to geese. The window tracery is exceptionally graceful and much of the 14th-century glass survives. Among the fine brasses in the church is a headless figure in chain-mail with an epitaph which translates: 'Of earth was made and formed, and to earth returned, William de Echyngham was his name. God on my soul have pity.' Sir William died in 1389.

Not far from Etchingham is Haremere Hall (see p.27), a fine 17th-century manor open to the public as a shire-horse centre.

EWHURST GREEN

Map p.151, C4   *
9 miles N of Hastings off the A229

This pretty little village, built along a ridge south of the River Rother, has spectacular views across the valley towards Bodiam Castle (see p.22). The church is set in a beautifully tended churchyard, and forms an attractive group with a cluster of old houses round it. Near by, a group of oast-houses has been converted into houses, far better adapted than most.

The **Church of St James the Great** is a sturdy building, with a 12th-century Norman west tower built largely of local ironstone, and a curious wood-shingled spire which looks askew when seen from afar. Inside, the rounded nave arcades are also Norman. The only major additions to the church date from the 13th century. On the west wall is a grotesque medieval carving of a man blowing out his cheeks, the only piece of decorative carving in the church. The richly glowing glass in the southern clerestory windows dates from the 1970s.

FAIRLIGHT

Map p.147, C2
3 miles E of Hastings off the A259

Fairlight consists of a few old coastguards' cottages up by the church, and a straggle of modern seaside houses running down the hill to Fairlight Cove. The lane by the

church leads down to the Hastings Country Park (see p.24).

St Andrew's Church is a big grey church in a magnificent situation, with a tall tower that is a landmark from both the sea and the countryside inland. It was built in 1845, on the site of a much humbler village church. Among the tombs in the churchyard is that of Richard D'Oyly Carte, founder of the Gilbert and Sullivan opera company.

FAIRWARP

Map p.149, B1
2 miles N of Maresfield on the B2026

Fairwarp is a small, relatively modern village on the southern slopes of Ashdown Forest. The Roman London–Lewes road cut through here, and the name Fayre Wharpe is mentioned as far back as 1519.

Christ Church is a handsome sandstone building, with an odd windowless polygonal apse, designed by Rhode Hawkins and built in 1881. Some fifty years later, the church had a lot of money spent on it by Sir Bernard Eckstein, in memory of his father who lived near by at Oldlands Hall. He added the chancel and tower and floored the building with pale Italian marble. In the churchyard are three memorials to the Eckstein family: one is a bronze statue of young Hermione Eckstein (1930); a second is adorned with bronze angels (1932); and the third, dated 1950, is a tomb-chest adorned with cherubs. All are signed by the same artist, Sir William Reid Dick.

FALMER

Map p.143, D2   **
4 miles NE of Brighton off the A27

Despite being split in two by the busy A27 and close to the Universities of Sussex and Brighton, this quaint village has managed to hang on to its identity.

Hurst Green, near Etchingham, looking south towards the Weald.

🏠 **St Laurence's Church***, originally built in the 12th century, but entirely rebuilt in 1815, stands in the southern half of the village, along with groups of flint cottages, around the green and pond, which serves as home to a number of ducks and geese. The churchyard is a designated conservation area for wild meadow flowers and grasses. A pedestrian bridge leads over the road to the other half of the village where an inn, a post office cum tea-shop and an unusual war memorial (a horse-trough filled with flowers) are to be found.

The **University of Sussex**, the first to be built after World War II, was designed by Sir Basil Spence and opened in 1962. It has a theatre, the Gardner Centre, where plays, operas and concerts are performed, while in the library the Barlow Collection can be seen, a display of ceramics, bronzes, jades and figurines depicting 3000 years of Chinese civilization.
Barlow Collection (University of Sussex):
Jan–Jul and Sept–Dec, Tues and Thurs 11.30am–2.30pm. Tel (0273) 678258.

FLETCHING

Map p.148, C4   * *
9 miles N of Lewes off the A275

The exceptionally appealing village of Fletching appears in Domesday as 'Flescinge'. It was known in medieval times for the manufacture of arrowheads and it was in Fletching's village church that Simon de Montfort spent a night of vigil before the Battle of Lewes, where he defeated Henry III.

🏠 **St Mary and St Andrews' Church** is a fine Early English building mainly dating from about 1230. Its Norman west tower, with later shingled broach spire, has small round-topped windows.
In the 18th century, the Sheffield Mausoleum was added to the north transept by John Baker Holroyd, 1st Earl of Sheffield, to house his family's remains. Buried in the mausoleum are the remains of historian Edward Gibbon who wrote

The Decline and Fall of the Roman Empire. Gibbon was a great friend of Holroyd's and spent the last few months of his life at Holroyd's house, Sheffield Park (see p.25). In 1880, the church underwent considerable restoration by John Oldrid Scott who added the unusually long chancel and built the lych-gate.
Monuments inside the church include a Jacobean pulpit and a decorative Perpendicular rood screen. There is a 14th-century brass to Sir Dalyngrige and his lady, shown under canopied roofs, and, in the south transept, a strange, 15th-century brass showing a pair of fashionable gloves in memory of glove-maker Peter Denot. The stained glass is Victorian.

Across the road from the church is a battlemented lodge and gateway to Sheffield Park. This used to be the park's main entrance, but public access is now through another entrance off the A275 (see also Bluebell Railway, p.32).
The L-shaped village street has a mixture of architectural styles including several Georgian houses. There are a couple of pubs, a post office and store, a cricket green and, next door to the church, Church Farm House, a particularly fine early 18th-century building in pale golden-hued brick.

FLIMWELL

Map p.156, E3
4 miles S of Lamberhurst on the A21

The hamlet of Flimwell lies right on the Kent border where the A268 crosses the main A21 Hastings road.

🏠 **St Augustine's Church** was built in 1839 by Decimus Burton, with the chancel and spire added in the 1870s. Inside, the walls are decorated with a mixture of stencilling, painting, tiles and mosaics. The pulpit is a hotch-potch of 17th-century woodwork.

One outstanding group of houses is a farm estate of Victorian steep-gabled cottages. They have Gothic windows, half-timbering and tile-hanging in much older Sussex tradition. Set well back from the main road, their front gardens resemble small allotments with neat rows of vegetables. Rising behind the cottages on the brow of a hill is the lattice tower and round receivers of a recently installed television relay and transmitting station.

FOLKINGTON

Map p.144, C4   * *
2 miles W of Polegate off the A27

The village, which nestles at the foot of the South Downs, is approached on a no-through-road.

♦ St Peter's Church lies in a pleasant grove and is built of flint and stone, with a small shingled spire; it dates from the 13th century although there is evidence of an earlier foundation. While it was considerably restored in 1870 and 1961, the elegant oak box-pews and old prayer-boards help the church retain its simple charm.

A memorial in the floor, below the altar, is to Catherine Thomas, 'a widdow before she died' in 1678 aged 23; a further reference is to her as a 'widdon', showing the illiterate hand of the stonemason. Other fine memorials to the Thomas family stand on either side of the altar and have painted crests. In the north wall is a memorial to Viscount Monckton of Brenchley (1891–1965) who lived in the Old Rectory.

Near by is a memorial to Violet Woodhouse (1871–1948) who did much to revive interest in early music in Britain: 'her playing of the harpsichord and clavichord revealed a forgotten world of beauty and imagination'. She is buried in the churchyard where the simple inscription reads: 'her genius brought the dead music of the past to life'.

Above the church, a footpath leads over the hill towards Wilmington 1 mile away and, straight ahead of the clump of trees above the churchyard, there are fine views of the South Downs.

FOREST ROW

Map p.154, D2
2 miles SE of East Grinstead on the A22

The village of Forest Row is strung out along the busy A22 London–Eastbourne road.

♦ The Church of the Holy Trinity is in the middle of the village and is very distinctive. Built by William Moseley in 1836, it has a tall thin tower topped by a spindly shingled steeple.

There is an attractive shopping centre, and one of the oldest village buildings is home to Powell and Partners, auctioneers and estate agents. Their illuminated lettering somewhat defaces the beautiful stone-built farmhouse, with its mullioned windows and ancient porch. The building is about 600 years old and dates back to when Forest Row was literally a single row of cottages forming a 'waste edge settlement' on the western fringe of Ashdown Forest.

♦ Kidbrooke Park, near by, was built for Lord Abergavenny in 1724. The park was redesigned in the early 19th century by famous landscape artist Humphrey Repton, when the house was owned by Charles Abbot, MP. Other famous owners have included Henry Freshfield, solicitor to the Bank of England, Sir James Horlick of the malted-milk drink fame, the Hambro family and, since 1945, the Michael Hall Rudolf Steiner School.

♦ Ashdown House, also a school, was built by Benjamin Latrobe in the late 18th century, in impressive classical style. Latrobe also designed Hammerwood Park (see p.18) and went on to emigrate to America where he won renown as architect of the White House and other famous buildings.

♦ Brambletye Manor, half a mile north-west of the village, is what remains of a fine Jacobean manor house. This was built in 1631 for East Grinstead MP Sir Henry Compton, and later purchased by

73

Sir James Richards. Sir James was accused of high treason and ran away to Spain in 1683 rather than face the consequences. The house has been allowed to deteriorate since then, but some of the towers and walls remain. The name Brambletye was adopted by an attractive mock-Tudor hotel (built in 1919) on the Lewes road.

FRAMFIELD

Map p.149, D2   *
2 miles E of Uckfield on the B2102

Framfield is a compact village with timber-framed and tile-hung cottages lining the road to St Thomas à Becket Church. This short road almost has the appearance of a village square.

♠ St Thomas à Becket Church is a long low building with a heavy Horsham slate roof. The church originally dates from 1288 but has suffered more than its fair share of disasters over the centuries. In 1509 it was largely gutted by fire and rebuilt. Then in 1667, the tower collapsed and more than two centuries passed before a new one was built (by Benjamin Ferrey who restored the church in 1892).

Inside the church, there is a simple brass to Edward Gage and his wife, dated 1595. A charming stained-glass window, designed by Jane Ross in 1962, depicts children picking flowers and playing. It was put here in memory of a dearly-loved vicar of the parish, Arthur Haire, who held office for 22 years. Out in the churchyard, a gravestone to Ann Leadner (d. 1825) is decorated with a terracotta plaque by Heathfield potter, Jonathan Harmer.

E. V. Lucas, prolific journalist and essayist (1868–1938), writes that in 1792, Framfield got together a cricket team from among its fifteen oldest inhabitants, whose combined ages totalled over 1000 years. Sadly, they never played a match as they were unable to find a suitably antique team of opponents.

FRANT

Map p.155, D3
2 miles S of Tunbridge Wells on the A267

The village of Frant is spread around a large, irregularly-shaped green. The houses are predominantly Victorian and neo-Georgian. The heart of the village is to the north where a short street leads to St Alban's Church. Frant's pretty Victorian station is 1 mile away at Bells Yew Green, a small hamlet grouped around a welcoming pub, the Brecknock Arms.

♠ St Alban's Church was built in 1821 in Perpendicular style with tall pinnacles on the tower, battlements, and a slate roof. Its slender windows have iron glazing bars, and the pillars inside are also iron. Several of the monuments predate the church including some 15th-century glass in the north and south windows and three 17th-century iron slabs.

♠ The Village School was built in 1816 and then rebuilt in 1852. It is incribed with an apt Biblical quotation from the Book of Proverbs: 'Train up a child in the way he should go; and when he is old he will not depart from it.'

FRISTON

Map p.144, D3   * * *
6 miles W of Eastbourne on the A259

♠ St Mary the Virgin Church, of early Norman origin, stands off the main road by a duck pond, one of the first to be listed in England (1974) as an ancient monument. Local tradition says that the mounting-block, to the right of the church entrance, was made from three stones taken from the pond in the Cromwellian era. A tapsell gate (on a swivel) leads into the churchyard; it is a reproduction of an early 19th-century design that allowed easier passage for funeral processions.

In the ancient porch are medieval graffiti carved into the chalk showing crude

Sheffield Park Gardens, near Fletching, are laid out around a series of lakes.

depictions of the Crucifixion and the fish symbol of the early Christian church. A very fine timber roof, of around 1450, surmounts the nave which has Norman features. The font is of winkelstone marble. By the door of the church is a memorial inscription to the composer and conductor Frank Bridge (d. 1941), a musical stave with the notes 'F' and 'B'.

The south transept contains a magnificent alabaster monument to Sir Thomas Selwyn (d. 1613) and his wife Elizabeth, of Friston Place; they kneel facing each other while six surviving daughters pray below. Between the parents lie three sons who died young. Opposite is a marble monument to Sir Francis Selwyn, with painted coats of arms; it tells of his seven sons and eight daughters. Remarkably, the family later died out.

In the churchyard is a plain, wooden cross marked simply 'washed ashore'; unknown members of the Merchant Navy drowned on active service lie to the south-east, poignant reminders of the coast near by. A bridleway leads south from the church onto the Crowlink estate (National Trust) towards the Seven Sisters.

FRISTON FOREST

Map p.144, D3   ⋆⋆
2 miles E of Seaford off the A259

Managed by the Forestry Commission, these 2000 acres offer a variety of woodland and forest walks, public bridleways and footpaths around the WESTDEAN area. The chalk downland below the forest is a water-catchment area for the public supply to Eastbourne.

Much of the forest had been eroded through farming and grazing in the early 20th century. The experimental planting of species began in 1926–7 and revealed beech to be the most suitable tree in the attempt to restore the quality of the soil. The beech trees were mixed with pines to support their growth in the early years. Furthermore, the plantings limited the exposure to salt air from the nearby

Cuckmere coastline. As the beech trees mature, so the pines are cut down to leave what will develop over the years into one of the largest beech woods in south-east England.

The Forest Walk⋆⋆ is just under 3 miles long. It skirts the grounds of Charleston Manor before continuing along Charleston Bottom, north of which is a Neolithic longbarrow, to return above Westdean to the car-park (through plantations of beech, cypress and sycamore trees). Part of the SOUTH DOWNS WAY passes through the forest and there is a Woodland Walk starting from the Seven Sisters Country Park (see p. 24).

Many smaller mammals, including rabbits, foxes and the occasional badger, as well as a variety of birds may be glimpsed. Occasional clay-lined dew-ponds provide much-needed water for animal life. There is also a profusion of plant species.
All year, daily at all times. Tel: (0323) 870280

GLYNDE

Map p.144, A1   ⋆⋆⋆
4 miles E of Lewes off the A27

A quiet, off-the-beaten-track village, Glynde is built up the side of a downland slope in the shadow of MOUNT CABURN. The narrow, tree-fringed road that skirts the hill was once the coaching road from Lewes.

🏠 **Glynde Place**⋆⋆⋆, the pride of the village, is a historic house dating from 1579. Always owned by ancestors of the present owner, Viscount Hampden, a house has stood on the site since the 12th century. The present building has a grand entrance flanked by a pair of ferocious winged dragons leading to a central courtyard and is built of flint, chalk and Caen stone. Inside are an Elizabethan staircase and panelled long gallery, antique furnishings, paintings by Rubens, Zoffany and Hofner, rare bronzes and fine needlework.

St Peter's Church, Hamsey.

♔ St Mary the Virgin's Church near by is an unusual Palladian building, once described as being 'in very bad taste'. Built of knapped flint by Richard Trevor, the Bishop of Durham, who owned the house in the mid 18th century, it has box-pews and hessian-covered interior walls. The bishop is buried in the church vaults.

The village is the birthplace of the black-faced Southdown sheep, bred by John Ellman in the 18th century, but now virtually disappeared from the downs. The great flocks of Australia, New Zealand and South Africa were developed from the breed. Ellman is buried in the churchyard. **Glynde Place**: Easter–Sept, Weds, Thurs and Sun (first and last of month) 2.15–5pm. Tel: (0273) 858337)

GUESTLING

Map p.147, B1
3 miles NE of Hastings on the A259

Guestling has no proper village centre; its ancient church, isolated and battered-looking, stands beside a farm down a side road.

During the Middle Ages Guestling was probably the meeting-place of the governing body of the Cinque Ports, known as 'Court Guestling'. It seems a strange choice, since the only one of the five ports within easy reach is Hastings; the other four – Romney, Hythe, Dover and Sandwich – are all a fair distance away on the Kent coast.

♔ St Laurence's Church was founded in Saxon times, and its tower, pierced with tiny round-headed windows, must have been built soon after the Norman Conquest. Between the north aisle and the chapel that leads out of it is an architectural rarity in the form of an ornate Transitional arch (marking the transition from Norman to Early-English style). It is so fine that experts suggest it was carved by masons taking time off from Canterbury Cathedral.

From the churchyard there are wide-ranging views south to Fairlight church and east to the restored windmill at Icklesham.

HADLOW DOWN

Map p.149, C3
3 miles E of Buxted on the A272

The hamlet of Hadlow Down straddles the main A272. Just south of the main road is the tourist attraction which draws most of the village's visitors, Wilderness Wood (see p.27), a family-owned and run working wood open to the public all year round.

♔ St Mark's Church was built by William Moseley in 1836, but it was virtually rebuilt in 1913 by Fellowes-Prynne. It is a mellow sandstone building with a battlemented west tower, topped by a slim, shingled spire with dormers. Where the nave and chancel intersect is a pretty little bell-cote.

HAILSHAM

Map p.145, A1   *
10 miles N of Eastbourne off the A22

Hailsham is a busy and ever-expanding market town, on a ridge above the Pevensey Levels, and the seat of Wealden District Council. Recorded as 'Hamelesham' in the Domesday Book, the town was renowned for its rope, twine and sack-making in the 19th century and was thus known as 'The String Town'. Some of Hailsham's older buildings can still be glimpsed despite the profusion of modern shopping arcades in the High St area and below the church in Market St. A market is held every Friday.

♔ St Mary the Virgin, of 13th-century origin but much altered, has a distinctive pinnacled tower of chequered flint and stone construction; until 1950, an evening curfew was tolled by its bells. The heads of a king and queen can be seen over the porch and at the west window. Behind the church stands a fine early 18th-century brick vicarage.

In the High St, nos. 22–24 are faced with mathematical tiles, used to resemble brick, and beyond the junction with George St is the Fleur de Lys, a mid 16th-century building later used as the parish poorhouse and as a Victorian post-office.

🏛 **Hailsham Heritage Centre★** is near by in Blackmans Yard off Market St. It houses a small but interesting display of memorabilia, including a reconstruction of a Victorian kitchen, local farming and industrial relics

The Lagoon in Vicarage Lane is a leisure complex with swimming pool and squash courts.
Heritage Centre: *May–Sept, Thurs–Sat 10.30am–12.30pm. Tel: (0323) 840947.*
Tourist Information Centre: *The Library, Western Road. Tel: (0323) 840604.*

HAMSEY

Map p.143, B3   *
2 miles N of Lewes off the A275

Virtually all that remains of this remote and mysterious hamlet are a few scattered farms and a Norman church. A prominent landmark, the church stands on a small knoll on an island in the River Ouse, which hereabouts is home to kingfishers, and can be seen for miles around. Founded by the Norman de Say family, the hamlet is thought to have been wiped out by the plague. Beside the road leading to the hamlet is a brick pillbox, one of several built to defend the Ouse Valley in World War II.

🛐 **St Peter's Church★** is lovely, with its square castellated tower decorated with gargoyles, and is often seen with sheep grazing among the gravestones. It was replaced by the parish church at Offham, but still has monthly candlelit services in summer. Inside is a canopied tomb to Edward Markwick (of 1538) and memorials to several members of the Shiffner family, killed in battles from the Peninsular War in 1814 to the desert war in 1941. The church is normally kept locked, but the key can be obtained from the nearby 400-year-old Hamsey Place Farm.

HANGLETON

Map p.142, D3   *
2 ½ miles NW of Hove off the A2038

Like several other suburbs of Brighton and Hove, Hangleton was once a medieval downland village. Before World War II it was described as 'a pretty country spot' and supported a population of little more than 100. Now, more than 11,000 people live there in extensive housing estates.

🛐 **St Helen's Church★** stands on high land in Hangleton, next to a large green which is thought to have been a burial ground for victims of the Black Death. The oldest surviving building in the Brighton and Hove area, it was originally built in the late 11th century, although what can be seen now was mainly reconstructed around 1300.

🏛 **Hangleton Manor★,** built in the 1540s, is the oldest domestic secular building in the area. Now a public house, it has changed little since it was built. Inside it has several 16th-century features, including an unusual staircase, carved stone fireplaces and a carved oak screen insribed with the Ten Commandments and a motto written with the use of only one vowel: 'Persevere ye perfect men. Ever keep these precepts ten.'
    In the manor's grounds stands a 17th-century, flint dovecote restored in 1983-7.
    At one time a railway ran via the village from Hove to the West Sussex beauty spot, Devil's Dyke. Now dismantled, the route between Hangleton and the Dyke is popular with walkers and cyclists.

HARTFIELD

Map p.154, D3   **
5 miles E of Forest Row on the B2110

The name Hartfield dates back to when Ashdown Forest was a royal deer-hunting park. The village, built along a dog-leg bend, is at the northern edge of the forest, close to both the Kent and Surrey borders.

It exceptionally pretty with tile-hung and half-timbered cottages and typical Sussex white weather-boarded buildings with haphazard red-tiled roofs.

Hartfield's main claim to fame is that it was home to A. A. Milne, creator of *Winnie-the-Pooh*. In 1925, the Milne family bought Cotchford Farm, outside the village, and their land stretched down to a Medway tributary known by several names: Mill Brook, Three Wards Brook, Steel Forge River, and Posingford Stream. In 1907, a little bridge was built over the stream, and local lore says that it was here that 'Poohsticks' was invented. The bridge was restored in 1979 by the East Sussex County Council.

In the 1920s, young Christopher Robin Milne used to visit Hartfield with his nanny 'Alice' on their weekly shopping trips. One of the shops he would have visited has jumped on the 'Pooh' bandwagon and called itself 'Pooh Corner'.

Pooh Corner is a delightful shop, well worth visiting with children. It sells all manner of 'Pooh' memorabilia, as well as traditional sweets from big old-fashioned glass jars, and tea and ice-cream in 'Piglet's Parlour'. The building itself, at the south end of the High St, is over 400 years old.

St Mary's Church, with its tall spire, is a magnificent local landmark. It stands up an alley at the southern end of the village and has a very unusual lych-gate: it once led into the churchyard beneath the overhanging first floors of a pair of Tudor cottages. Only one of these is now standing, although the old timber arch still spans the brick path – a yew tree grows where the other cottage stood. The church dates from the 13th century but has later additions. It is built of local sandstone and has old kingposts and tie-beams in the nave roof. The Rectory is a lovely Queen Anne house which is also used as the church hall.

Bolebrook is 1 mile north-west of Hartfield. This was once a large 16th-century mansion. It was owned by the Dalyngriges and later the Sackvilles.

What remains is the gatehouse with two octagonal turrets, an east-facing house which could have been the mansion's east wing, and a timber-framed brick granary. **Pooh Corner**: *All year, Tues–Sat 9am–5pm; Sun–Mon 2–5pm. Tel: (0892) 770453.*

HASTINGS

Map p.147, C1   * * *
5 miles E of Bexhill on the A259

If Brighton is the queen of South Coast resorts, then Hastings is their slightly eccentric great-aunt. Far older than Brighton – Hastings was one of the Cinque Ports, along with Dover, Hythe, Romney and Sandwich – it was a flourishing harbour town when Duke William landed along the coast at Pevensey in 1066. Throughout the Middle Ages it was one of the main contributors of ships to the English navy. It was sacked by the French in 1339 and again in 1377. Thereafter its naval importance declined, though it remained an important fishing port, as it does to this day.

The Victorians built squares and terraces of seaside houses, turning it into a summer resort, while the speeding-up of the railway in the late 19th century, enabled commuters to live there all the year round. The streets of Old Hastings, at the eastern end of the town, still keep much of their ancient seafaring charm. Elsewhere the town has expanded in every direction, linked to St Leonards on its west side, and absorbing the villages of Ore and Hollington into its modern outskirts.

Old Hastings grew up in the valley between the twin sandstone ridges of East Hill and West Hill, which run slantwise inland from the sea. The harbour originally extended well up the valley, along a stream called the Bourne, which now runs in a pipe under the modern street of the same name. But a great storm in 1287 blocked the creek with shingle, and the harbour took the form it has today. Though there is a protecting harbour arm, for greater

The Anchor at Hartfield.

safety, or maintenance purposes, the fishing boats are hauled up by winch on to the foreshore, known as The Stade.

♖ **Hastings Castle.**★★ The first castle built by William the Conqueror was on West Hill, where a wide grassy expanse gives a bird's-eye view of the whole town. Immediately after the Conquest, a prefabricated wooden castle was built there, followed by the present stone structure a year or two later. As much of West Hill and the castle was washed away in the storm of 1287, little remains, apart from a stretch of the curtain wall, the lower sections of the gatehouse, and part of the walls and tower of the Norman church attached to the castle. Outside the curtain wall a warren of passages in the sandstone may have been used as dungeons or, more probably, storehouses.

The castle's most recent showpiece is **The 1066 Story** – a dramatic audiovisual re-creation of the confrontation between Harold of England and William of Normandy, housed in a blue-and-white-striped replica of a Norman siege tent.

Down on the seafront, past the shops selling jellied eels, candyfloss and curios, are Hastings' most typical and striking survivals – the tall, black-tarred wooden 'Net-shops' where fishermen used to hang their nets to dry, before the days of manmade fibres. Their design is thought to go back to Tudor times. The **Fishermen's Museum** is tucked among them; built as a chapel in 1854, it is now lined with photographs of whiskered 19th-century mariners looking down on the main exhibit, the last of the Hastings luggers.

Near by, the **Shipwreck Heritage Centre** commemorates 3000 years of disasters at sea, with plenty of photographs of wrecks and displays of salvaged treasure. Visitors can also study today's busy Channel shipping on a radar screen.

The Sea Life Centre, which occupies a low, sprawling building complex by the harbour, gives an introduction to all aspects of marine life. It brings the aquarium concept up to date, with a glass-walled 'viewing tunnel', where visitors can look a shark or a giant ray straight in the eye, video displays, and a fish nursery where young of many species are reared.

St Clement's Caves★ burrow far under West Hill, a short way inland from the castle. Formed naturally by the action of water in the distant geological past, they cover 4 acres and were greatly enlarged and embellished during the 19th century with arcades and galleries. During the 18th century they were used by smugglers for storing contraband – a colourful era recalled by a series of tableaux forming the 'Smugglers' Adventure', full of life-sized figures going about their nefarious activities. Below the caves, narrow lanes lead steeply down past terraces clinging to the hillside, to the old centre of the town.

♜ **St Clement's Church**, just above the High St, is one of the town's two surviving medieval churches – there were originally no fewer than seven. Begun about 1270, it was largely rebuilt about 1390, after the French sack of Hastings. It is the town's borough church, and contains the mayor's pew, with a gilded rail along the top. In 1860 the pre-Raphaelite artist Dante Gabriel Rossetti married his chief model, Elizabeth Siddall, in St Clement's.

♨ The long, narrow High St is lined with old houses, many of them half-timbered, and is an antique-hunter's paradise. **The Old Town Hall Museum**★, about half-way along it, is the place to study Hastings' centuries of local history. It has displays on life through the ages, including the fishing industry, and on famous Hastings inhabitants, among them John Logie Baird, the inventor of television, who carried out some of his early experiments in the town. The dignified museum building was the town hall for most of the 19th century; its rounded ground-floor windows were originally an open market arcade.

From the High St, steep alleys (known in Sussex as 'twittens') lead to streets of tall terraced houses higher up the ridge. At the top of the High Street is the Roman

Catholic **Church of St Mary, Star of the Sea**. It has no tower and is built of rounded pebbles. Its founder was the Victorian poet Coventry Patmore (1823–96), who lived in the magnificent Georgian Old Hastings House across the road. Almost next door to St Mary's, a small tile-hung house is on the site of the home of Titus Oates, who in 1678 concocted the notorious 'Popish Plot', which claimed that Catholics were plotting to murder Charles II.

All Saints' Church. Earlier in his career, Oates was curate of this spacious building on a bluff across the main road. Like St Clement's, it was destroyed by the French, and rebuilt in the early 15th century. Its most striking feature is the wall-painting over the chancel arch, showing Christ seated on a rainbow, in judgement on the souls of the righteous and the wicked.

All Saints' St leads back to the seafront, parallel to the High St. (The Bourne, ugly and nondescript, was hacked through back gardens and alleyways in the 1960s.) It is also lined with fine old buildings, many of them once fishermen's cottages; one of them, the rickety-looking, timber-framed Shovells, was the home of the mother of Sir Cloudesley Shovell, the 17th-century admiral with the unforgettable name who drowned in a shipwreck in 1707.

Above and parallel to All Saints' St, the pretty little cottages of Tackleway face the grassy slopes of East Hill, at the edge of the Hastings Country Park (see p.24).

Late-Georgian and Victorian Hastings grew westwards along the coast from West Hill. The earliest seaside development was Pelham Crescent, below the castle, built in the 1820s, with a church (now disused) as its centrepiece; the spacious and dignified Wellington Square dates from much the same period.

The **Hastings Embroidery** is a modern version of the Bayeux Tapestry, housed near by in the Victorian Gothic Town Hall. Made in 1966 to mark the 900th anniversary of the Battle of Hastings, it shows great events of the past nine centuries.

The bustling **Pier**, along the seafront, was opened in 1872 as a place for holiday-makers to stroll and take the air; its clutter of buildings have been added down the years. The Conqueror's Stone, at its entrance, is said to be where William ate his first breakfast in England. West of the pier, Hastings merges imperceptibly into St Leonards at the wide, dignified Warrior Square.

The White Rock Theatre, across the road, is the town's main entertainment centre. Cream-painted and oriental-looking (Pevsner describes it as 'Spanish Mission style of America'), it was built in the 1920s. Under the auditorium, the Domesday Exhibition shows life as it was around 1066, complete with a 'talking head' of William the Conqueror. The original White Rock was a large outcrop, demolished in 1834 when the seafront was extended westwards towards St Leonards.

The town's main **Museum and Art Gallery** lies across the steep gardens behind the theatre. It houses some remarkable and evocative pictures of Hastings in former centuries, cases of documents and ship models, and a complete room removed from an Indian colonial palace.

Castle: Early Apr–Sept, daily 10am–5pm; Oct, daily 11am–4pm.

Fishermen's Museum: Late May–Sept, Mon–Fri 10.30–12am, 2.30–5pm, Sun pm only.

Shipwreck Heritage Centre: Easter–Oct, daily. Tel: (0424) 437452.

Sea Life Centre: All year, daily 10am–6pm (9pm in summer hols season). Tel: (0424) 718776.

St Clement's Caves: Late March–late Oct, daily 10am–6pm; winter, daily (exc. Mon) 10am–4pm. Tel: (0424) 422964.

Old Town Hall Museum: All year, May–Sept, Mon–Sat 10am–1pm and 2–5pm, Oct–Apr, Sun 3–5pm. Tel: (0424) 721209.

Hastings Embroidery: All year, Tues–Fri 10am–5pm. Tel: (0424) 722022.

Museum and Art Gallery: All year, Mon–Sat 10am–5pm; Sun 3–5pm. Tel: (0424) 721202.

Tourist Information Centres: The Fishmarket, The Stade, or 4 Robertson Terrace. Tel: (0424) 718888.

HEATHFIELD

Map p.150, D1
8 miles E of Uckfield on the A265

Almost the size of a town, Heathfield is an unremarkable modern village on the main A265. It used to be called Tower Street and grew up around the railway station on the old Polegate–Tunbridge Wells line (now closed). East of the town, hidden behind a wall, is Heathfield Park: over its wall there is a round, castellated folly called the Gibraltar Tower. This was built in honour of General Sir George Augustus Elliot, a Governor of Gibraltar, who successfully defended the Rock against the combined French and Spanish forces over a four-year period in the late 18th century.

At the south-eastern corner of the park is OLD HEATHFIELD, which has a church, a pub and a few cottages. At Cross in Hand, 2 miles west of the village (along the A265), there is a large road junction. On its central triangle is an old post mill which was moved from Uckfield, where it originally stood.

HELLINGLY

Map p.150, F1 ✱✱
1 mile N of Hailsham off the A267

⛪ **St Peter and St Paul Church**✱✱, founded around 1190, occupies a much older site. There is evidence that the oval churchyard, rising several feet above the surrounding road, was used in Saxon times (and possibly even earlier), as a 'ciric', or burial ground (the oval shape was a mystic symbol in early burial rites). It is certainly one of the best surviving examples in Sussex. Tile-hung cottages, some Tudor, closely follow the curve of the churchyard, which has four entrances. By the porch are two late 18th-century gravestones with terracotta plaques by Jonathan Harmer, who worked at Heathfield.

Much of the exterior shows Norman work with later additions and extensions.

Construction of the tower to replace the former spire commenced in 1836 and the church was extensively restored in 1869. On a buttress on the south wall is a scratch dial, now upside-down and moved from an earlier location. This was used to tell the time of the services.

The chancel, with fine Norman windows in the north wall and two Early English windows in the south wall, has a 15th-century brass of a lady on the floor, thought to be one of the Devenysh family who lived at the timber-framed and moated Horselunges manor house near by.

The transept, nave and side aisles contain ornamental capitals and windows of various periods. There is a blocked Norman doorway in the west wall of the north aisle, which may have been the original west door. In 1557, John Miller, the minister of Hellingly, was burned at the stake in Lewes for his Protestant faith. A memorial plaque above the west door commemorates the death of Queen Victoria and the rehanging of the peal of six bells in 1901.

HERSTMONCEUX

Map p.150, F2 ✱✱✱
4 miles NE of Hailsham on the A271

Originally the manor of the Monceux family (pronounced 'monsoo'), the village is today the adopted home of the Sussex trug: a hand-crafted, gardening basket made in the village for over 160 years from locally coppiced chestnut and willow wood. The firm of Thomas Smith, opposite the Woolpack Hotel, continues the tradition of its founder, who displayed his craft at the Great Exhibition in London in 1851; Queen Victoria became a valued customer and Smith walked the 60 miles to Buckingham Palace to deliver her order.

⛪ **All Saints' Church** ✱✱✱ lies 2 miles away, opposite the entrance to Herstmonceux Castle (see p.22), and is approached on the Flowers Green Rd. A mounting-block stands at the church gates. Probably Saxon in origin, the church

Hastings Beach.

is late 12th-century, with a shingled spire and later additions and extensions.

To the left of the altar is the magnificent canopied Dacre Tomb, of Caen, Purbeck and Bonchurch marble. The painted tomb, restored in 1970, shows two reposing knights in armour believed to be half-brothers of the Hoo family; the tomb may originally have been at Battle Abbey before being brought here and modified to suit the later memorial to Lord Dacre and his son, Sir Thomas Fiennes. A brass in the chancel floor commemorates their ancestor Sir William Fiennes (d. 1403) and offers 120 days' pardon for those who will pray for his soul. On the south wall is a memorial to the eccentric scholar Georgiana Hare-Naylor by the Danish sculptor Kessels; dated 1829, it was erected 23 years after her death in Switzerland, the original memorial having been lost at sea. Beside it is a memorial to the 1st Viscount Hailsham (1872–1950), former Lord Chancellor and Leader of the House of Lords, who lived near by and worshipped here. The font is late 14th-century and has an earlier broken companion. There are broad views over the Pevensey Levels from the churchyard.

HOOE

Map p.145, A4
4 miles W of Bexhill on the B2095

Hooe's odd name means 'spur of land' in Saxon; and this applies here exactly, as the village stretches along a low ridge, looking towards the sea above the flat expanse of Pevensey Levels. Such centre as it has is round the green of Hooe Common, at its northern end.

⛪ St Oswald's Church is well out of the village, past farm buildings down a lane hardly wider than a cart-track. Isolated above the fields, it seems unbelievably remote in time from the beach chalets visible in the distance.

The squat stone church dates mainly from the 15th century, although the north chapel survives from an earlier building. The chancel, set at an angle to the nave, is of the type known as a 'weeping chancel',

as it represents the angle of Christ's head on the cross. At one side is a dugout chest, carved from a single massive log, and said to date from the 13th century. The church is normally locked during the week because of vandals.

HORAM

Map p.149, E4   *
4 miles N of Hailsham on the A267

The **Merrydown*** cider and wine-making plant dominates Horam's centre. Founded in 1946, it is now an important local industry. Some 15,000 tons of local apples are pressed every year, and the juice matured in oak vats, to produce a range of ciders, wines and health foods. A reproduction cider-press, made from oaks brought down in the Great Storm of 1987, stands at the entrance.

🏛 The Sussex Farm Museum** lies near the village community hall and is approached by the road to the caravan and camping site. It houses an absorbing collection of artefacts from the period 1900–1950 grouped in a set of farmyard buildings. These show the changes in farming practice down the years; period room-settings with memorabilia explain social developments in the first half of the 20th century. Farm machinery, model carts and an exhibition of local crafts and traditions can also be seen.

The museum curator works as a blacksmith in the Museum Forge, specializing in reproduction armour, often used in TV and film productions. A nature trail leads from the museum and follows marked woodland paths.

Under the railway bridge below the hotel is a section of the Cuckoo Trail*, a 12-mile footpath and bridleway on the former railway track between Heathfield and Polegate. The site of the railway station which led to Horam's expansion in the 19th century is now covered by a modern housing development but the original platform can still be seen.

Merrydown: *Visits by appointment, Mon–Fri. Tel: (04353) 2401.*
Sussex Farm Museum: *Apr–Nov, daily 10am–5pm. Tel: (04353) 3130*

HOVE

Map p.142, E3   ***
1 mile W of Brighton on the A259

To the casual observer Hove may seem like a continuation of Brighton, but in fact it vigorously guards its own identity. The border between Brighton and Hove is marked on the seafront by the Peace Statue, which was unveiled in 1912 in memory of Edward VII, a frequent visitor to the town.

A much quieter version of its neighbour – sedate and genteel are words often used to describe the town – Hove is famed for its graceful Regency squares, broad tree-lined avenues and sweeping lawns, which give an air of spaciousness to the place. No fewer than 500 of its buildings are of national historic and architectural interest.

Its origins are much the same as Brighton's, and for centuries it was little more than a tiny fishing and farming village based around what is now Hove St. Like many villages on this coast, it suffered at the hands of French raiders, particularly in the 16th century. Little remains of this early period, other than a few fishermen's homes in Victoria Cottages, just off the seafront.

The first major development took place between 1825 and 1828 when Brunswick Square, which opens to the seafront, was built with its cream-painted terraced homes for the famous and wealthy, characterized by a succession of bow-fronted windows and Ionic and Corinthian columns. Through an Act of Parliament, the buildings must be painted every five years in a colour known as Hove Regency Cream.

Even more attractive than Brunswick Square in some eyes are elegant Palmeira Square and the adjoining Adelaide Crescent, named after Queen Adelaide, wife of William IV. Originally designed around 1830 by Decimus Burton, who (with his father James) was responsible for much of the architecture in St Leonards, Adelaide Crescent should have been a complete crescent overlooking the sea, but shortly after building started it ran into financial problems, and when work recommenced some 20 years later it was decided to open up Palmeira Square behind. One of the attractions of Palmeira Square is its beautiful working floral clock, which was unveiled on Coronation Day, 1953. Elsewhere there are numerous large Victorian villas, some based on Queen Victoria's home on the Isle of Wight, Osborne House.

Within a century Hove's population leapt from barely 100 to 30,000 and in the 1950s a number of isolated downland villages such Hangleton, Portslade and West Blatchington, were engulfed by urban expansion.

As well as its architectural delights, the town has some beautiful parks, among them Hove Park and St Ann's Wells Gardens, which has a perfumed garden for the blind and a brick dovecote. Located in a corner of Hove Park is the Goldstone, which is thought to have Druid connections.

St Andrew's Church★ was built in Waterloo St in 1827 by Sir Charles Barry who, with Augustus Pugin, went on to design the Houses of Parliament. It is regarded as the first example of Italianate architecture in England.

Another **St Andrew's**, in Church Rd, is the burial place of George Everest, who was appointed surveyor-general of India in 1830 and gave his name to Mount Everest.

Hove Museum and Art Gallery★, housed in one of the town's grandest villas, has one of the richest collections in the south-east. It features English paintings, including works by Gainsborough, Bonington and Duncan Grant (who lived a few miles away at Charleston Farmhouse, see p.16), miniatures and pottery, glass and silver, coins, medals, model ships and Victorian toys, while one room is devoted to the history of Hove. There are also regular temporary exhibitions. Particularly outstanding is the Jaipur Gate, a large wooden pavilion which stands on the museum's front lawns. Constructed in Rajasthan and sent to London in 1886, its intricately carved pillars and golden dome were re-erected in Hove in 1926.

The British Engineerium★★ was opened in 1975. After a century of use as a pumping station, supplying fresh water to Brighton and Hove, the building is now a museum to engineering, and houses hundreds of engineering models, printing presses, hand tools and some full-size working steam traction engines. The station's massive beam engine, and the famous Corlis engine (which won first prize at the Paris Exhibition in 1889), have been restored and are 'in steam' on Sundays and Bank Holidays.

Much of sporting life in the Brighton area centres on Hove; both Sussex County Cricket Club – the oldest county cricket club in Britain, formed in 1839 – and Brighton and Hove Albion Football Club have grounds here. There is also a top-class greyhound stadium (which has been holding meetings since 1928) and a seafront lagoon, which is popular with novice windsurfers.

A more recent addition to Hove's sporting activities is the King Alfred Leisure Centre, one of the first leisure complexes to be built on the south coast. It includes three swimming pools, water flumes, a sports hall, indoor bowls centre and a bowling alley.

Museum and Art Gallery: All year, Tues–Fri 10am–5pm, Sat 10am–4.30pm, Sun 2–5pm. Tel: (0273) 779410.
The British Engineerium: All year, daily 10am–5pm. Tel: (0273) 559583).
Tourist Information Centres: Town Hall, Norton Rd, te.l (0273) 775400; King Alfred Leisure Centre, Kingsway, tel. (0273) 746100.

ICKLESHAM

Map p.147, A2
6 miles NE of Hastings on the A259

Though battered by the traffic of the main road from Hastings to Rye, Icklesham still has plenty of old-style village charm. The back road from Pett brings you into the village past a restored windmill, to a fork where the roads splits into Workhouse Lane and Laurel Lane, both presumably survivors from Victorian times.

Icklesham first occurs in the records in 772, when it appears as 'Icoleshamme' in a land charter signed by Offa, King of Mercia. In early times it dominated the River Brede in the valley to the north, and was no doubt a prime target of the Normans immediately after their landing in 1066.

All Saints' Church★★ is a splendid Norman and Early-English building, which survived the Victorian restorers largely unchanged. The unusual central tower, capped by a pyramid roof, is in three diminishing stages. The way in is through a curious hexagonal porch at the west end. Inside, the nave arcading is round-headed Norman, with superb carving on the capitals, all of them different; the chancel is later, with pointed arches dating from the 14th century.

IDEN

Map p.152, C3
2 miles N of Rye on the B2082

Iden straggles along a network of roads, on a spur of land above the Rother Levels. The village is said to have been the birthplace of Alexander Iden, Sheriff of Kent, who in 1450 killed Jack Cade, leader of the Kentish rebellion against Henry VI.

All Saints' Church (usually locked) is up a lane off the main road, beside a cluster of ancient cottages. Unlike most churches, which were enlarged down the centuries, All Saints' was made smaller: where the south aisle once stood is obvious from the infilling of the present south wall.

Oxenbridge, Iden's oldest house, is a 15th-century timber-framed hall house at the northern end of the village. It probably gets its name from the Oxenbridge family of BREDE.

Herstmonceux Castle, one of the earliest in England to be built of brick.

IFORD

Map p.143, D3   *
2 miles S of Lewes off the A27

This peaceful farming village with a mysterious air lies in the Ouse Valley, hidden away off the unclassified road that links Lewes and Newhaven. Tractors rather than cars are more likely to be seen on its single road. Nowadays some way from the river, it was a busy herring-fishing port in medieval times. There are several large houses, including a 19th-century manor house built in Tudor style which can be glimpsed from various parts of the village, and a neo-classical house dating from 1828. Also worthy of note is a large cottage with mullioned windows which is thought to be the original 16th century manor house.

Near by are Swanborough Manor, parts of which date from the 13th century, and Northease Manor, once owned by Lord Abergavenny, which is now an independent school for children with learning difficulties.

St Nicholas' Church★, standing at one corner of the village, is a fine flint-built 11th-century Norman building which, despite major restoration in 1868, has changed little since it was constructed. Its font dates from around 1200, while its stained-glass windows are 19th- and 20th-century. From the churchyard there are lovely views across the water meadows, here known as the Brooks, to Firle Beacon and Mount Caburn.

ISFIELD

Map p.148, E4   * *
2 miles SW of Uckfield off the A26

In recent years, this straggling village has been known for its Lavender Line, the old railway station that serviced the Lewes to Uckfield line, a victim of the 'Beeching axe' in the 1960s. Under the Isfield Steam Railway Company the station was carefully restored to its former glory and decorated in the original Southern Railway colours, while a collection of steam-engines and vintage coaches helped recreate the period atmosphere. Unfortunately the station closed in the summer of 1992 and was put up for sale, hopefully to be re-opened to the public by its buyer. Next to the station is the Laughing Fish, a strangely named public house that was originally the village chapel.

St Margaret's Church★★ stands in isolation some way from the village beside the River Uck, close to the remaining earthworks of a medieval motte and bailey fortification which protected the point where the Uck flows into the Ouse. Dating from the 13th, 14th and 15th centuries, the church was largely restored in 1876. A carved slab from the tomb of Gundrada, daughter of William the Conqueror and wife of William de Warenne, which was originally at LEWES Priory, was discovered under the floor and returned to Lewes where it can now be seen at Southover church.

The pride of St Margaret's is the Shurley Chapel which contains some fine monuments to the Shurley family, who were prominent Sussex landowners. These include some brasses, but best of all is a magnificent tomb with alabaster effigies of Sir John Shurley (d. 1631), his two wives and their nine children. The Shurleys lived at nearby Isfield Place, a Tudor mansion which is said to be linked to the church by an underground passage and is thought to have been used in smuggling operations in the area. Unfortunately the house is not visible from the road.

A little farther to the west of the church is the line of the Greensand Way, a Roman road which ran from Lewes to Rochester. Also in the village are a large mill and a pound, recently restored, which was used to round up stray animals. Owners could get them back on payment of a fine.

JEVINGTON

Map p.144, C4   * *
1 1/2 miles SW of Willingdon off the A22

This unspoilt village conceals its origins well – there have been settlers here since prehistoric times.

The **Church of St Andrew**★★ is dedicated to the patron saint of mariners. The church tower is Saxon and traces of Roman bricks can be seen in the blocked up windows on its north and south walls. Inside, on the north wall below the tower, is a curious Saxon sculpture showing the risen Christ killing a beast with a sword – the triumph of good over evil. The chancel has an aumbry and a piscina with a ledge, used for washing the holy vessels. On the west wall of the chancel is a memorial to 'Nat. Collier M.A.' showing the year of his death as 1691/2. This reflects the confusion over the calendar style that was to be adopted at that time (whether the year began in January or in March). A tapsell gate with a style, in the south–east corner of the churchyard, leads back to the village skirting the grounds of Jevington Place.

Opposite the church lies Monastery Field, the site of a 14th-century monastic settlement devoted to the Saxon martyr St Lewinna. It is said that she was formerly buried in the church where her bones performed miracles for pilgrims.

The Hungry Monk restaurant was the home of 'Jevington Jigg', a notorious smuggler in the late 18th century whose gang operated locally, often in collusion with the church rector who lived opposite. The village houses still contain many hideaways for contraband.

Combe Hill★, north–east of the village, can be reached via a footpath opposite the Eight Bells pub. There are good examples of bowl and disc burial barrows from the time of the Neolithic settlement near by. During World War II, Churchill tanks were put through their trials here before entering service.

KINGSTON-NEAR-LEWES

Map p.143, D3   ★
1½ miles SW of Lewes off the A27

Nestling in a combe at the foot of the downs, Kingston comprised just a single street of cottages and farm houses,

a medieval church, a manor house and a village green until the 1920s. Since then, the village has expanded with modern housing attracting commuters and local University lecturers, though it has still managed to retain the atmosphere of a small downland village.

The Juggs public house in the centre of the village recalls the fishwives who used to walk over the downs from Brighton via Juggs Lane, carrying the fish their fishermen husbands had caught to sell at the market in Lewes. The juggs were the flat baskets in which they carried the fish.

Half-timbered **Kingston Manor** dates from the mid 16th century and was partly built from material taken from Lewes Priory.

St Pancras Church★ has an unusual tapsell gate, which swings open at a central axis at the entrance, while inside there is a Jacobean chest and a stained-glass window showing the beauty of the local countryside.

LAUGHTON

Map p.149, F2   ★
6 miles S of Uckfield on the B2124

The village sign shows that this is the 'village of the buckle' – the symbol of the Pelham family who once lived here. Sir John Pelham fought with the Black Prince at the battle of Poitiers in 1356 and helped capture King John of France – he received a buckle to add to his crest. Pelham buckles can be seen carved on churches throughout the county, including Laughton church.

All Saints' Church lies a quarter-mile to the south of the village and dates in part from the 13th century although it has been much restored. The church guidebook proudly points out the sealed slab of the Pelham crypt, under the chancel arch, as marking the resting place of two Prime Ministers, three Earls of Chichester, a Duke of Newcastle and a Bishop of Lincoln. Above the chancel arch are two funerary helmets. The chancel has two

tablets to the 6th and 7th Earls of Chichester, father and son, who died within a week of each other in 1926. In the churchyard, where there are fine views to the South Downs, stands a curious cast iron urn memorial dated 1823.

🏠 William Pelham built **Laughton Place** as his seat in 1534 but the family departed in 1595 for a new home at nearby Halland (now demolished). All that remains is the moated tower, which stands in open farmland outlined against the backdrop of the Downs, 1½ miles to the south-west of the village. The tower, of brick construction and now a private home, can be viewed from a distance by following the public footpath from Colbrans Farm to the west of Laughton.

LEWES

Map p.143, C3   * * *
8 miles NE of Brighton off the A27

The county town of East Sussex, Lewes sits at the edge of a spur of the South Downs, in a gap in the hills created by the River Ouse. The name comes from the Old English word, *hlaew*, meaning hill, and the town's strategic importance was recognized by the Romans, the Saxons and the Normans. In fact, Lewes became one of the first towns to be fortified after the invasion of 1066.

William the Conqueror gave Lewes and large tracts of the surrounding countryside to one of his companions-in-arms, William de Warenne, who built the castle on a prominence overlooking the town.

🏰 **Lewes Castle★★** was of the motte and bailey type and was unusual in having two mottes, one of which bears the substantial remains of the keep, from where there are panoramic views over the downs. The other motte, a grassy mound known as Brack Mount, can still be seen behind the Lewes Arms public house.

Between the two is a fine 14th-century barbican and a 300-year-old undulating

bowling green on what used to be the castle tilting yard. It is believed to be the only green of its type in the country, where the original game of bowls, as played by Sir Francis Drake on Plymouth Hoe while awaiting the Spanish Armada, is still played. Opposite the green, Castle Lodge was once the home of Charles Dawson, the man who perpetrated the Piltdown Man hoax.

🏠 **The Priory of St Pancras★** was also founded by William de Warenne and his wife Gundrada. This magnificent building was based on the great abbey of Cluny in Burgundy and when completed, late in the 11th century, its church was larger than Westminster Abbey. It lasted for more than 400 years until Henry VIII's dissolution of the monasteries in 1537, when it was largely dismantled, its stones used in the construction of other buildings in the area. Some parts of the old walls can still be seen behind Southover church.

Both William and Gundrada were buried at the priory and their caskets were uncovered in 1845 when the Lewes–Brighton railway was being built. Their remains are now buried in a chapel in Southover church, beneath Gundrada's black marble tomb stone, discovered during restoration work at ISFIELD.

After the building of the priory, the next major event in the town's history was the Battle of Lewes, which took place on 14 May 1264. It was to have a marked effect on the country's future. Henry III was on the throne at the time and proved to be fairly incompetent, wasting money and quarrelling endlessly with his barons, who rose up against him under the leadership of his brother-in-law, Simon de Montfort, Earl of Leicester. They finally met in a bloody battle on the downs outside the town, the barons won and Henry was forced to sign a treaty which effectively paved the way to parliamentary government. A memorial to de Montfort, in the form of a knight's helmet and decorated in bronze with scenes of the battle, was erected near the priory ruins on the 700th anniversary in 1964.

Lewes Castle was built by a companion-in-arms of William the Conqueror, not long after 1066.

The Georgian period proved the most prosperous for Lewes and, before Brighton appeared on the socialite's map, it was the fashionable place to be. Great town houses were built for the local nobility and medieval half-timbered houses were given Georgian facades, some of them with mathematical tiles, shiny tiles fitted to buildings to look like bricks. Even today, the main street has a strongly Georgian appearance, unblighted by the chain stores usually associated with modern high streets.

🏨 **Shelley's Hotel** is one of its more notable buildings. A Georgian mansion, it was converted from a 16th-century inn. The old inn sign, a nude Bacchus astride a barrel draped with grapes, now hangs at Anne of Cleves House. Also worth seeing are the **Crown Courts**, built in neo-classical style with figures representing Wisdom, Justice and Mercy, and the **White Hart Hotel**, a coaching inn since 1727 and meeting place of the Headstrong Club, an 18th-century political group. One of its members was the revolutionary Thomas Paine, who lodged at nearby Bull House and took part in both the American War of Independence and the French Revolution. He later wrote *The Rights of Man* and was forced to flee the country to avoid a charge of treason.

🏨 ℹ️ **Lewes House★**, which now houses the Tourist Information Centre, was (and might still have been) the home of Rodin's masterpiece, *The Kiss*. Edward Perry, who commissioned the work and exhibited it there along with other pieces of art, offered it to the council, but unfortunately town prudery had its say and the sculpture was eventually 'banished' to the Tate Gallery in London.

Each side of the High St are narrow lanes called 'twittens', a Sussex word derived from 'betwixt and between', all of which are worth exploring. One of them, Keere St, a steep hill surfaced with bricks and beach pebbles and lined with period cottages, is one of the town's prettiest streets. George IV, while Prince Regent, is said to have driven a coach and four

horses down the hill for a bet. One of the town's oldest buildings, a 15th-century half-timbered second-hand bookshop, stands at the top of the street.

Another interesting twitten is Pipe's Passage, which was once the sentry walk along the town wall, parts of which can be seen in Westgate St. Along the passage is a strange round house, formerly the base for the town's windmill. It was owned briefly by Virginia and Leonard Woolf in 1919 but they decided to buy Monk's House at RODMELL before they moved in.

Here and there are also hidden courtyards, one of the most outstanding being at Castle Antiques. Medieval half-timbered buildings round the pretty paved yard make a superb ensemble with the castle keep rising immediately beind.

⛪ **St Michael's Church** is close by. It has a mainly Georgian flint façade although its round tower, one of only three similar towers in all of Sussex (the others are at PIDDINGHOE and SOUTHEASE), dates from the 12th century. On its wall is a modern statue of the Archangel Michael. Inside is a monument to Sir Nicholas Pelham, who repelled a French attack at Seaford in 1545, and two 15th-century brass effigies.

⛪ **St Anne's Church★** is at the top of St Anne's Hill, charmingly lined with 18th-century cottages. It dates from the 12th century. Worth seeing inside are the basket-weave Norman font, a canopied, 14th-century Easter Sepulchre and a Jacobean pulpit.

Beyond the church, between the Black Horse and Pewter Pot pubs, a brass strip marks the Greenwich meridian. Farther on, near the edge of the town, is the grim Victorian structure of Lewes Prison. Much of the town's history can be traced at two museums, the Barbican House Museum next to the castle, and the Museum of Local History in Southover High St.

🏛 **The Barbican House Museum★**, which is administered by the Sussex Archaeological Society, documents the history of Sussex from prehistory to the Middle Ages through archaeological discoveries. These include extensive displays of tools and artefacts from earlier ways of life including the Roman, Saxon and Norman periods.

The Lewes Living History Model★
is next to the museum. It is a scale model of the town as it was 100 years ago, showing the breweries, iron foundries and riverside wharves that were once such a part of the town. A light and sound display also traces the 1000 years of the town's history.

🏛 **The Museum of Local History★★**
is housed in Anne of Cleves House, a large 16th-century timber-framed house given to Henry VIII's fourth wife as a divorce settlement, though she never actually lived there. It has kitchen, living room and bedroom displays with fine collections of furniture, as well as toys and games, Victoriana, Sussex ironwork and stone from the priory.

The Southover district of Lewes, beneath the castle and close to the priory ruins, is one of the most attractive parts of the town. At one end of Southover High St is Southover Grange and gardens.

🏠 **Southover Grange★★** was built in 1572 from stones removed from the priory, and between 1630 and 1637was the childhood home of the diarist, John Evelyn. Its beautiful walled garden contains some magnificent old trees and colourful floral displays. Near by is Lewes's answer to Brighton's sweeping Regency crescents, Priory Crescent, built around 1840.

At the end of the Georgian and beginning of the Victorian periods, a 'New Town' was built behind the castle in an area leading down to the river.

⛪ **St John-sub-Castro★**, built in 1839 in place of a Saxon church that stood on the site, incorporates an arch and a doorway from the old church. The churchyard, which stood on what was a Roman camp, is now overgrown, but among its more

interesting memorials is one to Finnish prisoners who died in the old naval prison after their capture in the Crimean War.

Just behind the church is an area known as the Pells, once the site of a paper-mill. The mill has disappeared now but the L-shaped canal that powered it is still there, surrounded by trees and a lovely place to stroll around.

The final part of Lewes is Cliffe, reached across the Ouse by an elegant hump-backed bridge, dating from 1727 and the latest to bridge this point in more than 800 years. From the bridge can be seen the grain stores of the old town wharf on one side and Harveys Brewery on the other.

In the 19th century, Lewes boasted no fewer than seven breweries and more than 70 public houses. Harveys, founded in 1790, is the last of those breweries and is housed in a handsome Georgian and Victorian Gothic building beside the river. Another brewery, the Star (in Fisher St), has now become an English Heritage funded arts centre.

⛪ **St Thomas's Church★**, at the far end of Cliffe High St, was founded in the late 12th century, probably by monks from SOUTH MALLING. Much of the building, though, dates from the 14th and 15th centuries.

At the end of the High St is South St, which until the late 1970s carried the main A26 and A27 traffic into Lewes and along the High St. Then a bypass was built, taking the A27 traffic south of the town, while the Cuilfail Tunnel was bored through the hill behind Cliffe to carry the A26 traffic.

Nowadays a quiet haven beside the Ouse, South St has the dubious reputation of being the scene of the worst avalanche disaster ever to occur in Britain. After two days of blizzards at Christmas 1836, a huge cornice of snow fell off the cliffs and crashed on to cottages below, killing eight of the occupants. The Snowdrop public house now stands at the site.

The biggest event in the town's calendar is bonfire night on 5 November, which is not so much to do with Guy Fawkes but more in connection with 17 Protestant martyrs burned at the stake in the town, victims of Queen Mary's purges in the 16th century. A memorial to the martyrs stands on the hill above Cliffe.

Every bonfire night the population of the town doubles to 30,000 for the highlight of the bonfire season, a peculiarly Sussex tradition which starts at Rotherfield in August. People come from across the country and even from abroad. As darkness falls all roads into the town are closed and numerous bonfire societies, their members colourfully dressed in exotic costumes, hold torchlight processions through the streets. The night culminates in huge bonfires and firework displays at various points around the town.

Museum of Local History: *Apr–Oct, Mon–Sat 10am–5.30pm, Sun 2–5.30pm. Tel: (0273) 474610.*

Lewes Castle: *Apr–Oct, Mon–Sat 10am–5.30pm, Sun 11am–5.30pm; Jan–Mar and Nov–Dec, Mon–Sat 10am–5.30pm. Tel: (0273) 474379*

Lewes House and Tourist Information Centre: *All year, Mon–Fri 9am–5pm; Apr–Sept, also Sat 10am–2pm. Tel: (0273) 483448*

Barbican House Museum: *All year, Mon–Sat 10am–5.30pm; Apr–Oct, also Sun 11am–5.30pm. Tel: (0273) 474379.*

Lewes Living History Model: *Easter–mid Sept, daily 11am–5.30pm. Tel: (0273) 474379.*

LITLINGTON

Map p.144, C3   *** ***
4 miles NE of Seaford off the A259

A popular centre for walks along the many local footpaths, the village sits on the eastern banks of the gentle River Cuckmere with woods behind and water-meadows below.

⛪ **St Michael the Archangel Church**, built of flint with a shingled spire and white weather-boarding, lies to the north and is of late Norman origin with later additions. To the right of the entrance is a 13th-century sundial used to tell the times of the services. The chancel has a fine sedilia and piscina and an Easter Sepulchre. In the churchyard is a memorial to General Charles La Trobe, the first Lieutenant Governor of the colony of Victoria in Australia, who recommended to Gladstone in 1846 that the transportation of convicts to Van Diemen's Land be stopped.

The group of flint, stone and brick buildings near by that now forms Church House Farm, was probably associated with the church and may well have been the home of the parish priest.

In the village centre are the **tea-gardens**, renowned far and wide for many years. Visitors may sit in the little summer houses and be served traditional afternoon teas by quaintly costumed waitresses; there are garden walks above the lawns.

A footpath by the Plough and Harrow inn leads down to a white bridge over the River Cuckmere, a haven for fish and wildfowl. To the south-west, outlined on the distant hill, is a white horse carved into the chalk by one James Pagden in the last century. The spire of Alfriston church can be seen to the north.

LITTLE HORSTED

Map p.149, D1   *****
1 mile S of Uckfield off the A26

This village tucked away beside the A26 near Uckfield is aptly named, comprising no more than a Norman church, some brick-built cottages and a school.

⛪ **St Michael's Church**, on a rise and with lovely views over the surrounding countryside, was restored in 1863 and features a belfry which is open to the church and a castellated tower topped by a curious turret.

🏛 **Horsted Place★**, a Victorian mansion built in 1850, stands across the road. The building's main influence comes from

As with many Sussex villages, Mayfield's high street is strung out along a hilltop site.

Augustus Pugin, who is known for his work on the Houses of Parliament, and the staircase in the house, hand-carved in oak, was his design. The library was the work of Lord Snowdon. In 1965, the house was bought by Lord Rupert Nevill, a friend of the Queen and Prince Philip, who were frequent visitors and often attended services at the church. Now a hotel and conference centre, the house is also home to the East Sussex National Golf Club, whose 36-hole course virtually surrounds the village. A rose bush in the grounds which has been entwined with a myrtle bush is said to have been grown from a sprig from Queen Victoria's wedding bouquet.

LULLINGTON

Map p.144, C3   ******
4 miles N of Seaford off the A259

On the minor road between Alfriston and Wilmington, the village church stands above the village and is reached by a brick footpath through private gardens. This is a magical and peaceful spot, with views to the South Downs.

ⓗ The **Parish Church**, described as one of the smallest in England, has a tiled roof, timber-boarding and shingled steeple. It is in fact the surviving chancel of a much larger building, whose outlines can be seen from the stone remnants to the west. The flint and stone church originally belonged to Alciston Priory, which in turn was controlled by the important monastic hierarchy at Battle Abbey. The destruction of the larger church probably occurred during the aftermath of the Civil War.

The north window is 13th century and is one of the oldest surviving parts of the building. There may have been earlier Saxon connections here. A solitary bell hangs in the tower and a harmonium nestles close to the altar.

Everything seems to be in miniature here (the church is some 16ft square and seats just over twenty worshippers) but it still hosts services, although no further marriages or burials are permitted

within the grounds. The church guidebook asks for information regarding an exact replica of Lullington church, supposedly built as a war memorial somewhere in the United States.

From the churchyard are fine views of Alfriston to the west, and the SOUTH DOWNS WAY crosses above the church on its course towards Wilmington.

MARESFIELD

Map p.149, C1
2 miles N of Uckfield, at the junction of the A22 and A272

The name Maresfield has nothing to do with horses: it derives from the Old English *mersc* or *mere* meaning marsh or pool, and *feld* meaning field. This rambling parish includes both Nutley and Fairwarp. It marks the southern apex of the triangle which forms the boundary of Ashdown Forest (the other points being Forest Row and Crowborough). Lying at the junction of two very busy main roads, Maresfield has great need of a bypass. It has some pretty tile-hung cottages and a tall, brick Georgian pub called The Chequers Inn which is built on a bluff with the ground falling away behind. Near the pub is a milestone which is not in fact of stone but, appropriately for the area, of cast iron. It is painted white and shows a distance of 41 miles from Bow Bells. Maresfield used to be a very important iron centre and had three iron foundries at the height of the industry.

ⓗ **St Bartholomew's Church** stands on the corner opposite the milestone. The oldest parts are Norman; a Norman window can be seen in the nave. The western end of the building is medieval, and the chancel and transepts were added by J. Oldrid Scott who restored the church in the 1870s. In the north transept is a pretty rose window. The pulpit is Jacobean. Over the north door is a finely moulded royal coat of arms of George III. Another reminder of the iron industry is an iron tomb slab to Robert Brooks, dated 1667.

MAYFIELD

Map p.150, B1   * * *
9 miles S of Tunbridge Wells off the A267

Mayfield is a large village in north-east Sussex with a lovely High St and raised red-brick pavements. In the middle of the pavement is a tall, village sign showing the figure of a girl referring to the origin of the name, *Maghfeld*, or Maid's Field. Mayfield is famous for the legend of St Dunstan's encounter with the devil. The saint, a blacksmith, was forging a horseshoe when the devil paid him a visit in the guise of a beautiful maiden (with the aim of tempting him off the straight and narrow). The saint spotted the cloven feet, however, and grabbed Satan by the nose with his red-hot tongs. The devil leapt away and in a single bound, landed in Tunbridge Wells where he plunged his burning nose in water to cool it. And that is why the waters of Tunbridge Wells have their healing sulphurous qualities.

⚑ The Catholic Convent of the Holy Child is the most outstanding feature, particularly if you approach Mayfield's centre from Rotherfield. Now a girls' school, the convent buildings form a group around the remains of Mayfield Palace, which was one of the great residences of the medieval Archbishops of Canterbury and an important church administrative centre. The most impressive building surviving from the palace is the magnificent 14th-century Great Hall which is now used as a chapel. It is vast, 70ft long and 40ft wide, and the roof is supported on three giant stone arches which rise from corbels on short shafts, supported by grotesque figures. Visitors to the convent are shown the famous tongs of St Dunstan, and his anvil.

Like many towns and villages in this area, Mayfield prospered during the height of the iron industry, and much of its finest architecture dates from that time. In the High St, Middle House is a splendid oak-beamed Tudor inn, the date 1575 carved into the barge boards. Twenty-five years before the inn was built, four Protestant martyrs were burnt at the stake here (during the reign of Catholic Mary I), and they are not forgotten by the community which has a thriving bonfire society.

⛪ St Dunstan's Church, not a surprising dedication, is set back from the main street and was mostly rebuilt after a fire destroyed it, along with much of the village, in 1389. It suffered more damage in 1621 when it was struck by lightning. The iron industry's importance is again seen inside the church: two cast-iron tomb-slabs are set in the floor of the nave, one whose letters have emerged from the casting back to front – perhaps the work of a novice foundryman? A view of the village and its church can be seen from high on Argos Hill, topped by a post mill and lying midway between Mayfield and Rotherfield.

MOUNT CABURN

Map p.143, C4   *
1 ½ miles E of Lewes off the A27

Mount Caburn is a distinctive hill rising to a height of 491ft just north of the A27 Lewes–Polegate road. Around 500 BC, the hilltop was occupied by a small farm, but then its strategic position was realized, overlooking the Ouse Valley, which at that time would have been a broad inlet of the sea, as well as routes through the downs. In about 150 BC it was fortified with ramparts, ditches and a wooden stockade. A 1930s excavation showed there were around seventy households there at one time and revealed coins, pottery and bronze jewellery. The fortress finally succumbed to the formidable might of the Roman legions.

Today, the earthworks at the summit are clearly visible and outstanding views extend along the Ouse Valley to the sea, east and west along the downs, and northwards into the Sussex Weald. It is a popular resting point for hikers walking up from Lewes or Glynde and, when the weather conditions are right, it attracts hang-gliders and para-gliders.

MOUNTFIELD

Map p.151, D2
3 miles N of Battle off the A2100

Mountfield hardly even qualifies as a village, as it consists of nothing except a church, a scattering of houses, and the big 18th-century Mountfield Court, glimpsed in the distance beyond parkland planted with wheat and studded with oak trees.

All Saints' Church, a small building with a stumpy Norman tower lower than the nave, is built on a site where pre-Christian worship was probably practised. It has no aisles, and the chancel is only 17ft square. The font is Norman, carved in the 16th century with shells and Tudor roses, and there are some faded remains of medieval wall-painting over the round chancel arch, from a 12th-century biblical scene to a Tudor Ten Commandments (only 'Steale' and 'Adulterie' survive). The 19th-century organ gallery was built in memory of Lady Brassey (see CATSFIELD).

Hidden away in woodland west of Mountfield is the huge factory of British Gypsum, the area's main employer. Towards Brightling is a vast underground gypsum mine, where the grey mineral is brought to the surface for processing, ending up as plasterboard, dental moulds, or additives for canned vegetables, flour and cosmetics.

NETHERFIELD

Map p.151, D1
4 miles NW of Battle on the B2096

Netherfield straggles for over 1 mile along a ridge, with no real centre and, surprisingly, no ancient church, though the village appears in the Domesday Book. The Victorians made up for this lack by building a complex of church and school at the eastern end of the village.

The Church of St John the Baptist was designed in the 1850s by Samuel Sanders Teulon. It is a Gothic-style sandstone building, with a tall tower jutting from its side. Inside it is entirely Victorian, with a stone pulpit and font also designed by Teulon. Several of the windows are of unusual yellow monochrome glass, decorated with outline engravings. In the north aisle is a lurid 17th-century, Italian painting of Salome holding the head of the Baptist.

For a comparatively recent church, the stonework is in poor condition, and needs a great deal of repair.

NEWHAVEN

Map p.143, F4   *
9 miles E of Brighton on the A259

Once just a tiny village called Meeching, Newhaven developed, literally as a 'new haven', after Seaford's decline as a port when its harbour silted up. A storm in 1579, diverting the River Ouse farther west, finally sealed Seaford's fate and led to the birth of a new port. Meeching itself had been known since Roman times and, in recent years, the remains of a Roman villa have been discovered. The site has since been covered by a new police station.

Ship-building developed and, in the Victorian era, there were great plans for Newhaven. It was expected to become 'the Liverpool of the south' and by 1880 it was the sixth most important port in the country. Somehow, it all came to nothing and now it operates as a small port with the occasional freighter, an often-troubled cross-Channel ferry link with Dieppe in France, a fishing fleet and a yacht marina. It has never been a holiday town – Dickens once described it as 'that most one-horsed town' – but it does have some areas of interest, including an old fort and maritime museum, a leisure centre, Seahaven pool and a ski school. Little remains of the old town other than the parish church and a hotel.

The Bridge Hotel, built in 1623 as the New Inn, changed to its present name

The cross-Channel ferry leaving Hewhaven Harbour.

101

when a drawbridge, built around 1775, replaced the ferry across the River Ouse. The old brewery of Thomas Tipper, which supplied ale to George IV in Brighton, is now incorporated into the hotel. Two of the hotel's more illustrious visitors were King Louis-Philippe and his wife Marie-Amelie de Bourbon, who arrived from France in 1848 as Mr and Mrs Smith after fleeing the second revolution.

⛪ St Michael's*, a 12th-century Norman church, has a fine beamed roof and unusual interior decor incorporating shades of blue and terracotta. In the churchyard is a memorial to the 105 men of HMS *Brazen* who lost their lives when the ship foundered off Newhaven in 1800. Thomas Tipper himself, who put up much of the money for the drawbridge across the River Ouse, is buried in the churchyard. His tombstone bears a carving of the bridge.

🏰 Newhaven Fort* is one of 72 coastal strongholds commissioned by Lord Palmerston in the 1860s to counter a threat of French invasion which never materialized. It is the largest of its type in East Sussex. Built into the cliffs beneath Castle Hill, it has gun-emplacements, mortar-batteries, magazines, a parade ground, casemates linked by a labyrinth of passages tunnelled in the chalk, and a military museum. It served as an important coastal defence during both wars and was used by the army until 1956, after which it fell into decay. It was restored in the 1980s and now has a children's assault course, picnic areas and access to Castle Hill Coastal Park.

As well as the major defensive role of its fort during World War II, Newhaven proved important in other aspects too. It was the main base for the disastrous raid on Dieppe in 1942 – there is a memorial to the many Canadian soldiers killed at the junction of Bridge St and the ring road – and, two years later, it was one of the assembly points for vessels and troops involved in the D-Day landings.

🏛 Newhaven and Seaford Historical Society Museum, on the West Pier, has a fine collection of old photographs, treasures salvaged from the sea and memorabilia from the two towns – as well as material and photographs relating to the history of the cross-Channel ferry service.

Garden Paradise is at the edge of the town, near Denton, and includes the Planet Earth and World of Plants exhibitions. The landscaped gardens have three lakes, a waterfall and a miniature train and temperature-controlled gardens showing desert and tropical-rainforest flora. Planet Earth recreates the earth's early years with lifesize motorized dinosaurs and simulated earthquakes.
Newhaven Fort: Easter–Oct, Weds–Sun (daily in school holidays) 10.30am–6pm. Charge. Tel: (0273) 517622
Garden Paradise: All year, daily 9am–5pm. Charge. Tel: (0273) 512123 and 513985
Newhaven and Seaford Historical Society Museum: Good Friday–end Oct, Sat–Sun and BHs, afternoons. Tel: (0323) 896724.

NEWICK

Map p.148, D4   *
3 miles W of Maresfield on the A272

The first thing you see as you approach Newick is a traditional village green with a distinctive fretwork sign on a tall post, showing the silhouette of the church. There is also a nice old long-handled water pump, dated 1837, with a lion's-head spout. The green is surrounded by mainly Victorian and Edwardian houses, and a signpost points you towards the old church, a quarter-mile up a narrow road.

⛪ St Mary's Church is a simple building with parts dating from Norman times. It is built in pale orange-gold sandstone and its squat tower is topped by a red-tiled pyramidal spire. The finials on the door surround are carved faces. The porch timbers are some 600 years old, and white doves fly in and out of the eaves. The stained glass in the chancel dates from about 1315. In the 19th century, the church was restored and the interior elaborately decorated with tiles and a painted frieze.

NINFIELD

Map p.146, C1   *
4 miles N of Bexhill on the A271

This village, which sprawls shapelessly across the top of a high ridge, has an unmistakable tang of the sea, which is only 4 miles away. Under trees by the main road are the old village stocks, made of Sussex iron rather than the usual wood.

⛪ The little Church of St Mary the Virgin is down a cul-de-sac, away from the village centre. Reached through a tunnel of trees, it still has its medieval lancet windows, though it was so drastically restored by the Victorians that not much survives from earlier than the 19th century. The brick porch, with a wooden sundial above the entrance, dates from 1735. Inside, the most noteworthy feature is the 19th-century clock mechanism, all brass cogs and blue paintwork, which thumps away like a steady heartbeat.

NORTHIAM

Map p.152, C1   * *
8 miles W of Rye on the A28

Northiam must be about the longest village in the county, straggling southwards for 2 miles from the River Rother. An old rhyme, comparing it with other villages round about, boasts: 'O rare Norgam, thou dost far exceed / Beckley, Peasmarsh, Udimore and Brede'. Nowadays it certainly exceeds them all both in extent and in interest for the visitor. Its name is an abbreviation of the medieval North Higham.

Fortunately for anyone walking through Northiam, its old centre is only about half a mile long, with an ancient house at either end: Great Dixter (see p.17) up a lane at its northern end, and Brickwall at its southern end. The main street is lined with a splendid collection of 18th-century weather-boarded houses, large and small: the finest of them is a grand three-storey building (now an estate agent's office), beside the small triangular village green.

Queen Elizabeth's Oak, the green's main feature. This ancient and battered oak tree, now almost branchless, gets its name from the story – probably authentic – that Queen Elizabeth I dined under it in August 1573, during her progress through Kent and Sussex. As her feet were hot and tired, she took off her green silk shoes and gave them to the people of Northiam. Near the tree is a smart village pump, dated 1907, and thus several centuries too late for the queen to have cooled her feet in its water.

⛪ St Mary's Church*, tucked away at the top of a slope beside the green, has a tall, slender spire, dating from the time when the Weald was heavily wooded and the easiest way to navigate cross-country was from one spire to the next. The base of the tower is sturdy Norman, built largely of brown ironstone. The church is unusually wide; the nave and aisles date from the 14th century, and the church was enlarged and restored in 1830–50. In the 1840s a mausoleum was built on the north side by the Frewens, a leading local family who lived at Brickwall. The first Frewen came to Northiam as rector in 1573, and the family bought Brickwall in 1666.

🏛 Brickwall* normally houses Queen Elizabeth's shoes in a glass case, although at present they are in a bank vault for safe-keeping. The house, now a boys' boarding school, gets its name from its most prominent feature – the high, brick wall, built about 1700, which runs round much of the garden. It is approached between a pair of impressive gateposts, and has such clean-cut and immaculately painted half-timbering that it looks almost bogus, though it is in fact clearly dated 1633.

The house is full of family portraits. The 17th-century Frewens were staunch Puritans, as is shown by such Christian names as Thankful and Accepted. Visitors are shown the front entrance hall, the music-room, which has a sumptuously elaborate plaster ceiling, and the dignified staircase.

The garden was originally laid out in 1680–1720 by Jane Frewen, who was also responsible for the wall round it. It still has its original layout of yew hedges and paved walks from the time of William and Mary;

a collection of flowers that Jane Frewen might herself have planted; and a new feature – a topiary 'chess garden', in which the pawns, knights and other pieces consist of contrasting yellow and dark green yew trained over metal frames.

Northiam played its part in World War II, as is recorded on a plaque at the entrance to the village playing-fields. In 1944, shortly before the Allied invasion of France, the prime ministers of Britain, Canada, South Africa and Southern Rhodesia met there to hold a conference and inspect the troops.

At the northern end of the village is a station of the Kent and East Sussex Railway, restored in 1990 as a result of one of Anneka Rice's television programmes. *Brickwall: Apr–Sept, Sat and BH Mons 2–5pm. Tel: (0797) 223329.*

NUTLEY

Map p.154, F2
3 miles S of Wych Cross on the A22

The hamlet of Nutley, in the heart of Ashdown Forest, is part of the parish of Maresfield (which also includes Fairwarp). It has a village shop, scattered houses, the Nutley Hall Rudolf Steiner Home, a church and a pub.

St James the Less Church was built in 1845 in grey stone. Its north aisle was added in 1871. The Shelley Arms is a large, well-proportioned 18th-century inn in grey and red brick. A mile north-east of Nutley is an ancient, working post mill complete with four sails (see Nutley Post Mill, p.34).

OFFHAM

Map p.143, C3 *
1½ miles N of Lewes on the A275

A tiny village of period flint cottages, a 19th-century church, a country house, two pubs, a tea-shop and a smithy, Offham was founded after the demise of HAMSEY.

It is known for having one of the first 'railways' in the south of England, a funicular railway operating from 1809 until 1870. Used to transport lime and chalk, quarried from a nearby pit, down a 1-in-2 slope to barges moored in the River Ouse 400ft below, it travelled through two brick tunnels beneath the road. As one loaded wagon descended an empty one was drawn up. The entrance to the tunnels, and four lime kilns, can still be seen in the car-park of the Chalk Pit Inn.

St Peter's Church, built in the style of the 13th century to replace the church at Hamsey, was opened in 1859.

⌂ **Coombe Place**, a fine country home tucked beneath the down's northern escarpment, dates from the 17th and 18th centuries, though a house has stood on the spot since 1492.

It was on Offham Hill, behind the village, that Simon de Montfort's men assembled before the Battle of Lewes in 1264. When the road through the village was being built in 1769, extensive human remains were unearthed, believed to be those of de Montfort's Londoners who suffered badly at the hands of Prince Edward's calvary in the early stages of the battle.

OLD HEATHFIELD

Map p.150, D1 *
Just S of Heathfield off the B2203

The old village of Heathfield used to be known for its Cuckoo Fair, held every year on April 14th. Tradition has it that an old woman would release a cuckoo from her basket at the fair, to herald the coming of summer. In Sussex dialect, this was called the Hefful Fair, from which Heathfield derives its name. The village consists of an old church, a splendid pub and some pretty weather-boarded and chequered brick cottages.

🏠 **All Saints'** is a large church built of Hastings sandstone. Parts of it date from

The post mill at Nutley, now restored to working order.

the late 13th century. It has a tower with a shingled broach spire and a 15th-century crypt. Much of the church was restored in the 1860s when all the windows were renewed. Inside, the kingposts and tie-beams can be seen. Out in the churchyard are two gravestones and a wall tablet decorated with terracotta plaques by Jonathan Harmer, son of a local stonemason.

♀ The **Star Inn** was built in 1348 to house stonemasons working on the church. Forty years later, it was turned into an ale house and, in the late 18th century, it was granted licences for wines and spirits. One of the inn's 18th-century landlords was George Brasher (a notorious cider drinker) whose ghost is said to haunt the Star. The building is in weathered sandstone and it stands in a beautiful garden which won a national award in 1987. The saloon bar is very welcoming and has heavy old beams and an enormous inglenook. The smaller bar has historic military uniforms on display.

OVINGDEAN

Map p.143, E2   *
3 ¹/₂ miles E of Brighton on the B2123

An unspoilt suburb of Brighton, Ovingdean was immortalized by Harrison Ainsworth in the novel *Ovingdean Grange*.

⌂ **Ovingdean Grange** dates from the 16th century but was given a new façade in the 19th century. Ainsworth's novel states that Charles II stayed at the Grange briefly, after his defeat at Worcester and before being put in touch with Nicholas Tattersell, the man who conveyed him to exile in France. There seems to be little truth in the legend. The Grange was the village's largest building until **Ovingdean Hall**, which is now a school, was built in 1786. For many years it was occupied by Nathaniel Kemp, uncle of Thomas Read Kemp who built Kemp Town in Brighton.

⌂ **St Wulfram's Church**★ is near the grange. This Norman building was damaged by the French raiders who attacked Rottingdean in 1377. Considered one of

the most attractive medieval churches in the Brighton area, it has a ceiling, rood screen and some windows by Charles Kempe, one of the greatest of the Victorian stained-glass window designers, who is buried in the churchyard. Magnus Volk, inventor of the Volks Railway in Brighton, is buried near by.

PATCHAM

Map p.142, C4   *
3 ¹/₂ miles N of Brighton on the A23

Another of the villages on the fringes of Brighton taken over by suburbia, Patcham still has a village atmosphere, especially around Church Hill and Old London Rd, despite the roar of traffic along the A23. Patcham Windmill (see p.34) stands beside the road over the hill to West Blatchington.

⌂ **All Saints'**, the Norman church, is rather ugly with its cement rendering but is noted for its 12th-century wall-painting of the Last Judgement, and the tomb of Richard Shelley, dated 1594. It stands at the top of the hill next to a massive tithe barn, 250ft long, now converted to residences. Opposite, in the grounds of Patcham Court Farmhouse, is a splendid, 17th-century flint dovecote, which contains about 550 nesting boxes.

Old cottages lead down to the Black Lion, a sprawling inn which replaced a similarly named inn in Old London Rd. The original, a large, brick building with a bay window, is now used as offices.

⌂ **Patcham Place**, a large house originally built by Baron de la Warr in 1588, stands opposite the Black Lion. It passed through the hands of several prominent Sussex families, including the Parliamentarian Anthony Stapley. He was one of 59 signatories to Charles I's death warrant, signed at the house in 1648. The imposing Queen Anne façade of black mathematical tiles was added in 1764. Since 1939 the house has served as a youth hostel.

Ⓜ On the downs, about 1 mile north of the village, stands an unusual war memorial.

Called the **Chattri**, it was erected in a
two-acre garden in 1921 and marks the
spot where Hindu and Sikh soldiers,
who died while in hospital at Brighton's
Royal Pavilion during World War I,
were cremated on a funeral pyre.

PEACEHAVEN

Map p.143, F3
6 miles E of Brighton on the A259

Planned by wealthy developer Charles
Neville during World War I as a 'garden
city by the sea' on the cliffs between
Brighton and Newhaven, Peacehaven was
originally to have been called Anzac-on-Sea,
in honour of the Australian and New
Zealand troops stationed in the area at the
time. Streets were laid out on a grid pattern
and plots sold at £50, £75 and £100.
Building started as soon as the war ended,
hence the change of name.

Today, Peacehaven is little more than
an extensive bungalow development
merging with the more recent Telscombe
Cliffs, with the Meridian shopping centre
as its focal point. Its cliff-top promenade is
largely unmade but half-way along stands a
20ft-high monument which serves as a
memorial to King George V as well as
marking the Greenwich Meridian.
*Tourist Information Centre: Meridian Centre,
Roderick Ave. Tel: (0273) 582668.*

PEASMARSH

Map p.152, C3
3 miles NW of Rye on the A268

Peasmarsh is a pretty switchback village,
strung out along the main road. Its centre
has recently been disfigured by a large
supermarket development. Its ancient core,
consisting of the Norman church and the
red-brick Georgian Peasmarsh Place next
door, is isolated down lanes 1 mile south of
the village.

**The Church of St Peter and St
Paul★** is worth hunting out. It is still largely
Norman, with a sturdy battlemented tower

capped by a broach spire. Inside, it has a
superb Norman chancel arch, carved with
stylized heraldic animals. The bells are far
older than most, as four of them were cast
in 1631. At the far end of the graveyard
under a large oak is a rare survival – a
battered wooden grave-board, now almost
totally illegible, of a type popular with poor
families 150 years ago.

PENHURST

Map p.146, A1 * *
5 miles W of Battle off the B2096

This tiny and idyllic hamlet is lost in the
lanes, miles from anywhere. It consists of
little more than a church, a manor house,
and a couple of large black weather-boarded
barns, one of which is now a craft shop.

The name Penhurst means 'head of the
wood' in Saxon, and goes back to the days
when the village was in the heart of the
Wealden Forest. In the Domesday Book it
was recorded as being 'worth 15 shillings',
and to have had 'two villeins with two
ploughs and one acre of meadow and wood
for two hogs' – hence the tree, peasants
and pigs shown on the village sign.

The **Church of St Michael the
Archangel★★** is an exquisite building,
built of sandstone between about 1340
and 1500. Its stumpy, tile-hung tower runs
the whole width of the building. Inside,
it still has its rough-hewn 14th-century
oak screen dividing the nave from the
chancel, and the hook on the kingpost
from which the Crucifixion was hung in
pre-Reformation days.

The **Manor House** stands on a hillock
above a small pond and forms a harmonious
group with the church. Partly of brick
and partly of stone, this tall, gabled house
was built about 1600 by William Relph,
a local ironmaster.

The lane west from Penhurst drops steeply
down to Ashburnham Forge: now just a
couple of cottages by a stream, but once an
industrial centre filling the woodland with
smoke and the sound of hammer on anvil.

107

A short way upstream is Ashburnham Furnace, last survivor of the Sussex iron industry, which closed down in the 1820s. (See also Ashburnham Place, p.14.)

PETT

Map p.147, B2
4 miles E of Hastings off the A259

Pett's modern houses and bungalows straggle for 1½ miles along an almost straight road, which, at its eastern end, swings steeply down to Pett Level – a wide expanse of reclaimed land, criss-crossed by canals and drainage ditches, which is a wildfowl haven.

The Church of St Mary and St Peter is summed up by Pevsner by the single word 'Dull'. Built in the 1860s for £2,000, it is only noteworthy for its tall, octagonal belfry and spire, and for the large gargoyles which peer down from it. On the north side of the nave is a modern, stained-glass window by Lawrence Lee, showing St Nicholas, patron saint of seafarers, with a lifeboatman.

PEVENSEY

Map p.145, C3   * * *
4 miles NE of Eastbourne on the A259

Pevensey Castle (see p.23) dominates this ancient town, which has been continuously inhabited since the Romans established the 'Anderida' fortress around AD 340. The PEVENSEY LEVELS to the north of the town were at that time submerged by the sea which extended towards Hailsham and Herstmonceux; the first settlements at Pevensey were built on a peninsula.

On 28 September 1066 Duke William of Normandy landed at Pevensey with his invasion force and 17 days later the Battle of Hastings was fought. The town and castle, with its massive Norman fortifications, grew in importance and Pevensey became a member of the Cinque Ports Confederation in the 13th century; its trade declined, however, as the sea retreated and the river silted up and by the 17th century its position as a trading port had been eroded. A walking tour of the town with its many listed buildings is best started from the main entrance to the castle near the car park.

The Mint House★★ is in the High St which runs east of the castle entrance. The 14th-century half-timbered building, now an antiques centre, occupies the site of an earlier Norman mint. Once the home of Andrew Borde, writer and Court Physician to Henry VIII, it contains several outstanding panelled rooms.

The Court House Museum★★ is further down the High St on the right, and was formerly the 'smallest town hall in England'. The town gaol and prisoners' exercise yard can be seen downstairs. The museum above houses a collection of local historical relics, including the original magistrates' benches and town weights and measures, the town beadle's uniform and a dinosaur's fossilized footprint.

St Nicholas' Church lies behind the High Street in Church Lane. Early English in style, but with Saxon origins, the church contains a fine Elizabethan tomb on the north wall; the lions below the recumbent figure of John Wheatley are from an earlier tomb. Pilgrims' crosses can be seen carved on the porch wall and a 12th-century crusader's tombstone is set into the chancel floor. The church was often used to hide smugglers' booty.

From here, Church Lane leads back to the public car park at Market Square.
Mint House: *Mon–Sat 9am–5.30pm. Tel: (0323) 762337*
Court House Museum: *end May–Sept, daily 10.30am–5pm (closed for lunch). No telephone.*
Tourist Information Centre: *Pevensey Castle, High St. Tel: (0323) 761444.*

PEVENSEY LEVELS

Map p.145, B2   * *
Between Herstmonceux and Pevensey, N of the A27

The 11,000 acres of wetland that lie between Herstmonceux and Pevensey are designated as a site of special scientific interest. In Roman times, when Anderida fort was built at Pevensey, much of the area was under the sea as can be detected by the suffix -ey (Saxon for island) in the names of local hamlets such as Rickney, Chilley and Horse Eye. In medieval times, salt-making was an important local industry. Some of the water-courses were still navigable by merchants in the mid 17th century.

To the north of the Levels rise the landmark spires of the churches at Herstmonceux and Wartling, and the domes of the former Royal Observatory in the grounds of Herstmonceux Castle (see p.22) are a startling addition to the skyline. The flat and peaceful marshes contrast dramatically with the nearby coastal resorts, downland hills and Wealden forest.

The area is a haven for flora and fauna, some protected in a Sussex Trust for Nature Conservation reserve. Agriculture has been practised since the sea receded and the rich pastures are patterned by a system of drainage ditches, many of them hundreds of years old.

The rushes and reeds that flourish by the marsh waters, which sometimes follow the line of the few roads across the Levels, are home to many species of birds, especially wildfowl, (several of which are winter visitors). Amongst the rarer plants found here are the water-violet and the water-soldier. The National Rivers Authority maintains the water quality of the area.

PIDDINGHOE

Map p.143, E4   *
1½ miles N of Newhaven off the A259

It used to be said of this delightful little village of flint-walled cottages on the River Ouse: 'At Piddinghoe they dig for moonshine'. This was a reference to the villagers' interest in smuggling spirits, which they would bury in the area until it was safe for them to be moved. Once a busy port, it now only harbours small boats and has the feel of a village 'miles from anywhere' even though Newhaven and Peacehaven are little more than 1 mile away.

⌂ St John's Church★, built on a bank above the river, is one of three churches in the Ouse Valley to have a round Norman tower and is thought to have been used as a beacon tower. The others are at Lewes and Southease. Rudyard Kipling immortalized the church's weather-vane in his poem 'Sussex', where he described it as a 'begilded dolphin'. Knowledgeable locals, however, maintain it is a sea trout.

Not far from the church, in the garden of Kiln Cottage, beside the Lewes–Newhaven road, is the only surviving bottle-shaped brick kiln in the country, last used in 1912 and restored in 1980. At the edge of the village, and close to the River Ouse, a disused clay-pit is now utilized by the Newhaven and Seaford Sailing Club and is often dotted with colourful sails.

PILTDOWN

Map p.148, C4
2 miles SW of Maresfield on the A272

In the 1920s, the pub at the hamlet of Piltdown was renamed after its most famous 'resident', the Piltdown Man. This find is now known to have been one of the biggest archaeological hoaxes of all time. The skull was unearthed by Charles Dawson in 1912. It had a human braincase and ape-like jaw and confused academics for some forty years. Thought to be the so-called 'missing link' between man and the apes, the find was given the name Eoanthropus Dawsoni.

Then, in 1949, Dr K. P. Oakley applied a new fluorine-dating test to the skull and started to expose the fake. Evidence based on carbon-dating methods identified the skull as that of a medieval man whose bones had been thickened by disease, and the jaw was that of a young orang-utan. The identity of the hoaxer has never been discovered.

The site of the find is in the **Barkham Manor Vineyard**. The modern winery produces award-winning English wine, and visitors can tour the vineyards and taste the wines. There is a shop and picnic area, and the premises are suitable for disabled access.
Barkham Manor Vineyard: *Easter–24 December, Tues–Sat 10am–5pm; Sun 11am–5pm. Tel: (0825) 722103.*

PLAYDEN

Map p.152, D3   *
1 mile N of Rye on the A268

Playden is Rye's northern extension, at the top of the hill down into the town. However, it still keeps a recognizable village centre surrounding the church. In earlier centuries it was known by the alternative name of Saltcote.

St Michael's Church**, well off the main road, has a tall needle spire covered in wooden shingles. The low tower is over the crossing, not at the west end – unusual in a small parish church. Apart from some later buttressing and a small vestry, it has hardly been altered since the Middle Ages. It was built about 1190 and is largely in Transitional Norman style, with a lofty roof that covers nave and aisles in a single sweep.

Inside, the most notable feature is the massive wooden ladder, dated 1686, which leads up into the belfry (now worm-eaten and not to be climbed on). There is a superb 14th-century wooden screen below the north tower arch, and a good Royal Arms of George III above the chancel arch. The west window in the north aisle is the only remaining Norman window in the church. Just over 3ft high, it is little more than an arrow-slit, and gives an idea of how dark the interior must have been before the windows were enlarged in the 14th century.

Below it, on the floor of the north aisle, is the church's greatest curiosity – a 16th-century stone slab carved with two casks and a pair of mashforks, the brewer's insignia. The inscription is in Flemish and commemorates Cornelis Roetmans, probably a Protestant refugee from Spanish persecution in the Netherlands, who fled to England to carry on his trade.

St Michael's has had its share of eccentric vicars. One 19th-century incumbent tested rocket-powered hydroplanes on the River Rother; while a 20th-century successor used to ride through the village on his motorcycle with his dog tucked under his arm.

From the churchyard there are wide-ranging views across Romney Marsh towards the sea.

PLUMPTON

Map p.143, B2   *
4 miles NW of Lewes on the B2116

This scattered village shelters beneath the steep northern escarpment of the South Downs and is just a short climb from the SOUTH DOWNS WAY. To most people passing through, Plumpton seems to consist of little more than a pub, the Half Moon, inside which more than 100 regular customers have been immortalized, raising their glasses, in a giant painting displayed on the wall.

St Michael's Church* stands across the fields, built of flint in Norman times with a tower added in the 13th century. 12th-century wall-paintings, uncovered in 1956, are just visible inside.

Plumpton Place*, a 16th-century moated mansion near by, was part of Henry VIII's dowry to Anne of Cleves. One owner, Sir Leonard Mascal, is thought to have introduced carp into England in Tudor times and bred them in the moat. The mansion is not open to the public, though it can be viewed from footpaths around the property.

Opposite the college a footpath leads to **Plumpton Plain**, where there is a Bronze Age settlement site with many tumuli.

Plumpton Green. An extension to Plumpton, Plumpton Green was established in Victorian times when the railway came to Sussex. It has been added to greatly in recent years. There is a modern flint church (built in 1893) while, next to the railway station, the National Hunt racecourse has one of the most picturesque settings in Sussex, with the downs as a backdrop.

Pevensey Castle, like the one at Lewes, was built shortly after the Norman Conquest.

POLEGATE

Map p.144, B4 *
4 miles NW of Eastbourne on the A22

Polegate lies on the route of the Roman road which ran west from Anderida Castle at Pevensey. The town centre, built around the railway station, has little attraction but two jewels can be found on the outskirts. The first is Polegate Windmill, (see p.34), a large tower-mill dating from 1817 and the only one of its kind in East Sussex open to public view.

⌂ The remains of **Otham Priory** are to the north–east of the town, on the edge of the Pevensey Levels (approached off the A22 down Otham Court Lane). They were founded in about 1175. Now part of a private house, the chapel can just be seen from the section of the Cuckoo Line footpath on the former railway track. The monks eventually moved to found the important community at Bayham Abbey (see p.20) near Tunbridge Wells.

PORTSLADE VILLAGE

Map p.142, D3 *
2 ¹/₂ miles NW of Hove off the A27

Formerly a downland village that dates back to Saxon times, Portslade Village has now been engulfed by the Hove suburbia which spread out between the 1930s and 1960s. Much of the old village survives, especially around the High St where there are several flower-bedecked, flint cottages and two pubs, the St George and the older Stag's Head, but no shops. One of the houses in the street, Kemps, is the oldest in Portslade, dating from 1580. The most prominent building in the village is the old brewery, also in the High St, which is now owned by a French engineering company.

⛪ **St Nicholas's Church★** is reached from a twitten opposite Kemps, and is a flint building with a stone roof, dating back to 1150. It has little stained glass, just one of St Francis and a tiny one of St Nicholas.

⌂ **The Manor House** was built near by in the 19th century , and is now a convent. It stands on the site of a 12th-century manor, the ruins of which are still visible.

ℹ **The Foredown Tower Countryside Centre★** is on the downs behind the village in a converted water-tower, all that remains of an isolation hospital that once stood there. The centre, opened in 1991, houses an exhibition about early downland life and features a camera obscura, one of the largest working examples in the world and one of only a handful in this country. It was originally made for the Gateshead Garden Festival in 1990 but now gives wonderful views of the South Downs and coast.
***Countryside Centre**: Apr–Sept, daily 10.30am–6pm; Oct–Mar, Thurs–Sun 10.30am–5pm. Tel: (0273) 422540.*

RINGMER

Map p.149, F1 **
2 ¹/₂ miles NE of Lewes on the B2192

A dormitory of Lewes, Ringmer still manages to retain the look and feel of a village, even though housing estates have been built in recent years and the population has quadrupled to around 5000 since the beginning of the century. In fact, Ringmer has one of the earliest settlements recorded in Sussex. It still has a village green, a huge one bordered by cottages and the church, where stoolball, a game invented by Sussex milkmaids more than 500 years ago, is played by teams of women. It also has two old wheel pumps. Glyndebourne Opera House (see p.17) is 1 mile south of the town.

⛪ **St Mary's Church** dates from the 14th century but has a 19th-century tower which replaced an earlier one that burned down. The tower was the work of William Martin, who is reputed to have built the first wooden-wheeled bicycle in England.

An unusual feature of the village sign is Timothy the Tortoise, who lived at the village in the 18th century with his owner, a Rebecca Snooke. Mrs Snooke was the aunt of famous naturalist Gilbert White who frequently visited Ringmer to carry out studies on Timothy, immortalized in White's work *The Natural History of Selborne*. The tortoise's shell is now in the Natural History Museum.

The East Sussex Gliding Club operates from a small airfield beside the B2192 north-east of the town.

RIPE

Map p.144, A2 ✱ ✱
5 miles W of Hailsham off the A22

A quiet and unspoilt village, Ripe parish was formerly known as Achiltone or Eckington.

St John the Baptist Church lies opposite the brick-built early 17th-century Eckington Manor. The church is constructed of flint and sandstone, and dates from the late 13th century, with a crenellated west tower added later. By the exterior west door are the carved buckle symbols of the Pelham family. There is an interesting two-seater sedilia in the chancel with scratched medieval lettering to the left – 'Sctus Sps' *(Sanctus Spiritus)*, 'Mtr dei' *(Mater Dei)* and 'Sancta Maria'. The east window has remnants of 14th-century painted glass; one pane is of a Tudor rose. Below the west window a stone stair leads to the bell-tower.

To the west of the tower lies the grave of Malcolm Lowry (1909–57) the poet and novelist, author of *Under the Volcano*, published in 1947 and based on his time in Mexico. He spent the last year of a troubled life at the White Cottage in the village (reached down the lane by the bus-shelter) where a commemorative blue plaque was erected 35 years after his death.

The sign for the Lamb Inn promises 'electric light in all bars, flushing water closets and wireless for your comfort'. Further down the village street is the extraordinary Old Cottage constructed of a variety of weirdly carved timbers, some depicting figures and heraldic devices – it has a matching garage.

ROBERTSBRIDGE

Map p.151, C2 ✱ ✱
5 miles N of Battle on the A21

Formerly called Rotherbridge, the little town of Robertsbridge grew up in association with a prosperous Cistercian abbey founded in 1176 (see also SALEHURST). It was a traffic nightmare until it was bypassed a few years ago, but it is now possible to enjoy its gently winding main street, which climbs from the river past a varied, yet harmonious, collection of half-timbered, weather-boarded and tile-hung houses. Some of them go back to the 15th century, and hardly any of them are more recent than the 18th century.

Fragments of **Robertsbridge Abbey** survive 1 mile to the east, down a lane off the bypass, including part of the refectory and the adjoining calefactory, or warming-house. The tall, gabled house near by incorporates the fine vaulted undercroft of the abbot's lodging. The abbey church, now vanished, lies below the fields towards the river.

Ripley's Museum of Rural Life, near the river at the bottom end of the town, carries on the long tradition of Sussex iron-working. Scrap iron lies in heaps outside the gate, and the entrance yard is dominated by a large cannon. The museum includes a Victorian kitchen complete with great iron range, an old-style grocery and hardware shop, and country bygones from mantraps to a pair of hop-stringers' stilts. The firm has its own working forge, and makes and sells every kind of iron fireback and firebasket, copying originals dating back to Tudor times.

The tile-hung **George Hotel**, at the top end of the town beside the war-memorial clock tower, was formerly a staging post on the London–Hastings road, but it is far older than the days of the stage-coach. A stone cellar survives from the first inn on the site, known as the Tunne, which was built in the 14th century. The landlords' names are recorded right back to one Isaac

Pooke, who was selling beer in the 1480s. The writer Hilaire Belloc stayed here at the beginning of this century, and the George has a framed photograph of him in old age, white-bearded and sitting by the fire.

Another pub, equally ancient, is the **Seven Stars**, half-way down to the River Rother. It may have been built by the Robertsbridge monks as a hostel for visitors or pilgrims.

Robertsbridge Abbey: Visits for parties only, by arrangement with the owner. Tel: (0580) 880441.

Ripley's Museum: All year, daily (except 24 Dec–2 Jan) 10am–4pm. Tel: (0580) 880324.

RODMELL

Map p.143, D3   ＊＊
3 miles S of Lewes off the A27

Lying between the downs and the water-meadows of the Ouse Valley, Rodmell was for many years the home of Leonard and Virginia Woolf, the writer. Their home, Monk's House (see p.19), is now owned by the National Trust. The village itself is one of the prettiest in East Sussex and made up of charming, half-timbered, flint and thatched cottages, as well as a Norman church with an ancient marble font, thought to be Saxon.

℞ **The Abergavenny Arms**, named after titled landowners who once lived in the area, was originally a 15th-century farmhouse but has been a public house for 300 years. Its lounge incorporates an 80ft well that used to supply water for the villagers, and some of the beams were taken from wrecked ships of the Spanish Armada. Like many other inns along the valley, it became the haunt of smugglers and Rudyard Kipling is reputed to have written *The Smugglers Song* while staying there.

The village still has a blacksmith and the large miller's house is more than 200 years old. The last miller, who died in 1926, is buried in the churchyard, beneath an old millstone.

At South Farm there is an old mulberrry tree, one of many planted in Sussex early in the 17th century, when James I was trying to establish a silk industry in the country. The leaves of the trees were used to feed the silkworms.

Near by, at an isolated hollow in the downs with the strange name of Breaky Bottom, is one of the most attractively located vineyards in England, where various white wines can be tasted in the courtyard of an old farm.

ROTHERFIELD

Map p.149, A4   ＊＊
3 miles E of Crowborough on the B2100

Rotherfield is a hilltop village of brick, weather-board and tile-hung cottages, centred on an irregular crossroads. The attractive main street runs on two sides of its centrally positioned church. The River Rother is said to rise in the cellar of one of the village houses and several of its tributaries spring near by.

⛪ **St Denys Church**＊＊＊ dates from the 12th century, but its dedication indicates that there was a church on the site some 300 years earlier. Bertwald, Duke of the South Saxons, was cured by the monks of St Denys, near Paris, back in the 8th century, and he built a church and monastery here in thanksgiving. The remains of the monastery are thought to be buried in a nearby field. The tower of the present church came crashing down on the night of the hurricane, October 16th 1987.

The interior of St Denys is outstanding. There is a superb waggon roof to the nave and a beautiful Perpendicular screen between the chancel and the side chapel. The pulpit is a fine piece of Jacobean carving, and the 16th-century polygonal font cover has folding doors like the one at TICEHURST. The five-light east window was designed by Burne–Jones and made by William Morris in 1879. It shows musicians surrounded by beautifully interwoven foliage. Some medieval frescoes

Rye, once on the coast, was cut off from the sea by the silting up of the Rother estuary.

survive including a 'doom painting' showing St Michael weighing the souls, with Christ and angels above. There is a sketchy wall painting depicting the village in 1711.

Argos Hill, with its old post mill, lies 1½ miles to the south-east, between Rotherfield and Mayfield. The panoramic views from the hill give a good impression of the surrounding hills that make up the Sussex countryside.

Map p.143, E2   *** ***
3½ miles E of Brighton on the A259

Lying in a dip in the cliffs, between Brighton and Peacehaven, Rottingdean has a small coastal front with a sea-wall promenade that links Brighton with Saltdean. The village has a long history, with the old part running inland along the High St up to the village green and pond overlooked by the church and several distinctive 18th-century houses.

One of the village's oldest buildings is Ye Black Horse Inn, dating from 1531. A number of half-timbered houses are to be found hidden away in its backstreets, but the modern coastal development has also encroached on the village.

Several famous people have lived in Rottingdean, including the Pre-Raphaelite artist Sir Edward Burne–Jones, the designer William Morris and the writer Rudyard Kipling, who described the landscape that surrounded him as the 'blunt, bow-headed, whale-backed Downs'. He lived for five years in a house called 'The Elms' overlooking the green, writing a number of his famous books and poems there before his annoyance at the number of sightseers invading his privacy forced him to move to the seclusion of Burwash. The attractive and extensive walled-gardens of the house are open to the public.

St Margaret's Church*, which has parts dating back to Norman times, was renovated in the 19th century and has five stained-glass windows by Burne–Jones, whose ashes rest in the churchyard.

The church has an interesting history having been burnt down, along with villagers sheltering there, by French raiders in 1377 during the Hundred Years War. Burn marks can still be seen on parts of the building today. Then, in the 1940s, Americans tried to buy the church to re-erect it in a Los Angeles cemetery. When the offer was refused, an exact replica was built instead. Prime Minister Stanley Baldwin married a local girl, Lucy Risdale, there in 1892.

The Grange Museum and Art Gallery** are housed in the old vicarage, a Georgian house with early 20th-century alterations by Sir Edwin Lutyens. It was once the home of artist Sir William Nicholson. The museum has a huge collection of toys dating back 150 years or more. One of its rooms is devoted to the life of Kipling and contains many books, letters, photographs and drawings.

Beacon Hill Windmill*, a late 18th-century, black weather-boarded smock-mill with large wagon-roof cap, stands on the cliffs just outside the village. Early this century it became dilapidated but, through the efforts of the writer Hilaire Belloc, it was restored in 1922. It can only be seen from the outside.

Rottingdean Cricket Club is one of the oldest in the country, with matches going back to 1758. They play on the green just north of the village.
Grange Museum and Art Gallery: *All year, Mon, Thurs and Sat 10am–5pm, Tues and Fri 10am–1pm and 2–5pm, Sun 2–5pm. Tel: (0273) 301004.*

Map p.152, D4   *** * ***
11 miles NE of Hastings on the A259

Crouching low on its hill-top, with the church tower at its summit and houses clustering all around, Rye still looks today very much as it did in the Middle Ages – from a distance at least. It is one of the gems of East Sussex, packed with summer tourists who come to admire its cobbled streets of half-timbered and Georgian houses, its medieval fortifications and its superb setting between rolling countryside and the levels of Romney Marsh, with the sea beyond stretching into the distance.

Although Rye is now a few miles from the sea, during the Middle Ages it was on a promontory, linked to the mainland by a narrow and easily defensible neck of land, with the wide estuaries of the Rivers Tillingham and Rother guarding it on either side. The Saxons called it *Atter Ie*, meaning 'on the island', which altered down the years to *Atte Rie*, and was finally shortened to plain Rye.

Like Winchelsea , it was an 'Ancient Town', linked to the Cinque Ports and responsible for supplying ships to the English fleet. In 1289, it was raised to the status of a royal borough. But from the 15th century on its importance gradually declined, due to a combination of raids by the French, the silting of the estuary and the build-up of shingle along the foreshore.

All the same, its fishing fleet remained important, and still survives today. (The boats unload their catches at the quayside by the Rother, on the eastern side of the town.) In the Middle Ages Rye had the monopoly of supplying fish direct to the royal table in London, by special carriers known as 'rippiers'. Before the start of an efficient postal service, the rippiers also acted as couriers for letters from the Continent to the London merchants, who often complained that their correspondence smelled of fish.

In Tudor times, Rye was still prosperous enough for Queen Elizabeth I to visit it on her royal progress through Sussex in 1573 (see NORTHIAM). She was so pleased with her reception that she gave the town the right to call itself 'Rye Royal'. In 1726, George I was blown ashore on Camber Sands, and stayed in Rye for four days (see Lamb House, below).

During the heyday of smuggling, in the 18th and early 19th centuries, Rye was notorious for its contraband activities. Its warren of ancient houses was ideal for hiding barrels of brandy or bales of lace, and whole streets had their attics connected so that smugglers could escape from house to house below the rooftiles.

St Mary's Church★★ dominates the town from its position on the crest of the hill. Its most notable feature is the pair of gilded 'quarterboys' or cherubs, who strike the bells of the tower clock on the quarters – but not, surprisingly enough, on the hour. (They are in fact fibreglass replicas; the originals, made in 1760, are kept inside the church.) Below the clock, the huge Perpendicular window of the north transept, filled with magnificent 15th-century tracery, pours light into the interior of the church.

The original Norman church, built about 1120, was largely destroyed by the French in 1377 and rebuilt in the 15th century. However, the round-arched Norman transepts survive, as do the nave arcades, which become gradually more pointed, and therefore later in date, towards the west end. The clock's 18ft-long gilded pendulum swings overhead in the north transept: it is well worth climbing the tower to see the mechanism made in 1560 for the then-high price of £31. From the top of the tower there are wide-ranging views over the town's red roofs, to the open country in one direction, and Romney Marsh and the sea in the other.

In the churchyard, outside the east end of the church, is Rye's most curious building – an elliptical brick structure, built in 1735 as a container for the town's water supply. The water was raised through wooden pipes by a pump, powered by two horses.

The **Ypres Tower**★★, a reminder of Rye's warlike past, lies south of the church, on the edge of the cliff on which the town stands. Built in the 13th century to guard against French attack, it failed in its purpose, as the French success in 1377 proved.

It gets its name from John de Ypres, who bought it in 1430 and lived in it. From the 16th to the 19th century it was a prison and is now the town Museum, full of exhibits ranging from pottery made in Rye since the 13th century, to the glasses worn by hop-pickers to protect their eyes. At its foot is the Gun Garden, which still has its complement of replica Elizabethan cannon trained out to sea.

The **Landgate**★, at the north-east corner of the town, is another impressive medieval survival. The last remaining of

Rye's three fortified gates, it was built in the 14th century, and still has its portcullis grooves.

From the Landgate, the main road winds through the centre of the town. East Cliff climbs up to the High St, and then curves down to sea-level again by way of The Mint – a reminder that in the Middle Ages Rye had the right to mint its own coins. The High St is full of remarkable buildings, among them the **Old Grammar School**, founded in 1636, whose unusual façade has tall pilasters carved in the brickwork, and Dutch-style gables.

Beside the steep Conduit Hill, just off the High St, is Rye's only monastic survival – a tall medieval hall that formed part of an Augustinian Friary, built about 1380. It is now a pottery. The well-known Rye Pottery, which has been in operation since 1869, is across the railway in Ferry Rd, on the northern edge of the town.

Between the High St and the church, the arcaded **Town Hall** looks across Market St, hardly wide enough to be a proper market square. Built in the 18th century, it is full of historical mementoes, including the town's four maces, and a gibbet in which the body of Rye's most notorious murderer, John Breads, an 18th-century butcher, was hung. This grisly relic is linked with the story of nearby Lamb House.

Lamb House★★★ (National Trust) is Rye's grandest town mansion. A magnificent Georgian house, it gets its name from its builder, James Lamb, who entertained George I there in 1726 on his involuntary visit to Rye (see above). Lamb came from a family which ran the town throughout the 18th century and, in his position as mayor, had fined John Breads for some misdemeanour. Thirsting for revenge, Breads lay in wait in the churchyard one night and stabbed to death a cloaked figure that he thought was Lamb, but was in fact his brother-in-law.

Lamb House has been home to two prominent writers: the American novelist Henry James, who lived there from 1897 to 1916, and E. F. Benson, mayor of Rye in 1934, whose Mapp and Lucia stories were set in the town of Tilling, closely modelled on Rye. The house is full of mementoes of Henry James, among them page-proofs of his novels and books by his contemporaries.

An earlier famous writer came from Rye. The playwright John Fletcher was born in the town in 1579, probably in the half-timbered house named after him just by the church. His name is generally coupled with that of his collaborator, Francis Beaumont, with whom he wrote some 15 plays.

Mermaid St★★★, round the corner from Lamb House, is Rye's most photographed street, cobbled and lined with medieval half-timbering and Georgian brickwork. The large Mermaid Inn, full of beams and inglenooks, is said to have been founded in the 11th century. In Georgian times it was the headquarters of a notorious and vicious gang of smugglers, who used to sit in the window with loaded pistols in front of them, in case they were surprised by the excisemen.

Strand Quay, at the foot of Mermaid St, looks out over the River Tillingham, now a quiet backwater where yachts lie at anchor. Its huddle of black-painted wooden warehouses have been largely restored. One of them, the **Rye Heritage Centre★**, houses a Town Model that forms the central feature of a sound and light show on the history of Rye.

Rye Art Gallery.★ Naturally enough, artists have flocked to Rye ever since Van Dyck came there in the 17th century. The gallery displays paintings by well-known artists such as John Piper and Graham Sutherland, along with works by contemporary artists, sculptors and craftsmen from the locality.

Rye is famous for its bonfire celebrations, formerly an excuse for wild revelry, and still among the most spectacular of such events in the South-East.
Ypres Tower Museum: *Easter–mid Oct, daily 10.30am–1pm and 2.15–5.30pm. Tel: (0797) 223254*

The Seven Sisters, one of East Sussex's most famous landmarks.

Lamb House: Apr–Oct, Weds and Sat only
2–6pm. Tel: (0797) 223763
Rye Heritage Centre & Town Model:
Apr–Oct, daily (and winter weekends)
9.30am–5.30pm. Tel: (0797) 226696
Rye Art Gallery: All year, Tues–Sat
10.30am–5pm (closed 1–2pm).
Tel: (0797) 222433
Rye Tourist Information Centre: Heritage
Centre, Strand Quay. Tel: (0797) 226696

RYE HARBOUR

Map p.152, D4   *
1 ½ miles SE of Rye off the A259

Reached down a narrow road, lined with
gravel workings and industrial buildings,
Rye Harbour has an unpromising approach.
But the village, built where the road fades
away above the shingle, has its own salty
charm, with its cluster of old fishermen's
cottages, several pubs, a Martello tower
perched up on a mound, and the usual
assortment of seaside bungalows.

The **Church of the Holy Spirit**,
a spiky, Gothic Revival building of about
1850, is well worth a look inside.
The magnificent woodwork of the ceiling
looks like an upturned boat, complete with
ribs, planking and huge cross-timbers.
On the wall is a list of the lives saved by the
local lifeboat – 128 in all since 1852.
A moving tablet commemorates the 17-man
crew of the lifeboat *Mary Stanford*, which
went down with all hands during a gale in
November 1928. In the churchyard behind,
a striking memorial to these same brave men
turns its back on the gravel workings beyond.

The **Rye Harbour Nature
Reserve**★★ covers much of the large triangle
of land bounded by the River Rother,
the sea and the Royal Military Canal.
Extending over almost 1800 acres, it is a
Site of Special Scientific Interest, taking in
tidal saltmarsh and creeks, the bank of the
river, the shingle beach and farmland
around Camber Castle.
The reserve has some of the finest
coastal shingle vegetation to be found
anywhere in England. More than 300 plant
species have been recorded, among them
seakale, with its blue-green cabbage-like
leaves, yellow horned poppy, and sea-pea,
which forms a carpet over the shingle.
Birds of every kind can be watched from
the hides dotted about the reserve. It has
breeding colonies of the rare little tern,
as well as common and Sandwich terns,
while oystercatchers, redshanks and ringed
plovers are common. Five species of gull
squabble and feed along the shore.
The reserve is on a major migration route,
and many species of wildfowl and waders
gather there to feed in winter. So far over
280 species have been recorded, of which
65 nest on the reserve. In summer,
marsh frogs, introduced into the Romney
Marsh area as recently as 1935, can be
heard croaking in the drainage dykes.
An information centre in the car-park
below the tower has panels on every aspect of
the reserve's geology and wildlife. Paths lead
round the edge of the reserve, and across
reclaimed pastureland to CAMBER Castle.

ST LEONARDS

Map p.146, D4   ★★
1 mile W of Hastings on the A259

St Leonards is now the genteel west end of
Hastings – the equivalent of Hove, west of
Brighton. Though the two have now
coalesced at the London Rd, St Leonards
was laid out as a separate development,
well away from the Hastings of the day.
Its creators were the architects James Burton
and his better-known son Decimus,
the designer of Hyde Park Corner,
who began a brand-new resort here in 1828.
By 1834 it was far enough advanced for the
young Princess Victoria to stay there with
her mother, the Duchess of Kent.
Its seafront centrepiece is the Royal
Victoria Hotel, which still bears the royal
coat-of-arms. It is now dwarfed by the
massive bulk of Marine Court next door,
a block of flats designed in the 1930s to
look like an ocean-going liner (Pevsner calls
it 'the Copacabana ideal'). Behind the hotel
is the Regency Masonic Hall, originally
the assembly rooms where concerts and
dances were held.

For their wealthy clients, the Burtons built a group of elegant Regency villas on either side of the oval and landscaped St Leonards Gardens, laid out round a small ravine with plenty of trees and shrubs. The market area to one side was called Mercatoria, while the cottages built for the washer-women who serviced the villas were known as Lavatoria Square.

The battlemented North Lodge, at the top of the gardens, was the home of the novelist Sir Henry Rider Haggard (1856–1925), author of *King Solomon's Mines* and *She*.

James Burton obviously liked what he had done, as he lived at Allegria Court on the estate from 1831 until his death in 1837, and is buried under a pyramid tomb in the disued burial ground.

Church of St Leonard. Burton's Gothic-style church was destroyed during World War II by a flying bomb. It was rebuilt in 1961 in plain modern style; its windows are filled with dark-blue stained glass, and its lectern is made from a ship's binnacle (compass housing). The pulpit, shaped like the prow of a fishing vessel, was made on the shores of the Sea of Galilee.

Modern St Leonards has swallowed up the Burtons' small nucleus, but it is well worth exploring as a unique example of a Regency planned town.

To the west, St Leonards shades imperceptibly into Bexhill. The Bo-Peep pub supposedly gets its name from the hide-and-seek played by the smugglers with the revenue men, long before there was any development here. The nursery rhyme 'Little Bo-Peep' is said to have been written by Old Humphrey, a well-known Hastings character in the early 19th century.

Sealh-Hurst, or 'Willow-Wood', and willows still grow down by the river. For centuries the Rother valley has been hop-growing country, and after some years when the EC bureaucrats frowned on English hops, the fields are once again green with hop tendrils clambering up their string-and-wire frameworks.

St Mary's Church* was built between about 1250 and 1400 by the monks of Robertsbridge Abbey for the inhabitants of nearby ROBERTSBRIDGE, which has never had a church of its own. Long and narrow, with a tall west tower, it escaped major alteration by the Victorians, although they cut the clerestory windows above the aisles to let in more light.

Below the tower is an extraordinary font, carved with salamanders round the foot. These creatures were associated with the Crusaders, and it is thought that the font may have been given to the church by Richard Cœur de Lion, after the Abbot of Robertsbridge negotiated his release from captivity in Bavaria in 1193. Another medieval curiosity is the monk's head, carved below the arch from the north aisle into the adjacent chapel; he is propping his chin on what appears to be a rabbit. Two unique 15th-century windows in the south aisle show the outline of birds drawn in brown on a green background.

Behind the church, a path leads between two massive oak trees straight into a hopfield, and from there down to the river.

The Salehurst Halt pub gets its name from a long-vanished station on the Kent and East Sussex Railway, the hop-pickers' line which once ran from Robertsbridge to Headcorn in Kent. (The station at NORTHIAM has been restored.)

SALEHURST

Map p.151, C3   *
5 miles N of Battle off the A21

This hamlet clusters round a church that seems unduly large for so small a place. Standing on a slope just north of the Rother, it gets its name from the Saxon

SALTDEAN

Map p.143, E3
4 miles E of Brighton on the A259

Like Peacehaven, Saltdean was a product of the inter-war years although more successful, some might argue. Its housing estates are grouped around a downland combe occupied by a park and putting green. They overlook the sea and enjoy access to the shingly beach and promenade by a tunnel beneath the coast road. The main centre of attraction is the 1930s-designed, freshwater-filled outdoor lido and toddlers' paddling pool. On the promenade is a similar style café. Standing at the highest point is the Ocean Hotel, built around the same period and now owned by Butlin's.

SEAFORD

Map p.144, DI *
9 miles W of Eastbourne on the A259

Until 400 years ago, the River Ouse flowed into the English Channel at Seaford, the busy port for Lewes. It was considered so important that, in 1544, it was granted membership of the Cinque Ports Confederation. But then the harbour silted up and a storm finally diverted the course of the river farther west to Meeching and the town's role as a port ceased.

Close to some of the loveliest coastal scenery in East Sussex, including the Seven Sisters and Seaford Head, Seaford became a favourite Victorian watering-place, although never achieving the fame of Brighton or Eastbourne. It now lives life as a quiet seaside town with fishing a popular activity from its shingly beach. Little remains of the old town.

St Leonard's Church dates from the Norman era but underwent major restoration work in the 19th century. Inside it has some rare pillar carvings. Also rare is the plaque on the telephone exchange in East St which bears the insignia of Edward VIII, who reigned for just a few months in 1936. In Church St stands what was the Tudor town hall, now much altered.

The beach at the western end of the town is called the Buckle in honour of Sir Nicholas Pelham who defeated French raiders there in 1545 – just days after they had sunk the pride of Henry VIII's fleet, the *Mary Rose*, at Portsmouth. A buckle forms part of the Pelham's coat of arms and recalls an earlier Pelham who received

the French King John's buckle from his sword in surrender after his capture at the Battle of Poitiers in 1356.

🏛 **Seaford Local History Museum★** is housed in the town's Martello tower. Built in 1806, it is the most westerly of a string of 74 that were built along the Kent and Sussex Coast to repel the threatened invasion from France during the Napoleonic Wars. On three levels, with a gun platform, garrison and magazine, it was restored in the 1970s and now has displays relating to the many shipwrecks that have occurred on this coastline. One night in 1809, within the space of a half a mile, no fewer than seven ships were driven ashore, with the loss of 31 lives. There are also extensive collections of office and home appliances and recreated shops and domestic scenes from Victorian times onwards.

Behind the tower stands the grand-looking **Corsica Hall**, said to have been built on the proceeds from smuggled Corsican wine. Originally at Wellingham, near Barcombe, it was dismantled and rebuilt at its present location on a small hillock which had been an island in the heyday of the port. Considerably altered, the house was owned by the father of Edward Fitzgerald, who became famous as the translator of *The Rubaiyat of Omar Khayyam*. It is now used as an education centre.
Museum: *All year, Weds and Sat 2.30–4.30pm, Sun 11am–1pm, BHs 11am–1pm and 2.30–4.30pm. Tel: (0323) 898222.*
Tourist Information Centre: *Station Approach. Tel: (0323) 897426.*

SEAFORD HEAD

Map p.144, D2 **
1 mile SE of Seaford off the A259

Between Seaford and the Cuckmere Valley, Seaford Head towers 282ft above the sea. It is an area of chalk downland and dramatic cliffs, with breath-taking views extending eastwards over the winding river to the famous Seven Sisters and westwards to Brighton. There is evidence, in the form of earth ramparts, that a Roman settlement existed here, but the only dwellings to be seen now are a row of coastguard cottages built in 1806 to overlook Cuckmere Haven, a popular landing place for smugglers.

The breezy vantage point is the site of a navigational beacon, but the adjacent downland is shared between a golf course and the Seaford Head Nature Reserve.

♣ **The Seaford Head Nature Reserve**★★, with 303 acres of grassland, salt marsh and shingle beach, is an important habitat for many birds, animals, insects and flowers, some of them quite rare. At low tide, the foreshore reveals a fine example of a wave-cut platform.

SEDLESCOMBE

Map p.146, A4   ★ ★
6 miles N of Hastings on the A229

The smart village sign beside Sedlescombe green shows the village's two main features: the church at the top of the hill to the north, and the little stone building that shelters the parish pump.

The houses grouped round the long, narrow green are a mixture of tile-hanging, weather-boarding and Georgian brick-work, making Sedlescombe the quintessence of an old Sussex village. Two of the oldest houses carry their dates – 1697 and 1737. The lead-covered pump, dated 1900, is long disused.

In Tudor times Sedlescombe was a centre of Sussex iron production, and there were more than thirty furnaces and forges within a 5-mile radius of the village. The most important was east of the village, off the back road to Brede. When the iron industry died out in the 18th century, gunpowder-making took over – still recalled by the Powdermill Reservoir near by.

♣ **The Church of St John the Baptist**★ is 1 mile or so to the north, well away from the village centre. Its churchyard is full of yew trees and guarded by giant Spanish chestnuts beside the entrance gate. The medieval church dates from the 13th century and has a sturdy 15th-century west tower, with a tall arch into the nave.

The iron-braced octagonal font has an oak linenfold cover, raised by a massive pulley, which dates from Tudor times.

By the door is a fascinating seating-plan of 1632, showing the allocation of the pews. It dates from the time when everyone had by law to attend church on Sundays, and any absentees would be easily noticed. The front pews were reserved for the Sackville family, and behind them sat the locals in descending order of importance, down to 'cottagers, youths and strangers' right at the back.

The **Pestalozzi Children's Village** is on the southern edge of the village, set in magnificent parkland. Here children, mainly from developing countries such as Zambia and Nepal, are educated up to a standard that will enable them to help their communities when they return home.

The **Sedlescombe Vineyard,** north of the church towards Cripps Corner, produces its wine organically, without any artificial fertilizers. Visitors can walk through two vineyards, separated by a stretch of woodland where a nature trail winds among the trees.

Pestalozzi Children's Village: Visit by prior arrangement only. Tel: (0424) 870444.

SELMESTON

Map p.144, B2   ★
6 miles W of Polegate off the A27

♣ **Selmeston Church** was restored in 1867 by its vicar, William Douglas Parish, the author of *A Dictionary of the Sussex Dialect*. Situated off the main road, in an oval churchyard, of Saxon and possibly earlier origins, it is a rough-hewn, flint construction with a short, shingled spire and a 'catslide' roof to the south. By the porch is the grave of F. S. Monckford (d. 1962) who was the originator of the international radio distress signal 'Mayday'. The interior has an Easter Sepulchre (later converted to a memorial monument) and unusual arcading, separating the nave from the aisle and supported on octagonal wooden pillars. There are several brasses in the

floor including one in the south aisle to Henry Rogers who died in 1639 – 'a painfull Preacher in this churche' – the attribute refers to his painstaking style.

In a sandpit near to the church, important archaeological remains were unearthed in 1933, revealing mesolithic and neolithic occupancy from over 5000 years ago.

THE SOUTH DOWNS WAY

Maps p.142, B4, to p.145, D1   * * *
Between Ditchling Beacon and Eastbourne

The South Downs Way is the Countryside Commission's first national long-distance bridleway and runs for nearly 100 miles between Eastbourne in East Sussex and Winchester in Hampshire. Opened in 1972, it offers limitless leisure possibilities for the walker, cyclist or rider along the chalk downland and heritage coast. A wide range of books, maps and leaflets describing each section can be obtained from local bookshops and tourist information centres.

Most of the route, which is well sign-posted with the acorn symbol, is within an Area of Outstanding Natural Beauty, and is easily accessible although suitable clothing and footwear should always be worn.

Firle Beacon (Map p.144, B1), with its triangulation point at 713ft, has a commanding viewpoint. A small car-park lies above Bo Peep farm, off the main road midway between Lewes and Polegate.

There are extensive views north to the Weald over the flat patchwork of fields and Arlington reservoir in the foreground, while to the north-west Lewes can be seen in the distant fold of hills, behind the Firle estate with its distinctive circular gamekeeper's tower built in 1819. Many prehistoric sites are located directly below and beside the Beacon area. To the south, Newhaven harbour can be seen beyond gently sloping fields of crops and grazing cattle and sheep, with Cuckmere Haven and the Seven Sisters to the south-

east. A popular spot for hang-gliding, it was here that the Southdown Gliding Club first met in 1922, the first such society in England. A radio mast stands to the west.

Ditchling Beacon (Map p.143, B1) stands at 813ft, the highest point in East Sussex, and is in the care of the National Trust. Ample parking facilities are near by. There is a series of signposted trails offering views of Leith Hill in Surrey, Mount Caburn and the Weald. Local archaeological sites at Newtimber Hill and Wolstonbury Hill can be included on the walk. Below the Beacon lies the village of Westmeston. The Sussex Wildlife Trust, together with the National Trust, has recently reintroduced sheep and cattle to the area, the first to graze there for nearly fifty years.

SOUTH MALLING

Map p.143, C4   *
¹/₂ mile N of Lewes off the A26

This small community, on a spur beside the River Ouse and isolated by a housing estate in the Lewes suburbs, was once part of the estate of the Malling Deanery, a fine red-brick mansion mainly dating from the late 17th century but incorporating some 16th-century features. The building was later converted to three homes, but its former coach house, a couple of workers' cottages, the new and old vicarage and the church make an attractive ensemble.

Sussex Police have their ultra-modern headquarters at the village, based in the grounds of Malling House, a Queen Anne mansion of 1710.

St Michael the Archangel★ is a flint-built church that looks medieval in appearance but dates from 1628, replacing an earlier one. A church has stood on the site since Saxon times when, in the 7th century, a monastery was established a little farther up-river, where Old Malling Farm is today. It was the first site of Christian worship in Sussex.

The South Downs Way offers magnificent views of the Weald.

In 1989, while the church's interior was being modernized, the coffin of Richard Russell was discovered buried beneath the floor. Dr Russell, the doctor responsible for putting Brighton on the map, was born in South Malling in 1687 and married the daughter of William Kempe, who lived at the Deanery. He died in 1759 but was thought to be buried in Brighton until his coffin was discovered. The victims of the Lewes avalanche are also buried at the church.

SOUTHEASE

Map p.143, E4   *
3 miles NW of Newhaven off the A259

In the days when the River Ouse filled the valley in which it lies, Southease was the most successful of the herring-fishing villages in what was then a broad estuary. Now it ranks as one of the prettiest villages in the valley, with ancient cottages surrounding the triangular green on which the small church stands framed by trees.

Southease Church* has Saxon origins, having been granted a charter by King Edgar in 966 (a copy is displayed inside). It has traces of ancient wall-paintings and a bell cast in 1280. Like two other churches, at LEWES and PIDDINGHOE, it features a Norman round tower. Its unusual organ was built in 1790 and is thought to be one of only four still in existence. The others are at York Minster, St Mary's, Westminster and Buckingham Palace.

SPITHURST

Map p.143, A4
5 1/2 miles N of Lewes off the A275

This tiny hamlet has a scattering of Victorian and more modern houses lining the quiet, wooded road just north of Barcombe.

St Bartholomew's is a fine flint-built church which dates from 1880. In the churchyard a recent grave bearing the name Konstantin is explained by the fact that on two Sundays every month the church is used

for Russian Orthodox services, usually attended by up to thirty people, most of whom are Russian exiles. The local Anglican vicar uses the church just once a month.

STANMER

Map p.143, C1   *
3 1/2 miles NE of Brighton off the A27

The name Stanmer comes from the Saxon *staen mere*, meaning a pond of stones since it is next to a rocky pool. Stanmer is a rare example of a farming village attached to an estate. It stands within the grounds of a Palladian mansion, Stanmer Place, near the University of Sussex. The undulating parkland, covering 537 acres of lawns and mature woods, is the scene of famous horse-driving trials held every May.

During World War II, the village was used for training Canadian soldiers in street-fighting and suffered a great deal of damage, but it has since been restored. It contains several flint cottages, a farm with a very long weather-boarded barn, and a tea-room.

Stanmer Place was built in 1724 and was once the home of the Pelhams, Earls of Chichester. It now lies empty though, in outbuildings, there is an interesting museum of agricultural bygones.

Stanmer Church is between the village and the house and dates from the 14th century, but in 1838 it was rebuilt in the Early English style following a fire. Inside is a memorial to Sir John Pelham (d. 1580) and his son Oliver, who died four years later. Outside there is the grave of a man who lived to the age of 117. Also in the churchyard is the old village well.

STAPLECROSS

Map p.151, C4
9 miles N of Hastings on the B2165

Although Staplecross is little more than a hamlet on a T-junction, consisting of a pub and a handful of houses, it has a certain historical importance.

During the Middle Ages and later, it was the central point of the Hundred of Staple, made up of the villages of Northiam, Ewhurst, Bodiam and Sedlescombe, together with parts of Brede, Mountfield and Whatlington. The hundred was a Saxon territorial subdivision; it is not certain whether it was so called because it contained 100 families, because it contributed 100 men-at-arms in time of war, or because its area covered 100 hides of ground (a hide varied from 60–120 acres).

STREAT

Map p.143, B2 *
5 miles NW of Lewes off the B2116

Little Streat, which appeared in the Domesday Book as Estrat, has been inhabited since the Stone Age. As well as comprising a few cottages, it has an Early English church which stands on a hillock and has good views of the downs and, next door, Streat Place, an Elizabethan flint-built manor house. Originally just a small farmhouse, it was given its grand E-shaped east façade in 1607. The sculptor John Skelton lives and works in the village.

To the south, on the north face of the downs, is a large V-shaped wood of beech, fir and lime trees planted to commemorate Queen Victoria's Golden Jubilee in 1887. Originally, it was intended the letters VR should be planted on the hillside, but lack of money meant the R had to be dropped.

TARRING NEVILLE

Map p.143, E4 *
2 miles N of Newhaven off the A26

In a picturesque leafy setting at the foot of the downs and close to the River Ouse, Tarring Neville is one of the smallest hamlets in East Sussex and a favourite subject of artists. At one time it was much bigger, but then the Black Death left its mark: it now has just seven cottages, two farms and a church scattered around a green. Its present population is about the same as when the Domesday survey was made.

St Mary's, the 12th-century church, is partly rendered and inside has an unusual octagonal font half-embedded in the wall.

From the church are views across to Piddinghoe, where brightly coloured sails can often be seen on the lake. Tracks provide access to the downs and a footpath leads across the water meadows to an ox-bow lake, where swans nest in springtime.

TELSCOMBE

Map p.143, E3 *
5 miles S of Lewes off the A259

This unspoiled little hamlet, virtually untouched by the 20th century, is isolated at the head of a combe in the South Downs, behind the modern housing development of Telscombe Cliffs and 2 miles from the Lewes–Newhaven unclassified road. The last squire, Ambrose Gorham, who lived at the 16th-century manor house in the village, refused to allow any development in Telscombe, and when he died in 1933 he left the estate to Brighton Corporation on the understanding that the rural state of the village be maintained. This has been done very well indeed with no evidence at all of modern encroachment. The manor house, now owned by the National Trust, is used as overnight accommodation by judges sitting at Lewes Crown Court.

St Lawrence's Church dates back to Saxon times and contains some fine medieval wall-paintings.

The village also has a youth hostel, housed in a terrace of three cottages knocked into one. Stud Farm, now a sheep farm and riding stables, was once occupied by racehorses and one of them, Shannon Lass, was a winner of the Grand National in 1902.

TICEHURST

Map p.150, A4 *
4 miles W of Hawkhurst on the B2087

Situated on a high ridge, Ticehust is an attractive tile-hung and weather-boarded village. The name comes from the Old English *ticce* , meaning young goat, and *hyrst*, wooded hill. To the north-west, the shores of Bewl Bridge Reservoir (see p.32) are within walking distance. When the reservoir was formed in the 1970s, the Southern Water Authority saved one of the village houses – the 500-year-old Dunster's Mill – from submersion by removing it, brick by brick, to a safe location.

Along the road to the village church is a charming row of shops fronted by an elegant Victorian arcade of delicate iron pillars.

⛪ St Mary's Church* dates mainly from the 13th and 14th centuries but was restored in 1879. During the restoration, a medieval stained-glass window showing Salome with her sons John and James, the Virgin and Child, and St Christopher was moved from its original position in the east window to the north wall of the chancel. One of the window lights is a 'doom window' depicting souls being carted to hell by wickedly grinning devils.

The exceptional 16th-century font cover is made of eight panels, four of which fold open to reveal ornate tracery carving both inside and out. There is a 14th-century brass of a knight in armour, only a couple of feet tall, and the figures of his two wives are smaller still. In the floor of the south chapel is an iron tomb-slab with the arms of the May family.

UCKFIELD

Map p.149, D1
9 miles S of Crowborough off the A22

Uckfield is situated on a south-facing slope with fine views of the South Downs. The oldest part of the town is at the top of the hill around the T-junction, from which the High St drops steeply downwards to the level crossing.

The best way to see old Uckfield is to take the Uckfield Town Walk. The Uckfield and District Preservation Society (who restored the ancient Nutley Post Mill, p.34) has produced a leaflet setting out the route. This can be obtained from Bridge Cottage.

⛪ Bridge Cottage**, near the level crossing, is a superb example of a medieval hall-house. Much of the original timber-work remains, including the kingpost timbers which are visible in the roof. It was built between 1380 and 1420 on a platform of clay, brought to the site to form a solid base as the surrounding land was marshy.

⛪ The long low **Church of the Holy Cross** was built in 1839 by William Moseley on the site of a medieval building. It incorporates the old tower, which was heightened and given a new shingled spire. In the churchyard is a vast and impressive cedar tree.

Apart from the old town, Uckfield is largely made up of modern development which spreads in all directions, practically linking it with Maresfield to the north-west.

The **Barnsgate Manor Vineyard** is at Heron's Ghyll, a couple of miles north along the A26 Crowborough road. It is a 56-acre farm commanding wide views of the Weald. A tour takes you on a walk through the vines with explanatory signs before leading to a museum of old and new methods of viticulture, and down to the wine cellar where the Barnsgate wines are matured. Finally, you can taste (and buy) the wines produced here. There is a restaurant, tea-rooms and a gift shop.
Barnsgate Manor Vineyard: All year, daily 10am–5pm. Tel: (0825) 713366.

UDIMORE

Map p.152, D2
4 miles W of Rye on the B2089

A village without a proper centre, Udimore straggles along the narrow, windy ridge that separates the River Brede from the Tillingham.

Place-name experts say that Udimore means 'Boundary of the Wood' in Anglo-Saxon, but local legend is far more romantic. The story goes that when the church was being built, the site chosen was

An 18th-century urn in the grounds of Stanmer Place.

an unsuitable one on marshy ground down by the river. One night a flight of angels miraculously carried the stones up to the top of the hill, chanting the words 'Over the mere! Over the mere!', which soon became altered to 'Uddimere', and finally to 'Udimore'.

🏛 **St Mary's Church** is a tiny building down a lane, tucked away beside farm buildings among the orchards. The nave survives from the original Norman church of 1170, while the chancel with its lancet windows is 13th-century. At some stage – perhaps in Victorian times – the south aisle was pulled down and the arcade gaps filled in. Inside, the capitals are crisply carved with Norman leaf decoration.

WADHURST

Map p.155, E4   *
6 miles SE of Tunbridge Wells at the crossroads of the B2110 and the B2099

Situated close to the Kent border, the pretty village of Wadhurst has a long High St of tile-hung cottages. At one time, it was very important as the centre of the Wealden iron industry.

The name Wadhurst dates the parish to Anglo–Saxon times and means 'Wada's settlement in the clearing in a wood'. Until the 19th century, the parish was divided into six 'quarters': Town, Bivelham, Faircouch, Riseden, Weeke and Cousley Wood.

🏛 **Church of St Peter and St Paul.*** Whereas many churches in this area have one or two iron slab memorials, Wadhurst's has thirty, demonstrating the scale of the local iron industry. The tall slender spire soars up behind the main street, reaching about 130ft. Its tremendous height has resulted in six lightning strikes over the years. The oldest part of the church is the Norman west tower; the rest of the building is Early English and later. The kingposts and tie-beams can be seen in the nave roof.

The iron slabs, dating from between 1617 and 1790, are the most famous and interesting monuments in the church.

Many commemorate the Barham family, who were local iron-masters. The oldest have simple repetitive designs of shields but, as the founders' expertise grew, so did the complexity of the designs, such as the ornate slab to William Barham in the chancel, dated 1701. There is also some modern iron-work in the church: the cast-iron cross and altar candlesticks were made in 1967, and the wrought-iron and glass screen depicting hops, flowers and lambs was given to the church in 1958.

In the church porch are several tablets to members of the Luck family, one decorated with a terracotta plaque by Jonathan Harmer, the potter son of a Heathfield stonemason. Two more of his plaques are in the north transept and in the sanctuary.

Next to the church is Church Gate House, a fine 18th-century Wealden timber-framed and tile-hung house with overhanging first floor. The big Queen Anne Vicarage which dominates the High St was built by the town's chief iron-master, John Legas.

At Cousley Wood, 2 miles north-east of the village, near the western shores of Bewl Bridge Reservoir (see p.32), is a very pretty 18th-century house called Ladyheads.

In the 1950s, the composer Sir Michael Tippett lived just outside the village, at Tidebrook Manor on the Mayfield road. Here he completed his opera, *The Midsummer Marriage*, and several important orchestral works.

At Pell Green, half a mile north-east up the B2100, is the Rehoboth Chapel; built in 1824, it is a pleasing symmetrical weather-boarded building with three round-topped windows interspersed with two doors. In the surrounding countryside outside the village are several oast-houses, testimony to the importance of hop-growing in the region.

WALDRON

Map p.149, D4   * *
3 miles SW of Heathfield off the A267

🏛 The **Church of All Saints**★★ is approached through a lych-gate, roofed with thick Horsham tiles, opposite the Star

Inn. Early English in style, with Victorian restorations, the church is notable for its very wide aisle and nave (unusual in the 13th century) and for its fine kingpost roof. Flagstones, memorials and brasses commemorate members of the local Dyke and Fuller families; the Fullers were ironmasters. Outside the porch is an early circular stone font that was discovered in a nearby field where it had been discarded, perhaps during the Civil War, and a tombstone with terracotta plaques by the Heathfield artist Jonathan Harmer.

St George's Vineyards★★, one of the leading local English wine producers, are just down the road from the church. There are audio and conducted tours of the vineyards which conclude with tasting the product. The tithe barn is a splendid timbered 11th-century structure which houses changing exhibitions of arts and crafts. Concerts, wine tastings and special events in the gourmet restaurant are held throughout the year at the vineyard. A range of local produce (including cheeses, honey and Sussex crafts) is on sale in the shop and visitors are even encouraged to 'adopt a vine'.
St George's Vineyards: Apr–Oct, daily 11am–5pm (rest of year varies). Tel: (04353) 2156

WARBLETON

Map p.150, E1 ★★
2 ½ miles SE of Heathfield off the B2096

🚏 **St Mary the Virgin Church**, approached through a lych-gate, is remarkable for its galleried manorial pew, dated 1722, which is reached by a stair from the aisle. The 13th-century church contains two fine memorials. The first of these is a brass, on the floor of the chancel, to a former rector of the church, William Prestwick (d. 1436) with an inlaid inscription in Early English lettering. He became Dean of St Mary's College, Hastings, and was 'a constant, patient, humble man, devout, urbane'. The second memorial, somewhat obscured in the chapel, is to Sir John Lade (d. 1740)

who served five times as MP for Southwark in London. Designed by J. M. Rysbrack, it is of marble with a pedestal bust and floral decorations. Fragments of early stained glass survive in the chapel window.

A former churchwarden, Richard Woodman, ironmaster in the parish, who lived where the modern graveyard now stands, publicly admonished Rector Fairbanke for 'turning head to tail' in his faith. Woodman was captured, imprisoned in Bishop Bonner's coal-house in Lewes and was burned along with nine other martyrs in June 1557.

To the south of the church is a tomb with a plaque in terracotta by the Heathfield artist Jonathan Harmer. It shows a mother playing with children; another Harmer plaque can be seen on a tomb by the east window of the chapel.

The group of cottages opposite the church gates once formed the village workhouse; the middle chimney is dated 1739. Next to these is the quaintly named 'Warbill-in-tun' pub. Local legend tells of a thirsty mercenary who opened a beer-barrel with his halberd or 'bill'.

The village of **Rushlake Green** lies 1 mile to the east. The popular Horse and Groom inn stands on the south side of the green which is surrounded by pretty brick houses and cottages.

WARTLING

Map p.145, A3 ★★
2 miles N of Pevensey off the A259

🚏 **St Mary Magdalene★★** church commands extensive views over the PEVENSEY LEVELS to the south and Pevensey Castle (see p.23) may be clearly seen. Built of brick and stone with a short, shingled spire, the church has a 13th-century chancel with later extensions. On the south exterior are a carved Pelham buckle and a Catherine wheel, believed to commemorate Katherine Pelham when the aisle was built in the 15th century.

A signature of a local craftsman, dated 1786, can be seen on a window behind the organ. The only known surviving cast-iron plaques by the Heathfield-based artist Jonathan Harmer (1762–1849) are displayed under the tower and show baskets of fruit and flowers. (He usually worked in terracotta.) The 19th-century, box-pews are complemented by a modern lectern in the shape of a heron; carved in elm from the Glynde Estate, it is a reminder of the nesting of herons near to the church for over a hundred years.

WEST BLATCHINGTON

Map p.142, D3   *
1 ½ miles N of Hove on the A2038

Since being swallowed by the post-war housing development to the north of Hove, West Blatchington shows little evidence of its origins as a medieval downland village. Unfortunately, its manor house was demolished after the war to make way for flats. All that remains of the old village is the early 19th-century hexagonal smock-mill (see p.35) with its small museum, and nearby St Peter's Church, which originally dates from the 13th century, but was restored in 1890 and considerably enhanced in the 1960s.

WESTDEAN

Map p.144, D3   * *
2 miles E of Seaford off the A259

The village lies tucked away from the road on the edge of FRISTON FOREST and is an ideal base for walks within the forest or further afield; car-parking is advised at the Forestry Commission enclosure as vehicular access to Westdean is difficult. Near the village is **Charleston Manor**, a Tudor and Georgian house in a beautiful setting; its gardens are occasionally open to the public in summer. (Tel: (0323) 870267)

All Saints' Church, on higher ground from the village, has a square, partially Norman tower under a Sussex 'cap'; there is a row of 18th-century box-tombs

in the churchyard. Inside is a splendid alabaster monument to William Thomas and his wife Anne, with angels on either side and a coat of arms above. In the chancel are a small piscina with an Easter Sepulchre and tomb canopy. The north wall has a further Thomas memorial with cherubs holding a spade and a torch. On the south wall is a bust by Epstein of the artist Sir Oswald Birley, who founded the annual local festival.

The Rectory is next to the church and dates from the 13th century. The Manor House of the parish lies below with the remains of a medieval dovecote.

WESTFIELD

Map p.147, B1
4 miles N of Hastings on the A28

The northern tentacles of Hastings reach out towards this red-brick, largely modern village, which straggles along the main road. Its old weather-boarded nucleus is on the byroad down to Guestling, round the Plough Inn. Westfield appears in the Domesday Book as Westwelle; at the time it included a pit for the ordeal of 'trial by water'.

The **Church of St John the Baptist**, crouching low behind trees at its southern end, is Norman built largely on Saxon foundations. The nave and chancel date from the early 12th century, while the squat tower with its massive buttresses is slightly later. The Victorians wrecked the ancient simplicity of the interior by adding a north aisle, but it still has its superb round chancel arch, with large squints cut on either side to give a view of the altar and the officiating priest. The iron-banded south door is dated 1542, the pulpit is Jacobean, and the tall wooden canopy over the 14th-century font was carved in the late 17th century.

The **Carr Taylor Vineyard**, on the byroad to Sedlescombe, is a flourishing vineyard and has a winery trail for visitors.

Telscombe, with the Downs beyond.

WEST FIRLE

Map p.144, B1   * * *
4 ¹/₂ miles SE of Lewes off the A27

A village with a feudal air hidden away at
the foot of Firle Beacon, a 718ft high-point
on the South Downs, West Firle is a
popular venue for film-makers. A winding
road leads up to the top of the downs,
from where the views extend to the
Channel in the south and to the Weald in
the north.

Firle Place (see p.18), a large country
house with a Georgian exterior hiding a
Tudor interior, has been the home of the
Gage family for 500 years.

⛪ St Peter's**, the little village church,
was built mainly in the 14th and 15th
centuries. It contains several tombs of the
Gage family, the most notable being that of
Sir John Gage and his wife Philippa,
which was sculpted in alabaster in 1556.
There are also some superb brasses,
including the splendid Bolney Brass which
shows Bartholomew Bolney with his wife
Eleanor. More recent is a memorial
window to the 6th Viscount Gage,
installed in 1985 and the work of the artist
John Piper.

At one time, the village had no fewer than
four inns, but when a new road bypassing it
was built in 1812, trade fell dramatically,
and now there is only one, the Ram.
Petty sessions used to be held at the inn.

WESTHAM

Map p.145, C2   *
¹/₂ mile W of Pevensey on the A27

⛪ St Mary's Church was possibly the
first built by the Normans in England
following the 1066 invasion and may have
served as a hospice for Pevensey Castle
near by. Original Norman work is found in
the south wall and in the Lady Chapel.
The crenellated flint and stone tower was
added in the 14th century when the
church was enlarged. The stained-glass

figures of apostles, at the top of the large
east window, are 15th century. In the floor
of the chancel are two tombstones marked
with large crosses; 14th-century in origin,
they were re-used some three hundred years
later. In the graveyard by the south wall, four
simple stones in the shape of a cross mark
the site of a plague-pit from 1666. 'Puttock
holes' which supported the scaffolding used
in the contsruction of the church can be
seen in the chancel walls and in the tower.

Among the former clergy of the parish
was Brian Duppa (d. 1662); tutor to
Charles II, and later Bishop of Chicester,
he is buried in Westminster Abbey.
William Leeke, who had fought at the
battle of Waterloo, served as curate from
1829, ministering to the local excisemen
based in the coastal Martello towers.

Two fine timber-framed houses, the Old
Dial House and the Oak House, stand near
the church gates and were built in the 15th
century. A path leads from the green by the
church through the Roman west gate into
Pevensey Castle (see p.23).

To the west of the village, at Stone
Cross, is a late 19th-century tower-mill
built of brick and with a replacement cap.

WESTMESTON

Map p.143, B1   *
5 miles NW of Lewes on the B2116

Westmeston is a village at the foot of the
downs near Ditchling Beacon. It consists
of several 17th-century cottages grouped
around an old church dedicated to St
Martin, patron saint of publicans. Ironically,
there is no public house in the village.

⛪ St Martin's Church* dates from the
early 12th century and, according to legend,
was built using stone originally destined for
Westminster Abbey. Part of the churchyard
is now a wildlife conservation area.

⌂ The west side of Westmeston Place,
a small manor house built in 1430, is
visible from the churchyard and incorporates
some fine Perpendicular style windows. It
was extended around 1882.

The village is linked with a series of ghostly goings-on, the most terrifying being the headless dog that haunts Black Dog Hill. The spirit of a monk is reputed to have been seen at Westmeston Place and, on certain days in May, the ghosts of Henry III's men can supposedly be heard with their horses fleeing the Battle of Lewes, which took place in 1264.

WILLINGDON

Map p.144, C4   * *
3 miles NW of Eastbourne on the A22

⛪ **St Mary the Virgin Church**, built of flint and stone with a fine tower to the west, stands above the busy main road and is Early English in style with possible earlier origins; the nave, with four lovely arches, font and chancel are 14th-century. The rood figures, showing the Crucifixion with flanking figures, are by Sir Ninian Comper and were dedicated in 1954; ancient tie-beams support the fine roof. A memorial to the left of the altar shows the kneeling figure of Sir John Parker (d. 1617), who was appointed by James I as Captain of Pendennis Castle in Cornwall. In the Ratton Chapel off the north aisle are further outstanding monuments to the Parker family; on the right is Sir Nicholas (d. 1619), recumbent in prayer with his kneeling children, and on the east wall there is one to Mrs Elinar Parker (d.1598). In the north aisle itself is a huge monument with an urn to Sir Thomas Parker (d. 1663), a Roundhead in the Civil War, which is is somewhat out of scale to the church. Fragments of carved pediments can be seen on the exterior of the tower's north wall.

Across the road is a group of almshouses with a Dutch gable dated 1857; to the right is 'The Hoo', a large house designed by Lutyens in 1902.

The village pump is a short walk away from Willingdon post-office on Wish Hill. It is housed in a curious shelter into which the knuckle-bones of cattle have been inlaid as a pattern, set among the flints on either side of the entrance.

WILMINGTON

Map p.144, C3   * * *
2 miles W of Polegate off the A27

From the village car-park, the Long Man of Wilmington (see p. 35) can be clearly seen. A footpath leads a quarter-mile up to the gigantic outline of a man holding a stave in each hand, of whose origin little is known.

⛪ The site of **Wilmington Priory★★★** was given by Robert de Mortain, half-brother of William the Conqueror, to the Benedictine Abbey of Grestain in Normandy. The first Prior was recorded in 1243; his chapel was in what is today the upper portion of the main house, where remnants of a 14th-century window can be made out. Carved heads of monks feature on the corbels of the vaulting within the gatehouse which once led to the great hall. The wellhouse court, with a 120ft-deep well, is the site of the original hall. To the east, steps lead down to the vaulted crypt which dates from 1300. The south-east wing and Tudor kitchen house a large collection of farming and kitchen implements together with items of local history, such as tubs used by smugglers.

The property is now in the hands of the Sussex Archaeological Society, and at time of going to press its future is uncertain, as it may be sold as a private residence to raise much-needed funds.

⛪ The **Church of St Mary and St Peter★★** was originally part of the Priory buildings. At its entrance stands a giant yew tree, reputed to be older than the 12th-century church. The Norman chancel, with splayed walls, has the surviving stone seats (used by the monks) and two aumbries are set into the east wall. On the north wall is an early stone figure which may depict the Virgin Mary. The North Chapel has an unusual stained-glass window showing ten species of bees and butterflies, some of them only found in Sussex. There are fine views from the churchyard to Firle Beacon (see SOUTH DOWNS WAY) to the west.

Between the priory buildings and the car-park is the old village pound, used to secure stray animals. It was restored in 1980.

WINCHELSEA

Map p.147, A3   * * *
2 miles SW of Rye on the A259

In the Middle Ages, Winchelsea, like Rye, was an 'Ancient Town', equal in status to the Cinque Ports, and responsible for supplying a contingent of ships to the English fleet. It stood originally on a shingle spit on the seaward side of today's town, but a great storm in 1287 which also affected the harbour at Hastings) carried away much of the spit, and washed away most of Winchelsea with it.

A new town was planned at once on the present hilltop site. Work began in 1288; streets were laid out and cellars dug at the King's expense, and wharves were provided on the banks of the River Brede below the town. Although Winchelsea was safe from the sea, it was attacked and plundered by the French no fewer than seven times in the 14th and 15th centuries. The extent of their destruction can be gauged from the fact that the town originally had 6000 inhabitants, now reduced to a few hundred.

⛪ The glorious **St Thomas's Church★★★** suffered like all the rest of the town. It is now just a magnificent fragment: tower, nave and aisles have all gone, and only the choir and side chapels are left. An idea of its scale can be got from the fragments of the transepts that remain west of the existing building.

Inside, its chief treasures are the canopied and pinnacled tombs on either side – three on the north, including a warrior in armour, and two even grander on the south. The southern pair are thought to be the tombs of Gervase and Stephen Alard, admirals under Edward I and II in the years round 1300.
The interior is lit by stained-glass windows dating from about 1930, which tell the story of Winchelsea in graphic form. At the back of the church is a large pre-Victorian box-pew, where whole families could have snoozed through the sermon unobserved by the vicar.

Wesley's Tree, on the west side of the churchyard, is a descendant of the ash under which the founder of Methodism preached his last open-air sermon in 1790. 'It seemed,' he wrote, 'as if all that heard were almost persuaded to be Christians'.

🏛 🏛 The **Court Hall★**, across the road from the churchyard, is one of Winchelsea's oldest buildings; it may date from the first days of the town. The lower floor was once the gaol; the first floor is now the **Museum**, full of relics of Winchelsea's history, including a model of the town as it was before the French destroyed it. Winchelsea is the smallest town in the country to have its own mayor and corporation; boards in the museum list all the mayors back to Gervase Alard in 1295. The 'Mayoring', when a new mayor is installed, takes place on Easter Monday.

Winchelsea still has its three medieval town gates, in varying degrees of repair. Visitors approaching from Rye come through the Strand Gate, above the river on the eastern side. On the north side, the Pipewell Gate guards the minor road across the Brede valley. It was here that Edward I's horse shied and jumped over a 30ft cliff while the king was in Winchelsea to review his fleet; by a miracle he survived. The third gate, the New Gate, stands forlorn at the southern end of the town, beyond fields where only bumps in the grass and a few arches remain from the days of the French raids.

Famous people who chose to live in the near-monastic calm of Winchelsea are commemorated by plaques on the walls of the houses. Among the writers who worked here were Thackeray, Ford Madox Ford and Joseph Conrad. The great actress Ellen Terry lived in a cottage beside the Strand Gate; the Victorian artist Millais painted his famous portrait *The Blind Girl* down on the marshes, with a

The early 19th-century smock-mill at West Blatchington.

rainbow overhead and Winchelsea on its hilltop in the background.

Winchelsea Beach, south of the town, is a ribbon of seaside bungalows and caravans. A massive sea-wall protects the land behind from the inroads of the sea, and the shingle beach, stretching down to sand at low tide, is chopped into small compartments by an array of wooden groynes.

WITHYHAM

Map p.154, D4
3 miles N of Crowborough on the B2110

Withyham is more of a hamlet than a village, having a short street of tile-hung houses, the oldest – Duckings – dated 1507, and a splendid early 19th-century pub called the Dorset Arms. The tiles on the pub are painted glossy white to the appearance of weather-boarding.

Withyham's strong links with the Sackville family make it something of an extension of Knole in Kent. The family members are buried in its church and Buckhurst Park, their home since the 13th century, lies just behind. Buckhurst is home to the De La Warr family, another branch of the Sackvilles.

St Michael and All Angels Church*, high on a hill outside the village, is reached via a steep lane leading up from the main road. It was largely rebuilt in the 1660s after being struck by lightning which, according to an eyewitness: 'came in at the steeple, melted the bells, and went up the chancel, where it tore the monuments of the Dorsets to pieces.' A sundial over the porch, dated 1672, was placed there when the rebuilding was completed.

The Sackville Chapel, inside, was completed in 1680. Below its blue-and-gold ceiling are funeral monuments to members of the family. The main piece is a grey-and-white marble tomb-chest to Thomas Sackville, son of the 5th Earl and

Countess of Dorset, who died in France in 1675 at the age of 13. It was carved by Danish sculptor Caius Gabriel Cibber and shows young Thomas, reclining on a mat and holding a skull while life-sized statues of his parents kneel in mourning either side. Among the other monuments is a simple, dignified tablet which reads 'V. Sackville–West C. H., poet.' She died in 1962.

WIVELSFIELD

Map p.148, D1 *
8 miles NW of Lewes on the B2112

The old village of Wivelsfield is more than 1 mile from its railway station, which lies in West Sussex and has been engulfed by Burgess Hill suburbia. The village became famous as the place where that great British institution, the Donkey Derby, was first held in 1951. Derbies have been held ever since, in the early days attracting such luminaries as Laurel and Hardy, and Charlie Chaplin. Now they are held every Spring Bank Holiday Monday with part of the proceeds going to a local hospice.

Great Ote Hall, close to the West Sussex border, is a 15th-century half-timbered manor house, said to be one of the best of that period in the county. In the 18th century it was the home of Selina Shirley, Countess of Huntingdon, the evangelical Methodist who built churches throughout Sussex. One of them, Ote Hall Chapel, built in 1778, stands in Wivelsfield, along with Baptist and Norman churches.

Wivelsfield Green, a short distance from Wivelsfield, is largely made up of modern housing estates, with a Victorian pub, the Cock Inn at the centre. As the name suggests, there is also a cricket green. Earlier this century, a famous nursery was founded here, which in 1930 created a species of Sweet William called the 'Sweet Wivelsfield'.

The Georgian exterior of Firle Place, West Firle, conceals the house's Tudor origins.

Road Map Symbols

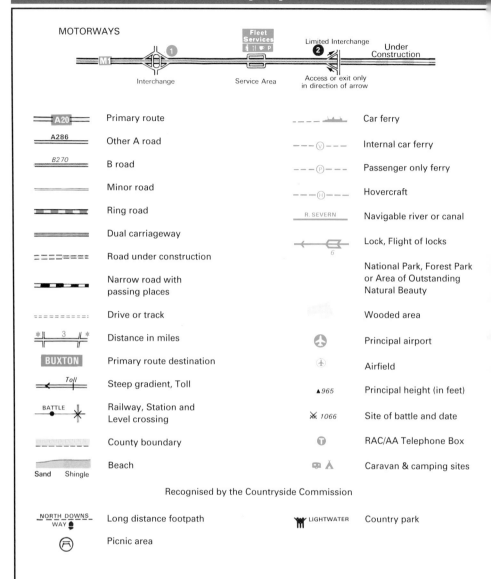

MOTORWAYS

Interchange

Service Area

Fleet Services

Limited Interchange

Under Construction

Access or exit only in direction of arrow

A20	Primary route
A286	Other A road
B270	B road
	Minor road
	Ring road
	Dual carriageway
	Road under construction
	Narrow road with passing places
	Drive or track
3	Distance in miles
BUXTON	Primary route destination
Toll	Steep gradient, Toll
BATTLE	Railway, Station and Level crossing
	County boundary
Sand Shingle	Beach

	Car ferry
(V)	Internal car ferry
(P)	Passenger only ferry
(H)	Hovercraft
R. SEVERN	Navigable river or canal
6	Lock, Flight of locks
	National Park, Forest Park or Area of Outstanding Natural Beauty
	Wooded area
✈	Principal airport
✈	Airfield
▲965	Principal height (in feet)
✕ 1066	Site of battle and date
☎	RAC/AA Telephone Box
	Caravan & camping sites

Recognised by the Countryside Commission

NORTH DOWNS WAY — Long distance footpath

Picnic area

LIGHTWATER — Country park

Scale 1:100,000 (approximately 1½ miles to 1 inch)

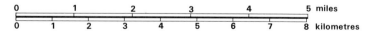

0   1   2   3   4   5 miles

0   1   2   3   4   5   6   7   8 kilometres

Cartography: George Philip Ltd
© 1991 George Philip Ltd

The representation in these maps of any road, drive or track is not evidence of the existence of a right of way. Based upon the Ordnance Survey maps with the sanction of the Controller of Her Majesty's Stationery Office, © Crown Copyright.

Tourist Symbols

🏢	Tourist Information Centre	□	Art collection	⚓	Historic ship
🅸	Tourist Information Centre Summer only	✖	Art collection/museum	🐘	Zoo
▪	House (N.T.if National Trust)		Ancient monument	🦌	Safari park
○	Garden	∴	Earthwork	�-	Farm park
◉	House & Garden		Windmill/Watermill	🐋	Aquarium/Dolphinarium
🏰	Castle		Other places of interest	🐦	Bird sanctuary/Aviary
▲	Cathedral	⊙	Roman antiquities	★	Viewpoint
✛	Abbey/Priory	🚂	Steam/miniature railway	⚑	Golf Course
✝	Church	⬤	Transport collection	BRANDS HATCH ▨	Motor racing circuit
✗	Museum	◈	Military museum	NEWBURY	Race course
⋈	Local museum		Maritime museum	JORDANS △	Youth hostel

Key Map

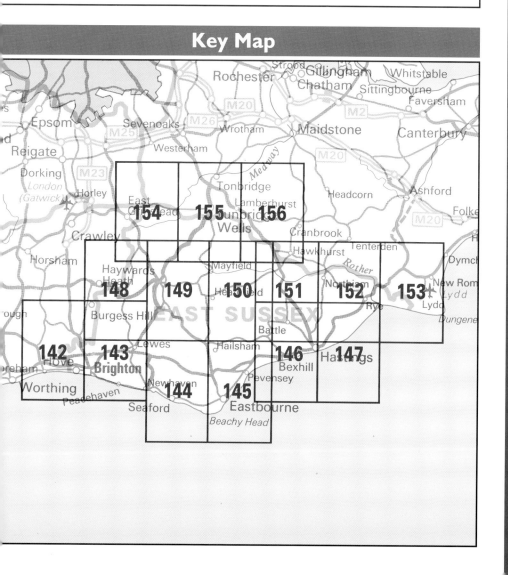

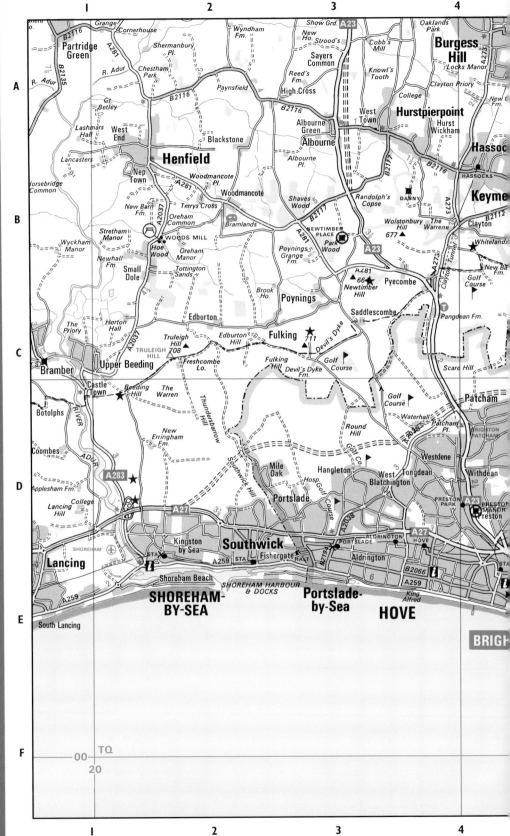

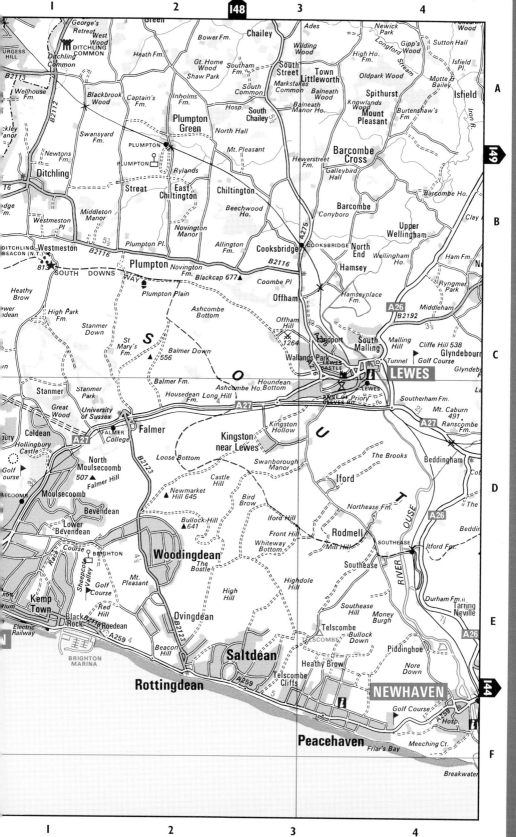

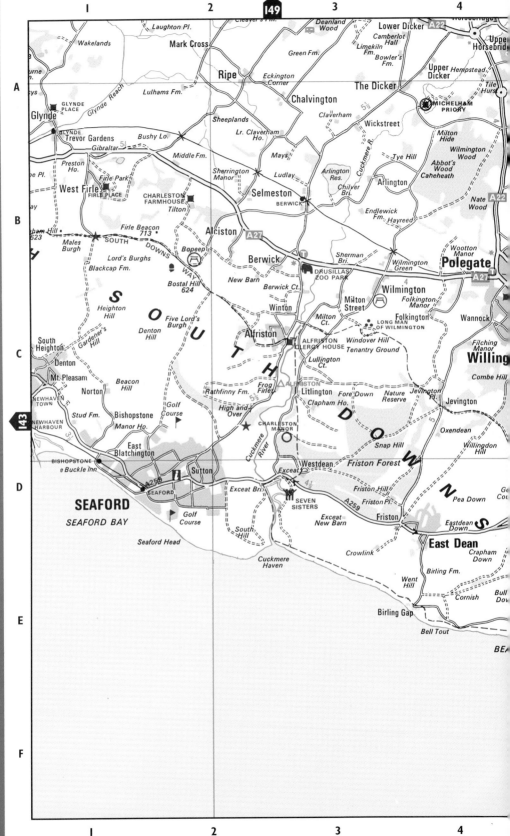

149

143

144

SOUTH DOWNS

SEAFORD

SEAFORD BAY

Polegate

Willing

East Dean

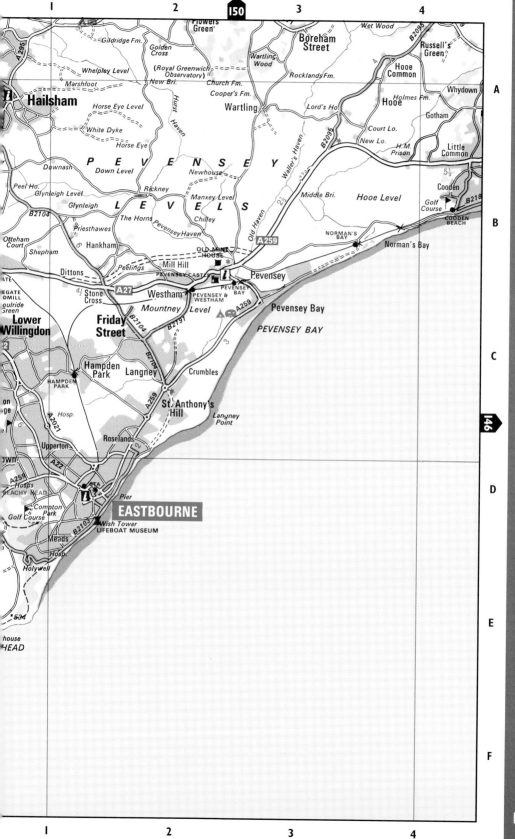

1   **2**   **3**   **4**

Flowers
Green

Gildridge Fm.

Golden
Cross

Wet Wood

B 2095

Boreham
Street

Russell's
Green

Whelpley Level

(Royal Greenwich
Observatory)

New Bri.

Wartling
Wood

Rocklands Fm.

Hoe
Common

Whydown

A 295

Marshfoot

Church Fm.

Cooper's Fm.

Holmes Fm.

A

i

Hailsham

Horse Eye Level

Wartling

Lord's Ho.

Hooe

Gotham

White Dyke

Court Lo.

New Lo.

H.M.
Prison

Little
Common

Horse Eye

B 2095

P E V E N S E Y

Down Level

Newhouse

Middle Bri.

Hooe Level

5½

Cooden

Downash

Peel Ho.

Rickney

Manxey Level

B 218

Glynleigh Level

Golf
Course

COODEN
BEACH

Glynleigh

L E V E L S

Chiley

Old Haven

B

Otteham
Court

B 2104

The Horns

Priesthawes

Pevensey Haven

NORMAN'S
BAY

Shepham

Hankham

OLD MILL
HOUSE

A 259

Norman's Bay

Dittons

Peelings

Mill Hill

PEVENSEY CASTLE

i

Pevensey

ATE

Stone
Cross

4½

A27

Westham

PEVENSEY &
WESTHAM

PEVENSEY
BAY

Pevensey Bay

EGATE
DMILL

A 27

Mountney Level

A 259

C

oulride
Green

**Lower
Willingdon**

**Friday
Street**

B 2104

B 2191

Pevensey Bay

P E V E N S E Y   B A Y

Hampden
Park

Langney

Crumbles

A 259

HAMPDEN
PARK

Hosp.

St. Anthony's
Hill

Langney
Point

on
ge

A 2021

Roselands

Upperton

A 22

A 259

D

Hosps

BEACHY HEAD

i

Pier

EASTBOURNE

Wish Tower
LIFEBOAT MUSEUM

Compton
Park

B 2103

Golf Course

Meads

Hosp.

Holywell

E

534

house
HEAD

F

1   **2**   **3**   **4**

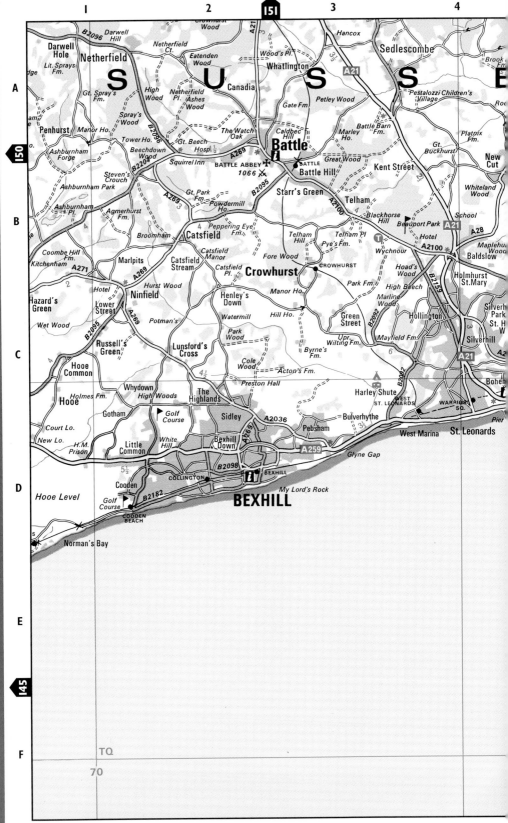

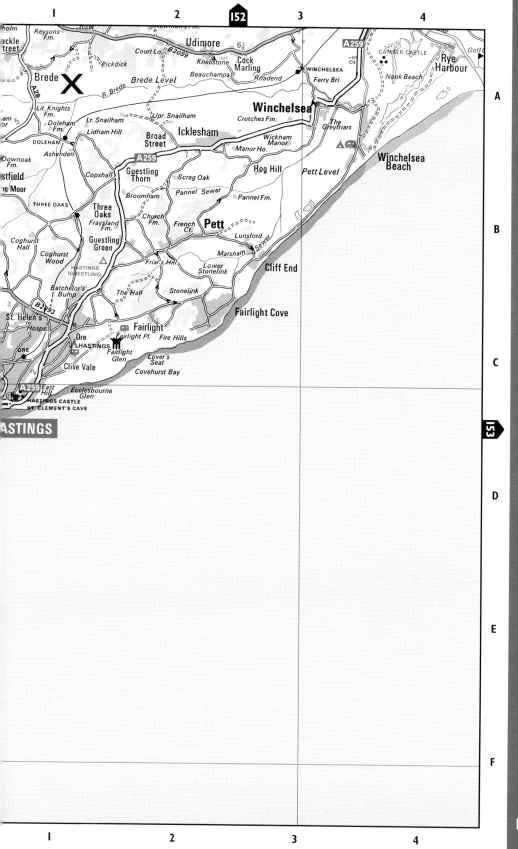

152

1   2   3   4

153

Reysons Fm.
Row
Udimore
B2089
Court Lo.
6½
A259
CAMBER CASTLE
Golf C
Pickdick
Knellstone
Cock
Marling
WINCHELSEA
Rye
Harbour
Brede
Beauchamps
Roadend
Ferry Bri.
Nook Beach
A28
R. Brede
Brede Level
Lit. Knights Fm.
Lr. Snailham
Upr. Snailham
Winchelsea
2½
Doleham Fm.
Lidham Hill
Crutches Fm.
The Greyfriars
DOLEHAM
Broad Street
Icklesham
Wickham Manor
Downoak Fm.
Ashenden
Manor Ho.
Winchelsea Beach
stfield
A259
7
ne Moor
Copshall
Guestling Thorn
Scrag Oak
Hog Hill
Pett Level
THREE OAKS
Broomham
Pannel Sewer
Pannel Fm.
Coghurst Hall
Three Oaks
Fraysland Fm.
Church Fm.
Pett
Coghurst Wood
HASTINGS (GUESTLING)
Guestling Green
French Ct.
Lunsford
Sewer
Friar's Hill
Marsham
Batchelor's Bump
Lower Stonelink
Cliff End
B2093
The Hall
Stonelink
St. Helen's Hosps.
Fairlight Cove
Ore
Fairlight Pl.
Fairlight
Fire Hills
ORE
HASTINGS
Fairlight Glen
Lover's Seat
Clive Vale
Covehurst Bay
A259
East Hill
Ecclesbourne Glen
HASTINGS CASTLE
ST CLEMENT'S CAVE

ASTINGS

A   B   C   D   E   F

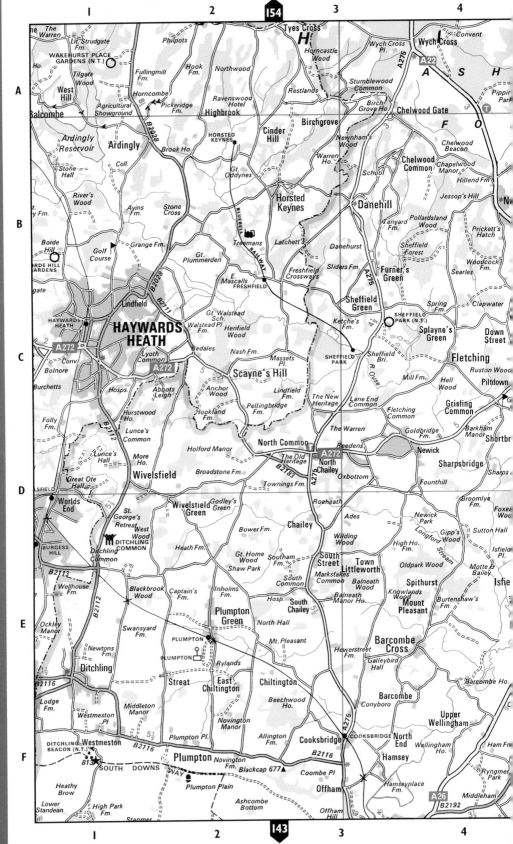

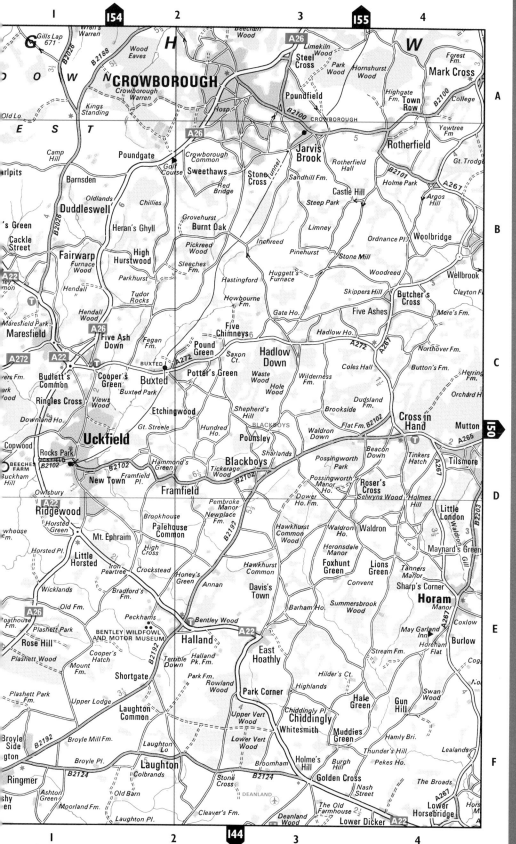

154 **155**

G W

O W

Gills Lap 671 · Wren's Warren

Wood Eaves

Wood

Beechen Wood

A26 Limekiln Wood

Steel Cross · Park Wood

Hornshurst Wood

Forest Fm.

Mark Cross

College

CROWBOROUGH

Crowborough Warren

Poundfield

Highgate Fm. · Town Row

A26

B2100 CROWBOROUGH

A

Hosp.

5

Yewtree Fm.

Old Lo

Kings Standing

A26

Crowborough Common

Poundgate

Golf Course

Sweethaws

Red Bridge

Stone Cross

Tunnel

Sandhill Fm.

Jarvis Brook

Rotherfield Hall

Rotherfield

B2101

Gt. Trodge

Camp Hill

A267

rlpits

Barnsden

Oldlands

Chillies

Grovehurst

Burnt Oak

Castle Hill

Steep Park

Holme Park

Argos Hill

Duddleswell

B2026

Heran's Ghyll

Limney

Woolbridge

Clayton F

B

's Green

Cackle Street

Fairwarp

Furnace Wood

High Hurstwood

Pickreed Wood

Sleeches Fm.

Inchreed

Pinehurst

Stone Mill

Ordnance Pl.

Woodreed

Wellbrook

A22

mon

Hendall

Parkhurst

Tudor Rocks

Hastingford

Howbourne Fm.

Huggett's Furnace

Skippers Hill

Butcher's Cross

Mere's Fm.

T

Hendall Wood

Maresfield Park

A26

Gate Ho.

Five Ashes

Maresfield

Five Ash Down

Fegan Fm.

Five Chimneys

A272

Hadlow Ho.

Northover Fm.

Herring Fm.

C

A272

A22

Budlett's Common

Cooper's Green

Pound Green

Saxon Ct.

Hadlow Down

Coles Hall

Button's Fm.

Orchard H

ers Fm.

T

Buxted

Potter's Green

Waste Wood

Wilderness Fm.

Dudsland Fm.

ark ood

Ringles Cross

Views Wood

Buxted Park

Hole Wood

Shepherd's Hill

Brookside

Flat Fm. **B2102**

Cross in Hand

Mutton

Downland Ho.

Etchingwood

Gt. Streele

Hundred Ho.

BLACKBOYS

Waldron Down

T

A265

Copwood

Uckfield

Rocks Park

Pounsley

Sharlands

Possingworth Park

Beacon Down

Tinkers Hatch

Tilsmore

BEECHES FARM

B2102

UCKFIELD

Hammond's Green

Framfield Pl.

Blackboys

Tickerage Wood

B2102

Possingworth Manor Fm.

Roser's Cross

Holmes

A267

D

uckham Hill

New Town

Framfield

6½

Dower Ho. Fm.

Selwyns Wood

B2203

Owlsbury

A22

Ridgewood

Horsted Green

Mt. Ephraim

Brookhouse

Palehouse Common

Pembroke Manor Newplace Fm.

B2192

Hawkhurst Common Wood

Waldron Ho.

Waldron

Little London

whouse m.

Horsted Pl.

Little Horsted

High Cross

Iron Peartree

Crockstead

Hawkhurst Common

Heronsdale Manor

Foxhunt Green

Lions Green

Tanners Manor

Maynard's Green

A26

Wicklands

Old Fm.

Bradford's Fm.

Honey's Green

Annan

Davis's Town

Convent

Sharp's Corner

Horam

Manor

oathouse Fm.

Peckhams

T

Bentley Wood

Barham Ho.

Summersbrook Wood

May Garland Inn

Coxlow

E

Plashett Park

BENTLEY WILDFOWL AND MOTOR MUSEUM

Halland

A22

Hoveham Flat

Burlow

Rose Hill

Cooper's Hatch

Halland Pk. Fm.

East Hoathly

Stream Fm.

Cog

Plashett Wood

Mount Fm.

B2192

Terrible Down

Hilder's Ct.

Swan Wood

No

Shortgate

Park Fm. Rowland Wood

Park Corner

Highlands

Hale Green

Gun Hill

Upper Lodge

Upper Vert Wood

Chiddingly Pl.

Chiddingly

Whitesmith

Muddles Green

Hamly Bri.

Lealands

royle Side gton

B2192

Laughton Common

Lower Vert Wood

Thunder's Hill

Laughton

Laughton Lo

Holme's Hill

Broomham

Burgh Hill

Pekes Ho.

The Broads

F

Ringmer

B2124

Colbrands

Broyle Pl.

Stone Cross

B2124

Golden Cross

Nash Street

shy en

Ashton Green

Old Barn

DEANLAND

Cleaver's Fm.

Deanland Wood

The Old Farmhouse 2½

Lower Horsebridge

Hors

A267

Moorland Fm.

Laughton Pl.

Lower Dicker

A22

149

144

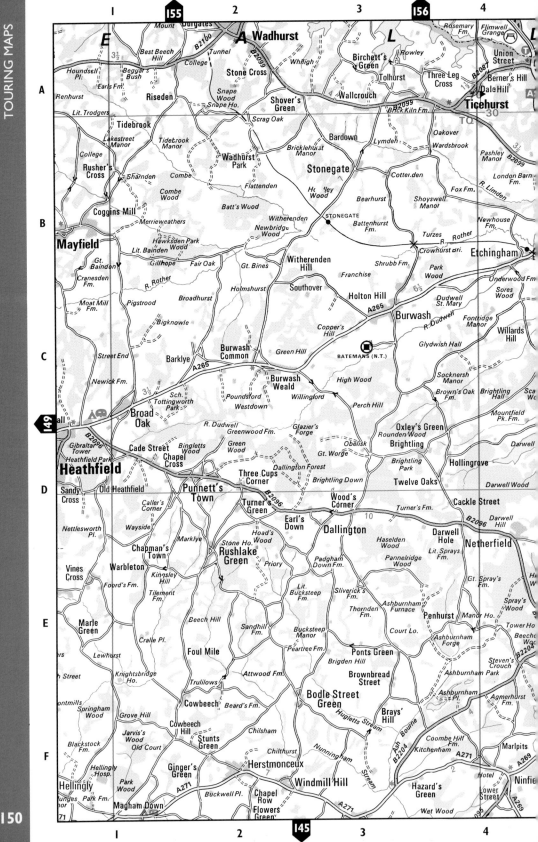

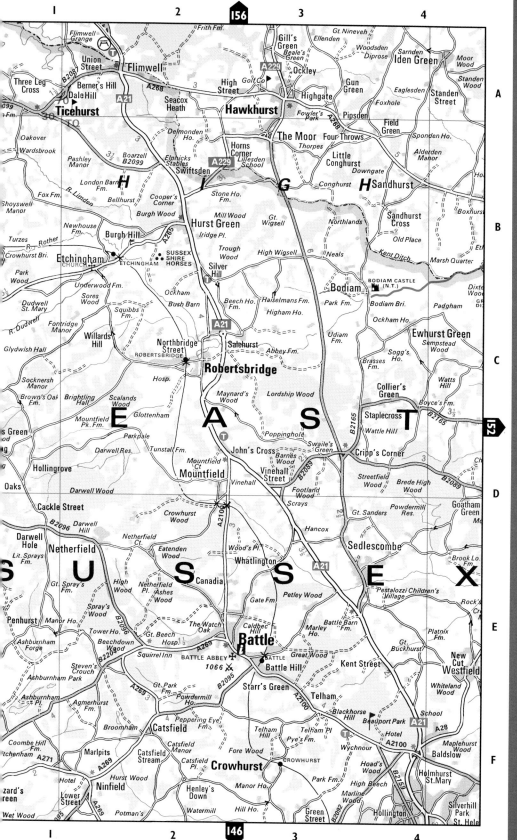

152

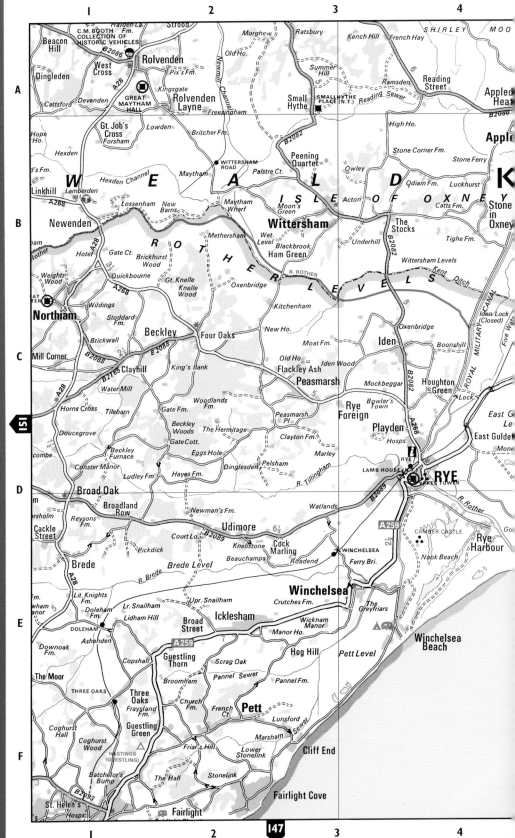

151

147

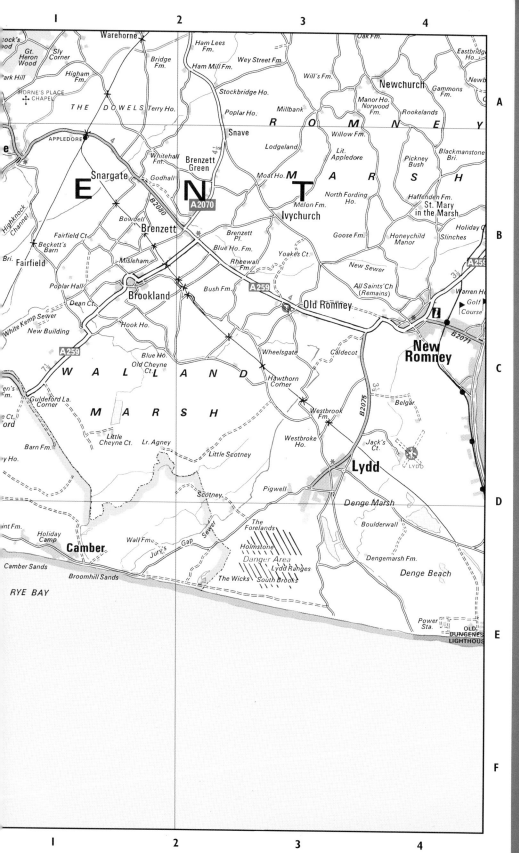

1 **2** **3** **4**

Warehorne
cock's
ood
Gt.
Heron
Wood
Sly Corner
ark Hill
Higham Fm.
Bridge Fm.
Ham Lees Fm.
Wey Street Fm.
Ham Mill Fm.
Will's Fm.
Oak Fm.
Newchurch
Eastbridge Ho.
Newb

HORNE'S PLACE
CHAPEL
Stockbridge Ho.
Gammons Fm.

THE DOWELS Terry Ho.
Poplar Ho.
Millbank
Manor Ho.
Norwood
Rookelands

A

APPLEDORE
e
Snave
R O M N E Y
Willow Fm.

Snargate
Whitehall Fm.
Godhall
Brenzett Green
Lodgeland
Lit. Appledore
Lit. Appledore
Pickney Bush
Blackmanstone Bri.

E
Highknock
Channel
N
Moat Ho.
M
A
R
S
H

Bri.
Fairfield
Beckett's Barn
Fairfield Ct.
Bowdell
Brenzett
Brenzett Pl.
Blue Ho. Fm.
Yoake's Ct.
North Fording Ho.
Melon Fm.
Ivychurch
Goose Fm.
Haffenden Fm.
St. Mary in the Marsh
Honeychild Manor
Slinches
Holiday C
A2259

B

Poplar Hall
Misleham
Rheewall Fm.
New Sewer
Warren Ho
Golf Course

Dean Ct.
Brookland
Bush Fm.
A259
Old Romney
All Saints' Ch (Remains)

New Building
White Kemp Sewer
Hook Ho.
Wheelsgate
Caldecot
New Romney
B2071

C

A259
Blue Ho.
Old Cheyne Ct.
W A L A N D
Hawthorn Corner
Belgar
B2075

en's m.
Guldeford La. Corner
M A R S H
Westbrook Fm.
Jack's Ct.

Ct.
ord
Little Cheyne Ct.
Lr. Agney
Westbroke Ho.
LYDD
LYDD

Barn Fm.
Little Scotney
Lydd
y Ho.
Pigwell
Denge Marsh

D

int Fm.
Holiday Camp
Scotney.
Boulderwall

Camber
Wall Fm.
Jury's
Gap
Sewer
The Forelands
Holmstone
Danger Area
Lydd Ranges
Dengemarsh Fm.
Denge Beach

Camber Sands
Broomhill Sands
The Wicks
South Brooks

RYE BAY
Power Sta.
OLD DUNGENES
LIGHTHOUS

E

F

1 **2** **3** **4**

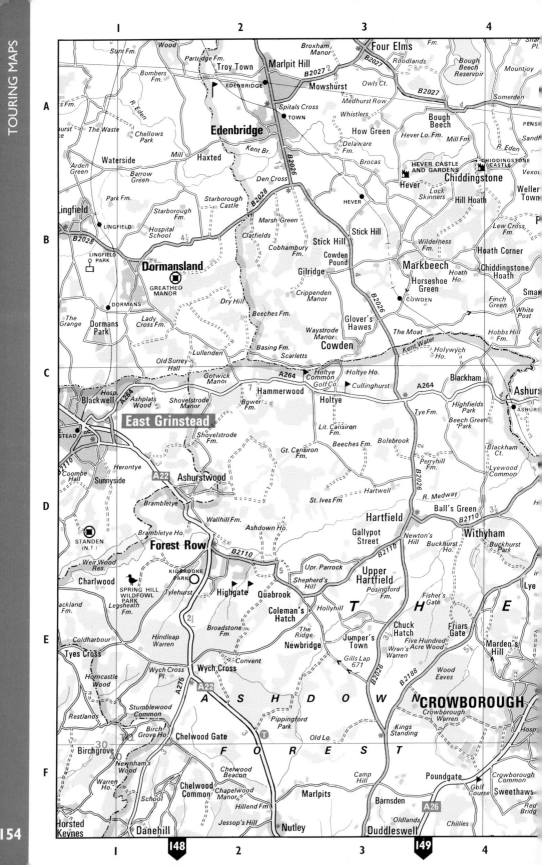

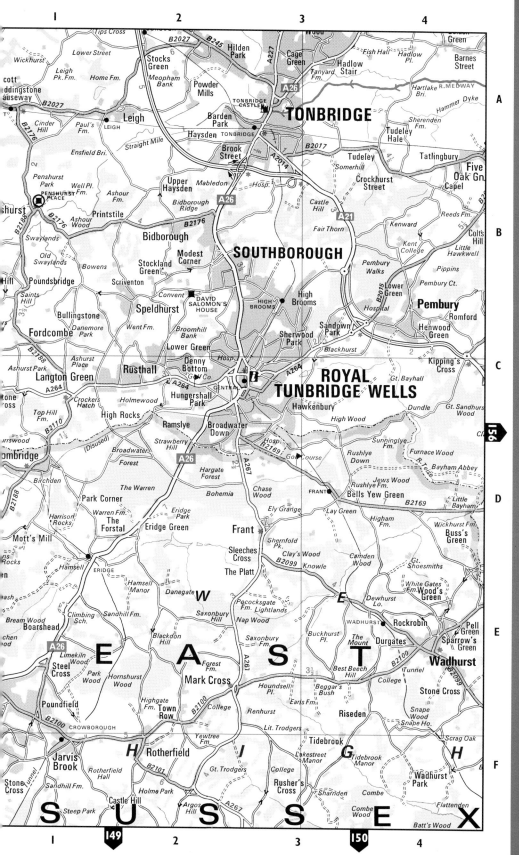

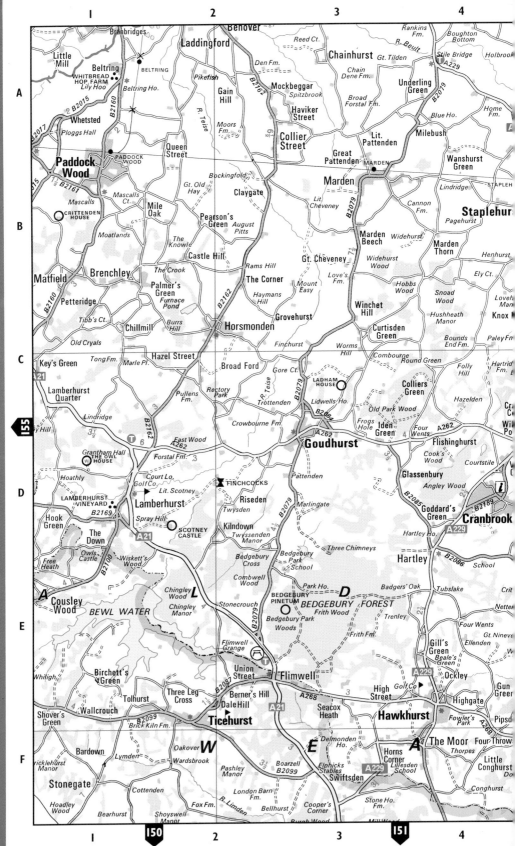

INDEX